PRAISE FOR
YOU SAY MORE THAN YOU THINK

"Driver puts her lessons to paper with straightforward prose and easy-to-use methodology. . . . Driver's advice will give readers immediate, effective results. . . . Sound examples (many drawn from her professional adventures), revealing exercises and self-tests, and a game sense of humor keep Driver's considerable expertise from overwhelming readers, making this an enjoyable and highly practical self-help." **—*Publisher's Weekly* (starred review)**

"I love books that educate and entertain. . . . [*You Say More Than You Think*] is funny, and I like the way it is crafted."
—Dr. Mehmet Oz, *Crain's New York Business,* **April 18, 2010**

"Insightful. A bold, powerful, mind-blowing book. . . . With Driver's 7-Second Fixes and playful exercises, in less than a week, opportunities and experiences will begin to open up for you that were simply not possible before."
—Debra Fine, bestselling author of *The Fine Art of Small Talk* **and** *The Fine Art of the Big Talk*

"Driver intimately knows her subject and is able to convey it in a way that tempts readers to partake in the lessons." **—*Library Journal***

"*You Say More Than You Think* is filled with interesting tidbits about common body language tricks." **—Rachel Saslow,** *Washington Post*

"Body Language Guru Extraordinaire Janine Driver divulges the moves that give you an edge." **—*Cosmopolitan***

"Brilliant! This book's insights will help you improve your communication skills, almost overnight."
—John Christensen, bestselling coauthor of *Fish! Philosophy*

ALSO BY JANINE DRIVER

You Say More Than You Think

The Revolutionary
Program to Supercharge
Your Inner Lie Detector
and **Get to the Truth**

YOU CAN'T LIE TO ME

JANINE DRIVER

with Mariska van Aalst

HarperOne
An Imprint of HarperCollinsPublishers

HarperOne

HarperCollins books may be purchased for educational, business, or sales promotional use. For information please e-mail the Special Markets Department at SPsales@harpercollins.com

HarperCollins website: http://www.harpercollins.com

HarperCollins®, 📖®, and HarperOne™ are trademarks of HarperCollins Publishers.

All photos and illustrations used by permission.

Library of Congress Cataloging-in-Publication Data

Driver, Janine.
  You can't lie to me : the revolutionary program to supercharge your inner lie detector and get to the truth / Janine Driver, with Mariska Van Aalst.
    p. cm.
  ISBN 978-0-06-211254-5
  1. Deception. 2. Truthfulness and falsehood. 3. Honesty. 4. Body language. I. Aalst, Mariska van. II. Title.
  BF637.D42D75 2012
  153.8—dc23   2012002472

  14 15 16 17 RRD(H) 10 9 8 7 6 5 4 3 2

CONTENTS

This book is dedicated to my refreshingly honest six-year-old son, Angus, who reminds me every day of the secrets to living a fulfilled life: love, laughter, cheese sticks, and LEGO Star Wars. I love you babe.

FOREWORD

FROM THE DESK OF JAMES J. NEWBERRY
Senior Special Agent, ATF (Retired)
Major, U.S. Army Reserve—Military Intelligence (Retired)
President and Co-Founder of the Institute of Analytic
Interviewing, Inc.
Certified "Truth Wizard"

She has done it again. Janine Driver's new book is powerful.

The techniques and tricks within her easy, step-by-step plan have the potential to strengthen your already strong, innate ability to spot liars—which Janine calls your "BS Barometer"—to create trustworthy relationships in all aspects of your personal and professional lives. And not surprisingly, when your world is filled with people who are honest and trustworthy, other trustworthy and honest people will feel compelled to connect with you, too—to make a purchase, to visit your blog, to pick you up at the airport (on time), and to treat your children and aging parents like family, protecting them as if they were their own. These true friends will be the ones who leap into action immediately and reach out a helping hand when you are drowning in stress, anxiety, and sorrow. Janine's unique book, *You Can't Lie to Me,* also inspires us to take action fast—which is exactly what we both did when I first met Janine nearly ten years ago.

In late 2003, early 2004, Janine tracked me down after spending more than ten years learning kinesics and analytic interviewing techniques from the manuals I'd helped put together as a senior special agent in the ATF (Bureau of Alcohol, Tobacco, Firearms, and Explosives). She'd seen my name in the manuals—my former students had collected anecdotes and secret tips I shared in class and edited them into the student guides, calling them out as "J.J. Newberry Moments." After reading these little teaching nuggets for more than a decade, Janine decided she wanted to meet me. True to Janine form, once she made that decision, she instantly dug in and did her research. After she heard a tape of a radio interview that I'd done, she was determined to accomplish her goal: to track me down.

The phone rang in my remote cabin one afternoon in late December 2003. The answering machine picked up. "Hi, Mr. Newberry! I'm Janine Driver. I'm an industry operations investigator and a training program manager in ATF headquarters and I'm running the interviewing program up here. I've been seeing these J.J. Newberry Moments of yours in my textbooks for over a decade, and I want to meet the source. I want to talk to you about what I need to do to become the next J.J. Newberry. I'd like you to be my mentor."

I spent the next two weeks investigating and calling random people I still had contact with at ATF. Who is Janine Driver? What's her legacy at ATF? Who was this obviously passionate investigator who'd sought me out specifically? I called her current bosses' bosses, her former bosses' bosses. I heard tales of her key work as a public information officer at New York City's World Trade Center and her powerful contributions on the award-winning explosives team out in Hartford, Connecticut, where she helped uncover explosives companies that were illegally manufacturing contraband M80s and illegally importing highly volatile explosives. I learned how Janine and an ATF special agent out of Boston conducted a complicated firearms investigation that resulted in the seizure of hundreds of thousands of dollars worth of illegally imported semiautomatic weapons.

At every turn, I heard things like "a natural" and "can quickly read people accurately" about her detecting deception abilities. I was glad I'd done my homework—Janine Driver was sounding like the real deal.

Two weeks after Janine's surprising message, I was headed to Washington, D.C., to train U.S. Customs officers in analytic interviewing and detecting deception. U.S. Customs officers enforce the laws of the United States of America for every person or object that enters or leaves the States. Their interviews can result in the prevention of undocumented immigrants or other people from entering the country unlawfully and may result in the detection and confiscation of contraband guns, drugs, and fraudulent documents. Since Janine worked in ATF's bureau headquarters in D.C. and my background research on her left me intrigued, I called her. "Janine, this is J.J. I'm coming to D.C. in two days to train U.S. Customs officers with Dr. Mark Frank. I'd like you to come meet us for breakfast."

At 7 A.M. sharp, she bounced in smiling, armed with a million questions, and stayed with me for the day. During that exclusive six-hour training session, I watched Janine quickly absorb all the information eagerly and ask brilliant questions. She even learned a dangerously simple deception detection technique that day that she reveals here within the book—but we can't tell you which one it is because it's the number one most effective technique used by Customs to spot someone who 100 percent has something to hide. (We wouldn't want to give that away, would we? Just know it's in here!)

Best of all, Janine made me laugh. A *lot*.

I told her I would be her mentor and that she'd be my final protégée. But I had one rule: "Janine, if I mentor you, then you have to guarantee to mentor others."

That day was the beginning of a beautiful friendship. I started out as Janine Driver's mentor, but, after watching her in action, I soon realized I had become the student. Janine has the remarkable ability to read people's body language and detect deception. Although Janine is not listed as one of the "Truth Wizards" (Dr. Maureen O'Sullivan, who tested the wizards, passed away from cancer before she could ever test her), she is, in my opinion, highly skilled enough to be one. Janine also has two other critically important abilities:

1. She can take any complex, hard-to-understand material and make it fascinating and educational; and

2. She's a total riot.

In our deadly serious world, you often don't see that combination.

While many of the students I've trained remain exclusively in the law enforcement world, Janine is one of the few who has successfully decoded and packaged the information for readers like you. Janine has carefully crafted these techniques without giving away any top-secret governmental techniques, adapting them for personal and business settings, so you can save your own life and the lives of people you love.

Out of all the top-secret security clearance people I've trained and mentored, Janine's the playful one—she takes heavy techniques and the way that they must be used, and she injects them with humor. She coined the term "the belly button rule" (a.k.a. "navel intelligence"), brought awareness of "naughty bits" to the corporate world, and now introduces the "BS Barometer"—all fun, creative, easy-to-understand terms for complex, serious concepts. This playfulness allows her methods and tools to seamlessly cross over into the business world and into the dating, marriage, and keeping-our-children-safe worlds, too.

These days, when I read Janine's two books and watch her instruct others, I am in awe. Janine's ability to read people is surpassed only by her ability to transfer her knowledge and ability to others. I was thrilled to see how well she'd translated that in her first book, *You Say More Than You Think*. And now, with *You Can't Lie to Me*, I am blown away. I feel like I am the student reading manuals with little "Lyin' Tamer" gems throughout it.

Janine has learned my stuff and she's made it her own, adding continually along the way. And I know that she expects you to do the same. So whatever you do, learn from the Janine Driver way—and then make it the Kyle way or the Kevin way or the Karen way. Do it *your* way.

Janine and I have each other's backs, and we appreciate the security that loyalty and friendship provide for us. We want that same thing for you: if your ultimate goal is to find someone to trust, someone who cares about you—you're in luck. You're about to uncover your own hidden potential to read others accurately. To find out how to develop your own abilities to spot trustworthy friends and allies, look no further than this book.

You'll learn to surround yourself with people who have your back—and who inspire you to be a better version of yourself. Keep your eyes open, and it will happen sooner than you think.

Now go work out and strengthen that killer BS Barometer of yours!

Oh, and have fun!

YOU CAN'T LIE TO ME

INTRODUCTION

People never lie so much as after a hunt,
during a war, or before an election.
—OTTO VON BISMARCK

DID YOU SEE YOUR NEW BOSS give that little shoulder shrug while she said, "What you're doing contributes to the team and company's success. Your work makes a difference."

Or hear that practically-perfect-in-every-way babysitter say, "Just ask any of my previous families—they all love me. I know they'll tell you that I'm dependable and trustworthy."

Did you happen to notice that your new girlfriend put a smiley face at the end of her handwritten "I'm happy I met you!" note?

In all of these examples, you might find yourself being lied to. But can you spot it? Even the most intelligent and observant among us can miss telltale signs of deceit and manipulation and fall victim to some unscrupulous folks out there. Whether the opportunist is a conniving ex-wife, a cutthroat coworker, a slick salesperson, or just an irresistibly sexy cheater, we need to be prepared.

But learning how to spot a liar is not a matter of becoming more paranoid. Nope, not at all. In fact, the skill that we most need to develop is how to look for the *truth,* not the lie. Because here's the secret: more trusting people make better lie detectors.

People who don't trust never really develop the skills to tell whether someone is lying or not—because they assume everyone is. The cost, of course, is never having any authentic or satisfying relationships. If no one can be trusted, how can you truly bond with someone? And then what kind of life do you live? A sad one, to my mind.[1]

Research has shown that, in contrast to conventional wisdom, people who score higher on measures of trust not only spot lies more easily, they're better at general assessments of other people, make better hiring decisions, and focus on the most important details that hint at other people's trustworthiness. They follow up on their suspicions, but they assume most people are innocent until proven guilty.

And here's the ultimate irony: people who lack trust in others are *more* willing to hire liars and are *less* likely to be aware they are liars.[2] People who show little trust in others suffer tremendous costs, especially in fewer genuine connections with other people.

So while other deception detection experts teach you to be suspicious, I want to do the opposite: I want you to enjoy *more* trust and to have better relationships. I want to get you back to that sweet spot between the gullible toddler and the bitter divorcée. I want you to learn how to trust your own gut again and to stop second-guessing yourself. When you learn the process I spell out in this book, you'll tap into your own innate lie detection ability—what I call your "BS Barometer"—and you'll have all the tools and the knowledge to spot harmful liars quickly. That way, you can relax, trust your instincts, and enjoy getting to know people.

The BS Barometer is a collection of your brain's oldest instincts, long used to spot the virtues and ethics within others—and within ourselves. But our BS Barometers have been taking hits for years, decades—even for centuries. Take, for example, George Washington's famous proclamation to his father about his favorite cherry tree, "I cannot tell a lie, I did it with my little hatchet." The truth? This is a total myth! Little Georgie never said that! That line was the concoction of Washington's biographer, the equivalent of a Revolutionary-era PR hack, to make Washington seem like he was such an honorable, honest guy, he wouldn't even lie as a child. So even a lie about lying itself can become a commonly accepted truth, simply by being repeated often enough.

Our BS Barometers have taken a beating, worn down from these constant exposures to BS and lies. We are now at a moment in history when we almost don't expect to hear the truth anymore—we are so used to being lied to that we are often wildly out of touch with reality. But that's no recipe for a satisfying authentic life. And that's exactly where the *You Can't Lie to Me* program comes in: While you may have lost some of your native ability to spot liars, using this program will re-calibrate your BS Barometer to spot the real truth, not the accepted reality of the truth. You'll strengthen your BS Barometer so it can once again perform at the height of its abilities. You'll build your self-confidence, because the stronger your BS Barometer, the more happiness and peace of mind you'll have. Your BS Barometer will automatically keep you at arm's length from potential manipulators, so you'll be free to bring more open, authentic people into your life. Not only will you be a natural at detecting deception, you'll also be a lot happier—because you can now confidently recognize the *real* truth.

WHAT'S AT STAKE?

Here's the thing: on the road to that happiness and confident trust, countless valuable resources—time, energy, money, affection—can be squandered because of fraud and deception. We've seen how very smart people can wind up at the mercy of charismatic BS artists. After all, we saw the handiwork of Tiger Woods, Governor Marc Sanford, and Bernie Madoff all in the span of *one year*. Since then, we've been through Anthony Weiner, Casey Anthony, and Justin Bieber's baby mama. We've seen public officials exposed as plagiarists. We've seen title-winning coaches exposed as child molesters. We've seen internationally renowned researchers get busted fabricating decades of "results" in gold standard scientific journals.

We see new, ever-more-shocking examples of bald-faced lying every day. But why? Consider these statistics:

- 80 percent of lies will go undetected.[3]

- Nine out of ten people who apply for jobs overemphasize, or downright fabricate, positive traits about themselves.[4]

- Between 66 and 80 percent of college students admit to having cheated at some time in their school careers.[5]

- Since 1991, lifetime infidelity among men over sixty has doubled. In women, it has *tripled*.[6]

- About 20 percent of men and 15 percent of women under thirty-five have cheated on their partners.[7] In those ages eighteen to twenty-five, the percentage is closer to 30.[8]

- Adult men and women lie in one out of every five social interactions; for college students, that number is one in three.[9]

Imagine—one out of every five (or three!) times a person opens his mouth, he's probably lying.

Those odds are definitely not in our favor.

But what if you could learn how to detect a lie the moment it starts (or even before)? What if you had a test that tipped you off the instant a lie was being told? An innate lie detector so powerful it becomes an unconscious skill, applicable with any person, in any situation, to help you uncover the truth before the lie takes hold of you?

Let's imagine how it could change your life.

Regardless of another person's intent to deceive you, *you* would always hold the power. *You* would know whom to trust, and who gets shown the door. *You* would regain control. You could look anyone straight in the eye, and your whole being would calmly and confidently say, "You can't lie to me."

I have spent nearly two decades teaching hundreds of thousands of people— chiefs of police, titans of industry, suspicious housewives, jaded lovers—how to use the New Body Language to charm clients, bust criminals, and succeed on the battlefield of love. In this book, I uncover hundreds of proven winning techniques that have been used by federal agents and law enforcement officers to catch the most egregious liars in the most outrageous crimes. You'll learn tricks used by the world's best investigators to target history's smartest con men (and con women!).

I've integrated all these tools into one easy step-by-step plan that quickly takes all the second-guessing out of detecting deception and gets you straight to the truth. You'll gain an understanding of the favorite tricks of master manipulators, so you can effortlessly protect yourself and not get sucked in. Learning to spot manipulation *as it is happening* will make you the first—instead of the last—to know when things aren't right. Because sometimes, a moment of manipulation can change the course of a person's entire life.

Manipulators Do Leave Scars

I have been in this lie detection business for several decades now. Every so often, someone asks me, "What got you into this, anyway? Why deception? Why spend so much time looking for bad guys?"

I usually make some kind of cheeky answer. "I started off at ATF—the Bureau of Alcohol, Tobacco, Firearms, and Explosives," I'll say. "My dad says it's because I just wanted to combine my favorite hobbies into a career."

That's usually good for a laugh. Which I'm grateful for, because it allows me to gloss over the true reason—which happened about eighteen years prior.

In 1976, I was six years old. Those were the days of free-range kids—my mom had no idea where I was for most of the afternoon. The town was safe. Everyone knew everyone. What could happen?

In those days, we weren't worried about bike helmets, let alone about "swimsuit areas" and stranger danger. No one was talking about kids getting molested—it was just unheard of. And in the days before Megan's Law, certainly no one was thinking that a nice guy in the community was a pedophile.

I was playing outside, climbing a tree I'd climbed a thousand times. An older man I knew from around the town called me down from the tree. We were going to play a fun game! Although I was curious, I remember hesitating a couple seconds because I was having so much fun climbing the tree. But this guy, whom I'd seen hundreds of times, who'd been at parties and barbecues, who waved to me whenever I rode past him on my bike, conned me out of the tree and led me into a shed.

Twenty minutes later, right after the streetlights came on, I was headed back to my house, with the course of my life forever changed.

He told me to come back after dinner; he said that "the game gets much better." But I never got a chance to go back. Right after dinner, my mom gave me a bath, and while the water was running, she asked me what I did that day. I told her the truth.

When the child psychologist arrived at my home, later that night, with a box of crayons and a pad of paper, she kindly asked me to draw a picture of what happened in the shed. We know now that when children are untruthful about an event, often the picture will not match the story. Well, my picture had the tree, the shed, the chair in the shed that stood against the left side—I had even colored the man's shirt the same color and pattern of the one he was wearing when the police knocked on his door hours afterward.

The psychologist told my parents that taking the pedophile to court and forcing me to testify would do me more harm than good. So they never had him arrested.

I get it—they were all trying to protect me. Unbeknownst to me at the time, my parents warned all my friends' families, and the man became a total outcast in the community thereafter. Of course, with the benefit of several decades of life experience, I realize that prosecuting the guy would've been better for everyone—especially me.

But I probably would be a different person today if we'd confronted him head-on. The scar of that day is still with me, still part of my story. In the years since those awful moments in the shed, I've mastered the very thing that all children who have endured trauma learn to do so well:

I've learned how to quickly spot the bad guys.

To this day, whenever I pass that shed, I can feel my fists curl up, as if I can somehow go back in time and stand up for my six-year-old self. But because I can't, I am now driven by the need to protect other vulnerable people.

I followed my gravitational pull into law enforcement. The real reason I joined the ATF wasn't to crack jokes about drinking, smoking, and shooting—it was to help keep guns away from little kids, to make sure people couldn't profit from the selling of guns to bad guys. And I was determined.

During my federal law enforcement training, I mastered skills and procedures that brought down sophisticated forgers, manufacturers of contraband explosives, and international gun dealers. My supervisors saw that I had a knack for deception detection techniques, and I was tapped to be a trainer for other investigators and special agents, teaching hundreds of subtle tricks that even some of the most senior agents didn't know.

Combining my drive to protect people with my newfound expertise helped me discover my life's purpose: to empower and educate as many people as possible with what I know, what I see, all I've learned. To save lives.

Teaching My Life's Purpose to You

Since then, I've taught everyone from housewives to police chiefs to jilted lovers to crowds of 5,000 people at the Future Business Leaders of America and executives at Fortune 500 companies such as Coca-Cola and Procter & Gamble. The demand for my presentations led to the formation of the Body Language Institute (BLI; www.bodylanguageinstitute.com), an educational forum to share my approach with the world. The BLI's mission is saving lives through boosting credibility, confidence, and careers.

Then, in 2010, I brought my knowledge about many aspects of nonverbal communication to the public in the *New York Times* bestseller *You Say More Than You Think*. Teaching readers how to use the New Body Language to get what they want, my first book shares all the secret techniques needed to read and fix any interpersonal situation "in the boardroom, barroom, or bedroom" in seven seconds or less.

Still, for years, my students—everyone from top female business executives who want to have peace of mind that at least one person in the office has their backs, to pilots who want to spot suspicious behavior when people board their planes, to middle managers and new moms who second-guess their gut instincts and as a result waste dozens of hours a week or put themselves, or others, in dangerous situations—have asked that I collect all I know about wrangling the truth into one book. Now I'm ready to lay all that really juicy stuff out on the table, to reveal everything I know about getting to the truth. The book you hold in your hands gives you a front-row seat to my always-sold-out course, "Detecting Deception," and it's the book I was born to write: *You Can't Lie to Me*.

In the pages of this book, I distill years of behind-the-scenes knowledge, cutting-edge science, and dramatic case studies into the simple, effective BS Barometer program that teaches you how to get the *real* story—in any situation. My techniques use the very same brain processes targeted in today's sophisticated lie detection technology, such as polygraphs, fMRIs, and ultra-cool infrared eye scanners. But, despite the billions of dollars spent developing and operating these absurdly awesome tools, *no machine ever built* has been proven to exceed the abilities of well-trained human "lie detectors." The simplicity and effectiveness of the BS Barometer program will prove to you that the only equipment you need to bust a liar is right between your ears.

You'll learn to combine three professional disciplines of deception detection—the New Body Language, verbal and auditory tells, and Statement Analysis® (created by U.S. Marshal Mark McClish)—into one integrated, easy-to-use, practical program. *You Can't Lie to Me* will teach you to:

- Use the subtle, effective techniques employed in police stations, federal agencies, and by successful investigative journalists around the world

- Decipher nonverbal language clearly and accurately, without giving the other person a clue to what you're doing

- Identify the most common temperamental and emotional responses of chronic liars and manipulators

- Master dozens of fascinating tricks and insider secrets of interrogation

- Detect the subtle "leaked" clues and problem hot spots in people's inconsistent behavior—*before* they have a chance to wreak havoc

- Hear the vocal variance, or see the microexpression fluctuation, that can help you identify "angry liars"

- Spot deception in all media—phone calls, emails, Facebook posts, handwritten notes, even drawings

- Learn from cautionary tales of savvy people who were deceived as well as inspiring, instructive stories of my students who reclaimed their power from people who had taken advantage of them

We won't just study liars—we're going for the truth!—so we'll look for honest people, too, and spot the differences between liars and honest people. Once you've powered up your own internal BS Barometer, you will:

- Outsmart disloyal coworkers—and beat them to the plum promotions

- Start relationships on the right foot—and avoid wasted months of worry, confusion, and pain

- Deposit at least ten more free hours a week in your personal life account

- Negotiate purchases with confidence—and avoid being "taken" for hundreds or thousands of dollars

- Stop feeling paranoid—by automatically surrounding yourself with honest people

- Protect your aging loved ones—and their nest eggs—from unscrupulous con artists disguised as trusted caregivers

- Hire loyal workers whose experience and résumés you can trust

- Stop lying to *yourself*—and live a happier, more productive, more passionate life

You Can't Lie to Me will change the way you look at job applicants, coworkers, dates, salespeople, money managers, siblings, friends, lovers—anyone from whom you deserve the *truth*.

GeTTING WITH THe PROGRAM

In the pages of this book, you're about to learn a ton of information, much of which you'll later want to access in high-stress situations. Now, you might be one of those people who can absorb massive amounts of information with no problems—lucky for you! I'm not one of those people. That's why I've created a TCB approach—a Taking Care of Business program to help *everyone* beef up their own internal BS Barometers more easily by learning the five-step process of detecting deception:

Step 1: Gathering Intel. You'll learn to get a fast snapshot of a person's normal behavior, sometimes in less than two minutes.

Step 2: The Wiretap. You'll learn to apply Statement Analysis to quickly spot words and phrases that suggest there's something more to the story.

Step 3: The Stakeout. You'll learn to study their nonverbal facial faux pas, and you'll notice any suspicious variations from this baseline of behavior.

Step 4: The Full Body Surveillance. You'll learn to decode the entire body's micromovements, which will set up your BS Barometer for success with all the information you'll need throughout your upcoming interrogation.

Step 5: The Interrogation. You'll learn to synthesize all the data you've collected, zeroing in with a few carefully crafted questions that get you *right* to the truth.

Throughout the book, while I teach you this process, I also present a series of exercises to help prepare your brain and increase your retention of the information as you go. The more you can absorb now, the faster you can put this information to work in your day-to-day life, and the sooner you enjoy more trusting, secure, loving connections.

Ultimately, you'll turn this process back on yourself and consider the most important question: How have I been lying to myself?

And, more important: How will I use my newfound power to draw more truth to my life?

This unique ability to protect yourself and the people you love, as well as to surround yourself with more honest people, will change into something far more powerful over the long haul.

You'll stand straighter and face life with more courage.

You'll feel stronger and more confident in uncertain situations.

You'll develop richer, more trusting, more authentic relationships.

You'll transform how the world sees *you.*

Take your best shot, world, you'll say. *You can't lie to me.*

PART 1

POWERING UP YOUR BS BAROMETER

THE TRUTH ABOUT LYING

All power corrupts, and absolute
power corrupts absolutely.
—**LORD ACTON**

IMAGINE THIS SCENARIO: you are about to become a mother for the first time. You and your husband prepare your home as you eagerly await your little baby boy's arrival. Just a month before you're due to bring him home, you are selected by your peers to win the highest award possible for a person in your profession. In a very public celebration, your entire industry's community surrounds you to exuberantly shower you with praise and accolades.

During the most touching moment of your acceptance speech, you turn to your husband and declare, "This is all worthwhile because of you—you showed me what love is."

After a whirlwind celebration party and lots of congratulations from all your friends and colleagues, you ride home with your man, holding hands and smothering him with kisses. After you make love in the bed you've shared for five years, you drift off to sleep, blissfully aware that you have had, hands down, the best day of your life.

And that's where the dream ends.

You wake up to find out that, while you've been slaving away on extended business trips, your husband has been having unprotected sex with a professional stripper—and she's decided she needs to tell the whole world about it.

You may not be Sandra Bullock. But you could imagine what Jesse James's betrayal felt like—the ultimate sucker punch to the gut.

We've *all* experienced a sucker punch at some point—and if not quite at this level of evil, still hurtful. Whether it was when your best friend stole your date for the junior prom or your closest colleague stole your idea at work, you've experienced that crushing moment when the realization of the lie and the betrayal sets in.

As painful as that was—how many *other* lies are you missing? Would spotting them help you avoid other drama or heartache down the road?

In this chapter, we take a look at some of the biggest truths and misconceptions about lying, and how both can lead even the most committed truth finder astray. We also take a quiz to see how strong your own BS Barometer is right now, before you start the *You Can't Lie to Me* program. Ultimately, once you've completed the program, you'll instinctively surround yourself with more genuine, authentic, honest people from the very first time you meet them.

FIGHT THE POWERS THAT BE

No, you may not be Sandra Bullock—but you can feel her pain. And you may also not be Kyra Sedgwick or Kevin Bacon—but you can imagine how it would feel if your entire life savings, money that you and your wife had worked together to save for more than twenty years, was stolen in one fell swoop by one horrible man.

When Bernie Madoff was caught in December 2008, he had a shocking $65 billion in fictitious investments in 4,900 client accounts. All told, his investors—including charitable foundations, Holocaust survivors, hundreds of unlucky widows and pensioners—lost about $20 billion of real principal.[1]

Twenty *billion* dollars of their hard-earned money. Mysteriously *gone*.

For years, this infamous Con King was somehow able to look hundreds of people in the eye without arousing suspicion, all the while knowing he was robbing them blind. Madoff stuffed his pockets and walked away whistling, without ever seeming to feel a twinge of guilt.

Who could do such a thing? How could anyone who treated others that way live with himself?

And how do these people get away with it?

Now, not just your average scumbag can pull off a scam on the order of $20 billion and bilk thousands of "marks." But plenty of people can easily lie without thinking twice.

In fact, every person lies. Even you. Probably more than you realize.

Sometimes we lie to protect other people's feelings. *(Delicious fruit cake, Aunt Suzie!)* But sometimes we lie solely to benefit ourselves. And, because you're an honest human being, you probably feel guilty about this kind of lying—which is what makes you so bad at it.

But chronic liars don't have that problem. Nor do sociopaths. Nor, it turns out, does your boss. Now, you may like your boss (or even be the boss), and this might have you shaking your head and saying, "Nope, not true." But bear with me a bit. . . .

You've heard the expression "Power corrupts," right? Well, you might be surprised to learn how *easy* it is for people in powerful positions to lie straight to our faces. Not just those folks who sit in the corner office: anyone who holds power over you—whether his grip is on your paycheck, your mortgage rate, or your heart—can lie to you as easily as tell you the truth.[2]

Here's how it works: when people in power lie, they focus on rewards more than on costs—they spend much more energy thinking about what they stand to *gain* than what they stand to lose.[3] This laser focus on rewards protects them from anxiety and makes it easier for them to lie through their teeth. (And Bernie Madoff sure had a lot of "reward" going on, didn't he?)

People in power enjoy the exact opposite neurobiological effects that people who lie do.[4]

- Lying raises the toxic stress hormone cortisol; power lowers it.

- Lying increases negative emotions; power increases positive emotions.

- Lying hampers your ability to think; power enhances your cognitive function.

All the physical and mental benefits that come with power can make unscrupulous people in power almost immune to guilt, allowing them to lie all the time without ever getting caught. Recently, a group of Columbia University researchers showed just how strong and immediate this "power" effect can be.

In a study of forty-seven women, researchers put some participants into windowed offices. These women were told they were "leaders" who controlled the salaries of their "subordinates" (who were stuck in dark and dreary cubicles in the hallway).[5] Then the researchers planted $100 bills in nearby piles of books and left. Computers on the workers' desks randomly asked half the leaders and half the subordinates to "steal" the money—and then asked them to lie about it.

The researchers tested the subjects' cognitive functioning and took saliva samples to measure stress hormones. They also studied videotapes of their interviews to assess their behavior. They were looking for tiny shoulder shrugs and increased rate of speech, two of the more likely signs of deception.

Another group of the researchers, with no clue as to whether the women were liars or leaders or neither, asked all the participants some basic questions. They wanted to establish what the subjects looked like when they were being truthful—to define their "baseline" behavior.

Then, with all the baseline data in place, the researchers asked all the leaders and subordinates whether or not they stole the money. As they answered, the researchers retested them and analyzed the data.

The results were shocking.

The low-power subordinates who lied showed *all* the expected signs of deception: slower thinking, higher stress hormones, shoulder shrugs, and faster speech.

The high-power liars?

Nothing. *Nada.* Not even a twitch.

The researchers found *not one detectable physical difference* between the higher-power liars and their truthful peers.

After the fact, the liars were asked how they felt about lying. Did they feel bad or guilty at all? But only the liars in lower power positions felt bad. The powerful liars did not feel a thing.

Power acted like conscience Teflon—not only did their dominant position allow them to lie more easily and persuasively, they felt no guilt or remorse.

Researchers are finding more and more evidence that power appears to give its owners a physical and cognitive high that completely blunts and disguises any negative effects of lying. Lie, get away with it, get what you want, and don't feel a thing—hmm, I could see how that might get slightly addictive!

This power imbalance might affect honesty even in situations that are meant to be positive and protective:

- A teacher with a student

- A doctor with a patient

- A parent with a child

Texas Judge William Adams was caught on a webcam beating his then-sixteen-year-old disabled daughter. After she was caught downloading a pirated videogame on the computer, Adams lost it, barged into her bedroom, and began to beat her with a belt. The mom also joined in on the horrific beating. Both parents yelled obscenities at the young girl for twenty minutes while she pleaded with them to stop. That young girl's name is Hilary Adams, and seven years later, now twenty-three, she spoke out about the video. When he was confronted about the video, Judge Adams said, "It looks a lot worse than it actually was." As a judge, it seems that Adams felt too powerful and above everyone else to feel any remorse or regret, let alone worry about what would happen to him.

Now, let's put this lying superpower into an even more morally questionable context:

- A terrorist who believes his glory waits on "the other side"

- A politician who knows a few well-placed words will win voters' trust (and elections)

- An accomplished pickup artist who only wants one thing—and knows exactly what to say to get it

- A "harmless" old neighbor—who also happens to be a pedophile

But powerful people aren't the only liars—sad sacks lie, too.

WHY WOULD I LIE TO YOU?

We've seen that liars with power are addicted to potential rewards. They're only thinking of what they have to gain.

Now, on the flip side—for those without the power—what motivates them to lie?

Simple. *What they have to lose.*

Lying, cheating, stealing, and manipulating are definitely not the sole purview of the powerful. Desperate times call for desperate measures, and, for many, these are quite desperate times. When your job or your relationship is on the line, lying can sometimes feel like a necessary act of survival.

Researchers believe that deception started this way, as a result of natural selection. You might call it "survival of the fibbers." About twelve million years ago, primates started deceiving each other in order to survive during times of dwindling resources. (There can be only one top banana!)

Twelve million years is a long time for fibbers to learn their trade. But for just as long, we've been trying to spot them. Why haven't we learned how to by now? How do we still get duped by another's deceit?

THE BS BAROMETER READING

AT THE SENATE HEARING

Authoritative palm-down gestures are often used to tell a child to stop from running in the street or to back down a subordinate. Essentially, this move is used to tell us to stop, back down, or calm down. When you calmly confront the potential liars in your life and they bring out this "talk to the hand" motion, ask yourself, "Why does she not want me to get to the bottom of this situation?" "What is he holding back?" "What is she hiding?"

On February 10, 2006, former Federal Emergency Management Agency (FEMA) director Michael Brown displays an aggressive palm-down hand gesture while testifying before a Senate Homeland Security and Government Affairs Committee hearing in Washington, D.C., on his mishandling of rescue operations during and after Hurricane Katrina. **(Getty Images)**

BS Barometer Reading: Full of It

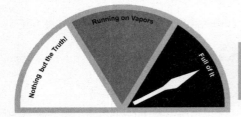

KEY

Total BS: Full of It

Partial BS: Running on Vapors

BS-Free: Nothing but the Truth!

Thanks to *TIME* magazine, the world quickly learned more about Michael Brown's disastrous decisions—and shockingly, his reaction to Katrina was just one of them. *TIME*'s exposé revealed that Brown had falsified his professional credentials for years. Among other bold lies were claims to have overseen emergency services for an entire town when he was, in fact, just an intern, and to have been chosen "Outstanding Political Science Professor" at a law school he merely attended as a student—thus beginning an illustrious career of untruths.

You might be surprised to learn, we used to be much better at spotting the "bad guys/gals" than we are now. Our brains have incredibly sensitive danger detection systems, way better than anything modern science has yet to cook up. We have very powerful instincts, but because of our concern with being polite or not wanting to be "paranoid," we've taught ourselves to disregard them.

Then there are the times when we *think* we know what signs to look for, but we don't have the right tools to detect deception—which can make us even *worse* lie detectors than pie-eyed Pollyannas.

For example, have you watched a television show about body language and then thought you now know what signs to look for in a liar? Think again. In a Michigan State University study of 108 people who watched the recent Fox television show *Lie to Me,* a different drama, or no program at all, those who'd watched *Lie to Me* were no better at detecting deception than the other participants—but they were more likely to accuse *honest* people of being liars. The researchers concluded that watching the show *Lie to Me* increased people's suspicion of each other and simultaneously *reduced* their ability to detect lies.[6]

Kind of the opposite of what we're going for, right?

Old Body Language practitioners may be partially to blame for these false accusations. As I discussed in my first book, *You Say More Than You Think,* the Old Body Language is a set of stock definitions of specific body movements that certain experts believe telegraph people's internal thoughts. The Old Body Language practitioners seem to think spotting a wrist flick here and an eye blink there can turn you into a mind reader.

Nothing could be further from the truth.

THE TOP TEN MYTHS ABOUT LYING

People tell lies for a million personal reasons, but most boil down to one of three essential needs:

1. To protect ourselves

2. To avoid tension and conflict

3. To minimize hurt feelings[7]

Now, if everyone lies, and we all know we all lie, why is it still not easy to detect these lies? Again, there are many individual reasons, but they, too, boil down to three realities:

1. Many of us don't *want* to know the truth (denial is a powerful de-motivator).

2. Many people are really good at covering up lies.

3. Most of us are looking for the wrong deception signals.[8]

We are able to investigate and identify *probable* lies with a fairly good degree of accuracy if we know the correct process to follow. But before we learn how to use the BS Barometer, we have to understand what may have kept us from seeing the lies all these years. As the study just mentioned and others have shown, false belief makes a person an even worse judge of deception than the person who believes *everyone* is telling the truth. What are some other common myths standing between us and the truth?

The Myth: Liars have shifty eyes. Let's say you notice your boyfriend is answering a rather pointed question with "shifty eyes." His eyes dart side to side and up and down every time you ask if his ex, Stephanie, was at the bar last night. Instantly you think, "Busted!"

The Reality: Not so fast. You wouldn't believe how many people think "shifty eyes" or a lack of eye contact definitively means someone is a liar. But it's simply not true. A recent metastudy revealed that twenty-three out of twenty-four peer-reviewed studies found that eye behavior is not a positive indicator of deception. No scientific evidence proves "shifty eyes" are a sign of deception.[9] [10]

The biggest thing we must look for in a person's eye movement is a *deviation* from normal behavior. Is your boyfriend nervous by nature, a person who struggles to focus on a conversation? Is he a rapid and frequent blinker, or does he wear contacts? Do his eyes generally have a "shifty" quality? All of these could play in to his ability to control his roaming eyes.

The Myth: Liars never make eye contact. (Alternate: Liars make constant eye contact.) A few of you may believe that liars make excellent eye contact during a fib, in an overt effort to lend credibility to their story. Most of you think that a liar will make little to no eye contact during the deed, a subconscious reaction to his own guilt that happens beyond his control and serves as a dead giveaway. (Indeed, when psychologists at Texas Christian University surveyed more than

2,500 adults in sixty-three countries, more than 70 percent believed liars make less eye contact than truthful people.)[11]

The Reality: You're both correct! And, of course, you're both wrong. Again, what's important is that we watch patiently for a *change* in a person's normal behavior. The minute your aggressive, believes-in-consistent-eye-contact girlfriend starts staring at the floor or avoiding your loving gaze, you know you have a problem and you need to act fast.

The Myth: Liars giggle like schoolgirls. Many of us believe that a poorly stifled giggle is a neon sign pointing to a big fat lie. However, we all know people who laugh when nervous, anxious, or scared. (My husband does this, and it drives me crazy—and *not* in a good way.)

In 2009, CNN producers Tracey Jordan and Ilana Rosenbluth invited me to be a deception detection expert contributor to their shows *In Session* and *Headline News (HLN)*. In one heartbreaking trial highlighted on *In Session,* "Celia" had been molested and raped at gunpoint by her father starting when she was fourteen years old. Fast-forward many years, and she and her brother had both been accused of killing their parents.

On the stand, Celia was questioned about her ordeal. While talking about her father and the horrific torture she endured, she *giggled and laughed* almost the whole way through.

Was she lying about the abuse? Did she delight in having murdered her parents?

The Reality: No way. Celia just had never told the story out loud before. In Celia's case, finally giving a voice to this trauma in a crowded courtroom was not only embarrassing, it caused the old pain to rise to the surface.

Moments after giggling, she glanced down and burst into tears. Big, huge face-flooding tears. Massive sadness simply erupted from this poor girl.

In cases like this, laughter can be a defense mechanism, used to suppress the harshness of the underlying emotion. Although seemingly inappropriate at the time, her laughter did not signal deception but rather the mortification of reliving those moments.

Sure, liars will often laugh—but not everyone who laughs is a liar.

The Myth: Liars scratch their noses. You may not realize this, but your nose contains erectile tissue. What this means is that just like our "naughty bits," the tissue in your nose can become sensitive when stimulated, and it may tingle or itch during times of stress. Such as when you're lying through your teeth.

The Reality: Rather than a foolproof sign of deception, this nose itch reaction can reflect a basic human response to acute stress, the "fight-or-flight" reaction. When you're in a situation in which you're threatened (anything from a dark alley mugging to being caught with your hand in the cookie jar), your blood rushes to your extremities, giving your legs energy to run and your arms energy to fight. When you do neither, the blood will rush back to your head, engorging those nasal tissues and making your nose itch like crazy.

Yet, touching our noses is apparently a common pastime. Dr. Mehmet Oz has said that men and women consciously touch their noses an average of five times per hour. So, does this mean we are all lying, all the time?

Nope. It simply means that we like to touch our noses! We must couple this "sign" with many others, compare it to a baseline, and then start asking the powerful questions way before we can reach our conclusion.

The Myth: Liars tend to squirm and jiggle. Ever notice people who are constantly in motion? They're rubbing their necks, picking at their cuticles, bouncing their legs, wringing their hands. Drives you nuts—and it can make you think something's up.

The Reality: Most likely, nothing's up. These "pacifier" actions do just that: they pacify and soothe unconscious nervous energy. Self-touch gestures such as these often have perfectly logical explanations. Lots of men will play with their cuticles or rub their fingers through their hair just before a big date—it's called "preening," and it has its roots in evolutionary biology, to prepare males to woo potential mates. My sister will twirl her hair when she is working on a big problem—it helps with her concentration. My former communications director, Jake, used to bounce his leg about a hundred times a minute. Mr. Fidgety, that one. Drove me bananas!

My point is, these individuals are simply exhibiting behaviors that fit with their baselines. But when people are being deceptive, these pacifiers can become "manipulators," designed to visually distract from the lie as well as to decrease liars' stress and to buy themselves some time. They increase in frequency and severity, often becoming extremely noticeable. Many liars believe their self-touch gestures convey believability and a humble nature, the nonverbal equivalent of "Shucks, ma'am, I have no idea what you're talking about!" But don't be fooled—when pacifier use jumps up during tense conversations, it's a sign of increased stress.

The Myth: Liars overwhelm you with details. (Alternate: Liars give too few details.) Some experts say you should be wary of too many minute recollections—that it means the person has overprepared for questioning in an attempt to appear as believable as possible. Others say that too few details indicate a lie because the teller simply hasn't thought his or her story through.

The Reality: Again, the truth is somewhere in the middle. We need to spot deviations. Maybe your friend is telling you a long-winded story, with lots of minute details (what color her nail polish is or what she ate for dinner). But when she comes to the part about running into your boyfriend at a club, the details stop. Maybe your boyfriend Bobby is usually just as long winded, but when asked about last Saturday night, he gets abnormally tight lipped. These deviations from normal behavior could be indicative of deceit.

A story should contain the same level of detail beginning to end, and a normally descriptive person should not suddenly hesitate to share. Additionally, watch out when people try to overwhelm you with unimportant facts, even if they're *very* interesting. So, if your Bobby wants to discuss the burger he ordered for dinner (Oooh, it had ketchup *and* mustard!? You don't say!) rather than the three hours he spent at the club, you know something's up.

The Myth: Liars pause often when telling lies. Sometimes people seize upon any slight pause with a dramatic accusation: "Aha! What's wrong—cat got your tongue?" If you are attuned to someone and trying to figure out if she's lying, any stumble is likely to feel like a lie.

The Reality: In any natural conversation, you'll experience pauses. When they make sense and reflect a moment taken for additional thought, it is unlikely deception is involved. When pauses (or a lack thereof) come at strange moments in a conversation, it should send up red flags!

Let's say I ask you about what you wore to work last Wednesday. If you answer immediately, "My red dress and black stilettos," I may rightfully wonder how you could answer so quickly. I, for one, have to look in the mirror to remember what I wore today, so the likelihood that I can remember last week's attire is zero. So for me, a reply that quick would be an instant red flag.

On the other hand, maybe last Wednesday was your birthday, and you were meeting your friends for dinner and drinks straight from work, so had come to the office dressed to the nines. Not only are you *not* lying to me, you had a very valid reason for recalling that "unimportant" outfit so easily.

The Myth: Liars are not very definitive. "I swear to God!" We've all said it. And some of us really mean it. Really!

The Reality: And then there are those who say it before absolutely everything they say.

"I swear to God, if it gets any hotter, I'm moving back to Boston."

"I swear to God, if she doesn't call back in five minutes, I'm breaking it off."

"I swear to God, if the Yankees don't win the series, I'm going to kill myself."

Okay, so if you're from Boston, that last one probably isn't you. But, this is where gathering baseline information becomes crucial. If this particular saying isn't part of the person's normal vernacular, pay attention when it comes out of her mouth during times of stress. Liars use this type of definitive phrase to try and *convince* us of their innocence, while a truth teller simply tries to *convey* his message. Unlike the liar, the truth teller doesn't have to work that hard at being honest.

The Myth: Liars repeat the question. Clearing of the throat. Turning the body. Repeating the question within the answer. All are examples of stalling techniques. Quite common in everyday conversation, but they are also signals highly indicative of deception.

The Reality: Many believe that, when being questioned, if someone repeats the question before giving their answer, it is a clear-cut case of deception. Example:

YOU: "Bobby, did you see Angela at the club Saturday night?"

BOBBY: "Did I see Angela at the club? I don't think so."

You should pay very close attention to what Bobby says after this repetition, but also bear in mind that there could be a simple explanation for his apparent hearing problem.

Perhaps you and Bobby are from different parts of the country and have different speech tones, rates, and patterns. If you are from Boston, like me, you probably speak quickly and without the benefit of certain consonants (who needs those *R*'s anyway?). If Bobby is from Louisiana, poor Bobby might be having trouble keeping up with your thick northeast accent. (True story: once when I was testifying in a courtroom, the judge had me repeat all of my answers twice. He and the court reporter were having a hard time keeping up because I spoke so fast.)

Men and women also have varying rates of speech. Women typically speak faster than men, who, from a strictly auditory perspective, have trouble keeping pace. Is it also possible that your companion has a legitimate hearing impediment, the background noise is getting in the way, or maybe you are mumbling just a touch?

Any of these extenuating circumstances might make someone repeat your question before answering. They may be honest souls who only want to answer truthfully. Or, they may be big fat liars stalling for time.

The Myth: Liars skip words. In chapter 5, when we cover something called Statement Analysis in great detail, you will learn that studies have shown that liars occasionally drop the pronouns in their speech. This happens because the liar realizes he is being untruthful, and knowing the difference between wrong and right, he tries to verbally distance himself from the action he is accused of. Example:

YOU: "How was your guys' night, Bobby?"

BOBBY: "Eh. Just went to dinner. Burger was good. Then to the club. Then back home."

The Reality: This absence of details—and even pronouns—is nothing alarming, if Bobby is typically pretty tight lipped. However, if Bobby usually shares enthusiastic stories of his escapades, with no detail left undivulged, then you may have an issue here as he departs from his norm. But many intelligent, communicative people, for one reason or another, do not include many pronouns in their speech. In the world of texting and instant messaging, pronouns have been rendered all but useless, for example. And the prior examples illustrate that pronouns are simply not required components for truthful sentence construction.

As you can see, determining myth from fact is not as straightforward as many people would have you believe. These myths cloud our perception, impede our judgment, and prevent us from seeing the truth. When we can recognize our very common stereotypes and judgment errors[12] and correct them, we strengthen our own internal BS Barometers.

THE LYIN' TAMER LITMUS TEST

Many people believe they can spot liars—but their BS Barometers are not quite as strong as they think they are. In the following quiz, we test your knowledge of nonverbal observation skills, Statement Analysis, and basic questioning techniques as well as general lie detection facts. Check the key that follows to see how advanced your lie detection skills are already. No matter where you stand at the start, you won't believe what a skilled BS Barometer operator you'll be when you finish this program.

1. **As you approach your daughter, she smells suspiciously like smoke. For the third time this week. If you were to ask if she had been smoking, which of the following responses is most likely to be truthful?**

   a. "No, Mom. Why do you ask?"

   b. "I WOULD NEVER SMOKE A CIGARETTE!"

   c. "It's gross, isn't it? The restaurant where we ate had people smoking outside. I had to walk right through it when I was leaving."

   d. "Never!"

2. **Uh-oh. The office rumor mill is at it again. And you suspect your close friend and colleague of being the culprit. Which response is a big, fat sign you are highly likely being *lied* to?**

   a. "Why would you ever accuse me of that?? No, I did not spread gossip about you to our boss."

   b. "Yeah, I was at Starbucks with our boss yesterday afternoon, we discussed the staff, but not you."

   c. "No, I wasn't talking badly about you to the boss—why are you asking me that? I thought we were friends?!" [tearing up]

   d. "[giggle] What?! Geez . . . don't be so insecure, it's not attractive on you. [giggle, giggle] After work, I took the metro to Chinatown; I bought a copy of *Cosmo*; grabbed a quick bite to eat; then I went to a movie by myself." [giggle]

3. **Research shows that approximately 95 percent of liars will do this when lying:**

   a. Shrug their shoulders

   b. Ask you to repeat the question

   c. Avert their gaze or look down

   d. Have a change in their pitch or tone of voice

4. **Uh-oh! You've been put on the spot! When asked a question you aren't prepared to answer, which of the following scenarios could be looked at as a "hiding hot spot" (or, as we'll learn about later, "backsliding")?**

   a. Sitting behind a desk during questioning

   b. Fidgeting with a pen while answering

   c. Suddenly bringing your hand to your neck dimple when responding

   d. Sitting with your hands folded during the entire conversation

5. **Which of the following is typically a sign of a *truthful* person? He:**

   a. Gives you more eye contact than usual

   b. Starts and stops his sentence, then changes direction and says something else

   c. Raises his tone of voice

   d. Has his arms on his hips, and they remain there when he responds

6. **Your boss is holding something back. You're petrified it means layoffs, no holiday bonuses, or the replacement of candy in the break room with granola bars. (Yuck.) Which of the following behaviors by your boss might indicate this?**

   a. Crossing her legs or wrapping her ankle around the foot of the chair

   b. Her normal amount of eye contact

   c. Wearing a turtleneck to work that day

   d. Using your name several times during the conversation

7. **You think your boyfriend might be cheating (that jerk!). When you ask him point blank, which of the following is a huge red flag?**

   a. He takes your hand into his.

   b. He starts blinking rather rapidly.

    c. He starts swaying in his chair.

    d. His voice remains steady and calm.

8. **Which one of the following behaviors is a huge clue indicating *deception?***

    a. The person remains calm and confident during questioning.

    b. She or he confidently looks you in the eye and gives you the answer you want to hear.

    c. She answers your question before you even finish asking it.

    d. His arms are crossed—and they stay that way.

9. **You suspect your child is lying. Perhaps it's something minor like he ate a Twinkie before dinner, or something more serious like drugs. What is the ideal statement for times like these?**

    a. "How many times do I have to tell you? Don't lie to me!"

    b. "Listen, you simply can't behave this way. Here is why . . ."

    c. "Don't ever do that again!"

    d. "I did that once in my day too, so I understand. However, I would prefer you be honest with me. We can get through anything."

10. **You just caught your significant other in a bald-faced lie. The first, and most important, step to take after you detect deception is:**

    a. Tell him you're not stupid and you *know* he's a liar.

    b. Simply state, "Don't lie to me because I know the truth already."

    c. Ask if there is a reason why she is uncomfortable answering your question.

    d. Blame it on intuition! Tell him you have a funny feeling and you just don't trust him right now.

11. **Is your son's new wife simply shy or a lying Lolita? To separate fact from fiction, first get her baseline. There are three times you need to be paying close attention. They are:**

    a. When she says, "I swear to God," crosses her ankles, and scratches her nose

    b. When she walks into the room, finishes her first answer only, and raises her voice

c. When she first hears the question, processes your question, and gives you her answer

d. When she clears her throat, does a shoulder shrug, and drops a pronoun when answering your question

12. **Research on deception illustrates that men and women lie with equal frequency. However, they lie about different topics. What are the top lies for each?**

a. Women lie to make themselves feel good; men lie to protect people's feelings.

b. Women lie to make other people feel good; men lie to make themselves look better.

c. Women lie to get something they want; men lie to avoid embarrassment.

d. Women lie to avoid embarrassment; men lie to get something they want.

13. **Finish this sentence: The average person tells one lie per . . .**

a. Sixteen conversations

b. Two conversations

c. Eight conversations

d. Four conversations

14. **In a weeklong study of thirty college students, deception researchers determined the most preferred method of lying:**

a. Phone

b. Using web-based messaging

c. Via email

d. Face-to-face

Answer Key

1. a	5. d	9. d	13. d
2. d	6. a	10. c	14. a
3. d	7. b	11. c	
4. c	8. c	12. c	

Your BS Barometer—What We Were Testing

Questions 1-2: Here we are looking at your ability to detect deception using Statement Analysis, or an individual's word selections.

Questions 3-8: This section helps you get an idea of your ability to detect deception by observing nonverbal communication cues.

Questions 9-11: These questions test your ability to prepare for and confront the master manipulators in your life—with tact and good judgment.

Questions 12-14: Here we test your general knowledge of the science behind detecting deception.

What Your Score Says About You!

12-14 Correct: You may be a natural!

You have the ability to notice indicators of deception, tells many of us let blow right over our heads. Your strong intuition gives you an advantage in life, and your observations allow you to sometimes spot deceptive behavior. Use *You Can't Lie to Me* to take your skills even further, help you successfully climb the corporate ladder, negotiate from a place of strength, and enjoy open, honest communication in your personal relationships. With more practice, you'll be able to quickly weed out those who don't play by the rules.

Your mantra: "Very few of us are what we seem." (Agatha Christie)

Your success killer: Always looking for the bad in people. Sure, right now it seems like nothing gets by you—but don't let this power go to your head. You might find yourself hung up on microscopic details and missing the big picture. Additionally, you may read people so quickly and correctly that you intimidate many who cross your path.

6-11 Correct: Stuck in the middle with YOU!

Have you ever studied hard for a test and still ended up with a "C"? You'd like to be better than the status quo, right? This isn't a huge problem, but it does leave room for improvement. You have an average-strength BS Barometer; you recognize the more obvious signs of deceit, but the small details tend to get by you. Sure, you can spot the obvious, which allows you to maintain fairly healthy relationships, but you still have work to do.

Wouldn't you love to get a perfect score next time? Let's ramp up that deception detector so we can eliminate liars and negativity from your life!

Your mantra: "In order to be a realist you must believe in miracles." (Henry Christopher Bailey)

Your success killer: Failing to recognize that your BS Barometer needs to be strengthened! At times, you may think your personal interactions are top notch—but you have a hard time seeing that you may have been lied to. I promise, it will shock you how much easier daily life will become the instant you are aware of the practices deceitful people try to pull.

0–5: Well . . . bless your heart.

We have a problem—a big one. You're not picking up on *any* signs of deception, big or small! Chances are, you are being duped by someone *right now!* We have to put a stop to it, *today!*

I am all for having empathy and compassion, which I guarantee you have in spades. There is nothing wrong with searching for the good in others. We should all probably do this more often. But it's a problem when your kindness to others hurts you. Simply put, if it leads to being taken advantage of, your niceness has become a liability.

Listen, you don't want to be that person everyone tries to get one over on! Aren't you tired of dating cheaters, cat sitting (yet again) for your ungrateful neighbors, or sitting idly by while you watch others garner praise and promotions at the office? It's time to tune your sense of observation up a notch and lead a new and improved life. The good news is that simply by reading and heeding my advice, you will significantly improve your score.

Your mantra: "If you're playing a poker game and you look around the table and can't tell who the sucker is, it's you." (Paul Newman)

Your success killer: Chances are good you are being duped on a daily basis. Big or small, lies are swirling around you all the time! I know it's truly tough to swallow, so choose to get excited that within the next hour alone, you'll know more about separating fact from fiction than all of your friends and family members combined! Tomorrow is a new day, just like Scarlett says. One in which you have Yours Truly in your back pocket, driving with you to success. Focus on the positive, your desire to improve!

7-SECOND FIX

THE FLIRTY FRIEND

(Baron Thrower II)

(Baron Thrower II)

The Problem: You have all-star good looks and a very happy marriage. However, you want your best friend to stop overly flirting with your husband.

The Fix: Take action fast with a smile, raise your hands, and playfully and powerfully say, "Listen to me, [pause] convince yourself fast [pause] to [pause] keep your hands off my husband, [pause] Angelina Jolie." This knockout approach will instantly get everyone else at the party to keep a close eye on your (supposed) BFF.

The Result: You can relax.

THE SECRETS WILL BE YOURS

Regardless of how you scored on the Lyin' Tamer Litmus Test, your ability to detect deception will only grow stronger after you learn all the secrets in this book—but it's crucial that you follow all the steps in order to succeed. Once you are properly trained, you won't have to rely on anyone else to protect you from the two-legged scorpions in your life—you'll spot them a mile away.

Let's turn to chapter 2 and take a look at how the BS Barometer process works, step by step. Detecting a lie isn't brain surgery—but it does take keen observation, top-notch listening skills, and a firm focus on the people you encounter. You'll get amazing results, I promise.

FRee InsTant RePLaY!

Your body is an amazing learning machine. It is designed to learn, adapt, and improve the tools, concepts, and ideas that you are exposed to faster than the most powerful computer ever created. From the time you were a baby, when you learned to roll over, crawl, and walk, your brain has been storing and reconfiguring information so that you can have access to it in an instant.

Readers of this book have the opportunity to allow their subconscious to automatically reinforce all the lessons they'll learn in this book. Visit www.you cantlietome.com and click the "Instant Replay" box. Find the link to the chapter you just read, turn your speakers on, and relax. Each instant replay will help solidify the concepts you just read. Whether this is the first time you used these new ideas, or it is the first time you are made aware of them, the faster and more intensely you reinforce the concept, the more use your mind and body will make of this information.

Detecting Deception Power Team member Oscar Rodriguez created these instant replays as a gift to you. (For more on the Detecting Deception Power Team, see page 46.) A hypnotist based in the Washington, D.C., area, Oscar's focus is on identifying what holds you back and overcoming its power over you. Whether it is a bad habit or a crippling fear, hypnosis is a powerful tool he uses to guide his clients to achieve their goals and destroy old limitations.

JUST RememBeR ...

- *People in power find it easy to lie, mainly out of greed.* And people without power find it difficult to lie but sometimes will do it out of desperation. When our BS Barometer starts to go off, we have to stay vigilant and ask ourselves, "What's in it for them?" And then, before we confront them, ask, "What's at stake for me?"

- *Your best tool is empathy.* The ability to put yourself in someone else's shoes will go a long way toward figuring out motives—and intentions.

- *No lie detection is foolproof.* You cannot see one or two body language signals or hear just a snippet of conversation and know whether someone is lying. And if you do believe you can, you're even worse at detecting deception than those who don't.

HOW THE BS BAROMETER PROCESS WORKS

Acting is like lying. The art of lying well.
I'm paid to tell elaborate lies.

—MEL GIBSON

W E'VE TALKED ABOUT THE myths surrounding lying and how they prevent us from finding the truth. But before we explore the five steps and
dozens of secret techniques of the BS Barometer that you'll use to *really*
bust those liars, I want to repeat—and have you absorb—one potentially uncomfortable fact:

You are a liar, too.

Everyone lies. Everyone. Almost every form of life on Earth has a means
of camouflaging itself, most often for self-preservation. The chameleon. The
worm. The house cat. The grasshopper. Even *plants* lie, for goodness sake.[1]

We cannot escape lying, nor would we ever want to, really. Society would
cease to function. Marriages would fall apart. Fights would break out in grocery
store checkout lines. Santa Claus would fall from the sky. You get the picture.
There *are* good reasons to lie to people.

Given that we tend to love Santa and peaceful shopping excursions, we will
never aim to bust *all* lies. What we need instead is a way to quickly sort the

healthy lies from the toxic ones. Learning to spot the clear-cut differences takes a period of focused training, which I outline in this chapter. Training your BS Barometer will give you the power to safely remove toxic liars from your life and guarantee better relationships with honest people—people (such as yourself!) who, yes, occasionally tell healthy lies.

Let's start by looking at where lying begins—for all of us.

A LIAR IS BORN

Lying is always about helping us get what we want. Sometimes what we want is selfish; sometimes it's kind. In fact, every lie can be placed along a continuum, from antisocial to prosocial.[2]

← **Antisocial ——— Selfish ——— Self-Enhancement ——— Prosocial** →

Antisocial	Selfish	Self-Enhancement	Prosocial
Lies that hurt others without helping you	Lies that hurt others to help you	Lies that help you without hurting others	Lies that help others

But as varied as our motivations may be, every point on this continuum contains a basic unavoidable fact of human nature: we want what we want, when we want it.

Lying is a totally normal part of human development. Learning to lie comes hand in hand with the moment when babies realize they are individuals. ("Other people might not believe the same things I believe? Huh! Maybe they want things I *don't* want!") Lying is such a natural part of our innate character that when kids are found to *not* be able to lie, it's typically because they suffer from a challenging disorder like autism.[3]

We don't grow out of the desire to "get what we want, when we want it" as we get older. Yet despite how useful lying is in this regard, brain imaging has proven that the baseline default for humans is to tell the truth. When we kick this default to the curb, we demand that our brains suppress our natural truth response—which is not comfortable for most people, especially the novice fibber. And the more we tell the truth, the harder and harder it is for us to lie.

Thankfully, most of us are raised with lots of practice in telling the truth. We're also raised in ways that breed a conscience. We learn to feel guilty when we lie, especially when we're trending toward the "selfish" (let alone the "antisocial")

Can Babies Lie?

Lest we think of our little cherubs as angels who would never dream of lying to us, think again! Our babies learn to lie before they learn to walk!

Age[4]	What It Looks Like
6–7 months	Fake laughter, either to be part of the group or in an attempt to get others to join in
8–9 months	Waits until Mom or Dad leaves the room to do something naughty—pull on the curtains, chew on a plant, and so on
	Uses "fake" cries to get attention, sometimes even stopping to listen for a response
9–11 months	Pretends to be deaf or not to hear a parent call to them because they're either doing something forbidden or want to keep playing without being disturbed—but the giveaway is that they will hold their bodies perfectly still, listening for the reaction to their "deafness" (kind of like teenagers)
11 months	Stares at parent or caregiver while doing something naughty, trying to "fake out" the caregiver
	Asks for a bottle but then pretends not to want it—and repeats this cycle a couple of times, with a glimmer in his eye
	Holds out arms for a hug, but then runs away when it is offered—repeats this endlessly
16 months	Turns her back and blocks a forbidden object or activity from your view
18 months	Hides behind the couch to do a forbidden thing
	Pretends to be hurt when others get hurt
2½ years	"I didn't want it anyway."
	"I don't care—I've been playing with it all day."
	"She did it! Not me!"
	"Daddy lets me."

Much as they have the ability to lie very early, little kids also have tremendous trust. Three-year-olds will believe anything told to them, particularly if the lie comes from a person standing right in front of them.[5] They also have a strong sense of altruism and an eagerness to share. At as young as fifteen

(continued)

months, babies will start to spontaneously help other people and notice an unequal distribution of food. The more surprised they are about the inequity of distribution of crackers and milk, for example, the more willing they are to share a toy they love—call it a sense of Baby Justice.[6]

These traits—honesty, empathy, a sense of justice and fair play—are as much a part of all of us as our propensity for lying. And with your strengthened BS Barometer, you'll be able to spot those kindred spirits much more quickly—so you can choose to share your crackers and milk with people who *really* care about their fellow human beings—especially *you!*

end of the lying spectrum. That guilt, combined with our brain's honesty default setting, can make us "leak" our feelings in all kinds of obvious ways: our posture, level of eye contact, uneven vocal tone, even our word choices.

Bottom line: for most of us, lying is hard work! Consider everything that's going on when you work up a lie:

- You have to have a clear memory and make a good plan in order to keep your story straight.

- You have to have a sense of what seems believable and what would instantly peg you as a liar.

- You have to watch the person as you're telling the story, to see if they believe you, without letting on that you're afraid they won't.

- You have to absorb their reactions and continually readjust your arguments based on any new incoming information from them.[7]

The combination of these factors increases what's known as your "cognitive load," the full range of demands on your brain at any one given time. (When you consider all this hard mental work, it's no wonder that certain parts of chronic liars' brains are actually bigger than honest folks'!)

But let's say, after years of your little boy nearly wetting his pants every time he tried to lie to you about stealing cookies, your now six-foot-tall teen tells you a new lie—about *not* sneaking booze. ("No way, Mom! I don't drink!")

And this time, you *don't* spot it. He gets away with it.

He's relieved—but also kind of intrigued. So, being the boundary pushers that most teens are, he lobs another one past you. Even better, this time the lie yields serious benefits: an extra 20 bucks from Mom's wallet or a secret rendez-vous with his girlfriend after lights out.

The lie is attempted again. And again it succeeds.

And so begins a very slippery transition from harmless lying into the smooth ease of toxic deception.

OUR PARENTS TEACH US TO LIE

Imagine telling your kids that the kooky and evil Dr. Doofenshmirtz in Disney's hit cartoon *Phineas and Ferb* is real. And when an airplane flies by in the sky, you look up and cry out, "Look. I bet that's one of Dr. Doofenshmirtz's crazy contraptions!" Sounds ridiculous right? Maybe not as crazy as you might think.

One study asked 127 parents their philosophy on lying. While 78 percent confessed they'd lied to their kids at one time or another, 74 percent had taught their kids that lying was wrong and would not be tolerated. Huh? Is that an instance of "Do as I say, not as I do," or what?

Parents lie to their kids *all* the time—about the Tooth Fairy, Santa Claus, Easter Bunny, even about the presence of candy in the cupboard. The real trick is, how do you break it to them gently when you've been lying to them for years?

When it's time to come clean, Jackson Peyton, Psy.D., a child psychologist from Washington, D.C., recommends a step-down approach for the Big Reveal: If your kid asks you, "Is Santa real?" turn it back on him: "What do you think?" If he responds, "I think he's real," he's not ready to give up the treasured childhood myth quite yet. Just continue on happily for a few more years.

But if he says, "I don't think he's real," rather than pull the rug completely out from under him at once ("Oh, thank God, now we don't have to hide your presents anymore!"), let him down easy: "Santa may not be a flesh-and-blood person, but for many he's a living symbol for the spirit of the season and the joy of giving." Or, "I think of Santa as the spirit of Christmas."

Bottom line: cut yourself some slack and stop feeling guilty about lying to your kids about Santa. After all—he's a nice introduction to the concept of the "white lies" we sometimes tell to help other people.

A LIAR IS MADE

When you look closely at it, becoming a good liar is a learned skill—one that, when mastered, has a nearly unlimited potential to be positively reinforced. The more often you attempt to lie and are successful at it, the more easily your brain and your body can adapt to the stress that comes with doing it, and the more convincing you are to the outside world. You continue to get what you want, when you want it. And, your lying becomes more automatic.[8]

This is where chronic liars end up. They have gotten so good at it that you never see them sweat. They seem so committed to their own lies it's almost as if they've convinced themselves it's the truth. When it comes to deception, practice really does make perfect.

Think about the con man in the movie *Catch Me If You Can*. Frank William Abagnale Jr. got so good at lying he was able to rake in millions of dollars while impersonating a Pan Am pilot, a Georgia doctor, and a Louisiana lawyer—all before he turned nineteen years old! He had mastered the stress of lying—in fact, the high of getting away with it became his drug, his addiction. His body never let on to any observers that he was the slightest bit nervous.

If you had been relying solely on the nonverbal "tells" of liars—a.k.a., the Old Body Language—to try and bust him, I hate to tell you, my friend, but that guy would've forged thousands of dollars of your checks and been headed to South America before you'd even see a single signal of his deception.

A LIAR IS CAUGHT

The Old Body Language is all about reading a person's stress signals as deception. But anyone looking for a sign of stress in Abagnale would've waved him right through security and into the cockpit because he didn't show any outward signs of stress.

Recent studies are proving again and again how inaccurate—and borderline dangerous—these kinds of presumptions are. Not everyone feels stress about lying, first of all. And even if they do, what does stress look like for them? It's a very individual thing.

That's why we have to do more—much more—than study nonverbal signals to bust liars and master manipulators. (To learn how small a part in lie detecting body language really plays, see the "BS Barometer Formula" on page 48.)

Our deception detection techniques have to become as sophisticated as the liars themselves.

A recent meta-analysis report by the FBI found that the most effective approach to lie detecting is a *combination* of tools. These tools are meant to capture "leakage" (unintentional communication) across multiple channels:

1. Facial expressions

2. Gestures and body language

3. Voice

4. Verbal style

5. Verbal statements[9]

Further, the researchers found that it's not simply this combination of signals but their deviation from the baseline, and how they are combined with each other, that make them an accurate reflection of deception. When these factors are considered in combination with each other—as when you deploy your BS Barometer—the accuracy rate jumps from just about a 50/50 chance (53 percent was the average in a meta-analysis of 206 other studies[10]) to an as-close-to-perfect-as-we'll-ever-get 90 percent.[11]

How about that?

The reason this combination of techniques is so effective is that it takes into account the first clues you have to a person's natural behavior as the starting point, but then it compares that person's behavior and thought process under stress. This approach can highlight inconsistencies, the behavioral and verbal "hot spots" that signal, "Hey, something important is going on here."

But we know that not all liars show those hot spots—these people are just *that good*. And people simply don't all react the same way to the same situations. That's when your BS Barometer really zeroes in for the kill: these interrogation techniques, culled from the secret playbooks of law enforcement agents and officers around the world, up the ante to increase the liar's cognitive load. That extra stress and burden of keeping all the varying strands of information straight is what finally does them in. These techniques blast away all the crutches that were helping the liar keep his wits about him—his every defense is blown.

The BS Barometer process seamlessly integrates the best investigative tools together into a method that's simple for you to use and impossible for the liar

7-SECOND FIX

THE MECHANIC

(Baron Thrower II)

(Baron Thrower II)

The Problem: To keep you and your children safe, it's crucial that you act fast, head to the mechanic, and get your car fixed. However, you don't want to spend all your money to get the job done right—you want a fair price.

At first, you (on the left) are getting aggressive with a palm-down gesture. You're trying to back down the mechanic (on the right) by facing him, but he's firm on the cost of the repairs. You need an effective move that works fast.

The Fix: Take immediate action. Instead of standing opposite or apart from the mechanic, move closer to his side. In less than a second, you are both on the same team. Next, mirror his moves, and increase rapport fast. Try an embedded command: "Work with me [pause] on the price to fix my car and I'll [pause and lower voice] decide now [pause and raise voice] whether to [pause and lower voice] move forward [pause] or not [pause] move forward."

The Result: Surprisingly, when done correctly, these easy-to-master moves will provoke your new mechanic-pal to help you keep more money in *your* pockets—instead of his boss's!

Bonus: Use the word *we*. "Where do we go from here?" "What do we need to do to get it to stop making that sound?" Great salespeople know the influential power of the word *we*.

to escape. You simply take stock of the situation, use tools from each of the five steps, turn up the heat, and before he knows what's happening—*bam!*

Busted.

THE NO-STRESS BS BAROMETER PROCESS

In our fast-paced world, when thousands of pieces of information are flying at us at the same time, we all need ways to reduce our stress. I think of it like the menu at the Cheesecake Factory: it feels like they have millions of entrées, appetizers, side dishes, and desserts—millions of them! Now, I guess the variety must appeal to some people. But when I'm faced with that many choices, I just shut down. I end up ordering the lemon chicken with mashed potatoes and carrots (my husband, Leif, orders the fish tacos) every single time I eat there, because I'm ridiculously overwhelmed with so many options.

I know I'm not alone—researchers have pointed to the ever-increasing amount of choice in our everyday lives as a core reason for anxiety. That's why I've worked so hard to streamline the BS Barometer process. This process takes you from "Huh?" to "Aha!" in just five moves, so you'll never second-guess yourself or make unintentional missteps along the way.

Let's take a quick look at each stage of the process, and how they work together:

Step 1: Gathering Intel

Okay, first things first. You must act fast and establish a baseline for a person's behavior, tone and pitch of voice, and word choices. This involves observing and noting certain nonverbal and verbal signals that are part of his general demeanor as well as his social norms. Perhaps, in the spring and fall, when the pollen is lining the trees and windows (and your pillows), your babysitter gets watery eyes and her nose is itchy—or maybe she's just always been fidgety. Maybe your new boss has had that stutter since toddlerhood and he's always called his car "the auto," his grandmother "Nana," and his mother's purse a "pocketbook." And yes, it's possible that your sizzling hot Match.com date avoids eye contact due to cultural demands—or it's because he's more auditory and he "lends you an ear." Sure, the people in your life may have weird habits (creepy ones even), but those may or may not indicate deception—they may simply be in their blood, part of their essential makeup.

I'll give you tips on how to keep the norming process very low stress, so you get the most accurate reading possible. You'll be studying them from head to toe, while running down a nine-point checklist. You'll size up their norms in mere minutes—but they won't have a clue.

Step 2: The Wiretap

Once we have the baseline sorted out, we drill down to expose the meaning *behind* the words. While body language has been the focus of lie detection for decades, recent research has proven that a detailed analysis of a person's speech may be much more accurate than an observation of nonverbal behavior.[12]

No matter how well formulated and executed a lie is, there will always be verbal indicators of deception lurking in and around the words a liar chooses. You'll learn what these are by asking key questions such as these:

- Is the person talkative and animated (your new BFF)—or flat-out refusing to talk?

- What specific verbal flags is she raising that should make you sit up and pay attention to what comes next?

Using a variety of dependable methods, I'll teach you the verbal discrepancies most often associated with lies: some are very common, but some are super sneaky and accompany whoppers you'd never expect.

Step 3: The Stakeout

Now that you've listened closely to the words, it's time to focus on facial faux pas and microexpressions. Can you spot the lightning-fast changes in facial expression? And do you know what flashes of forehead tension tell you? You're looking for those deviations from the baseline. When the person's expressions and gestures don't match the words coming out of his mouth, those are hot spots. Pay close attention or you might miss them!

Step 4: The Full Body Surveillance

When we focus on the nonverbal deviations from your subject's normal range of behaviors, I'll share many of the secrets of the law enforcement profilers, the most effective tricks and techniques they've used to determine suspects' body language hot spots (which we talked about earlier—the moments when change in a person's behavior betrays their nervousness or emotional leakage). What do shoulder shrugging and leg rubbing tell you? You'll read some common explanations—but I also teach you how and when those explanations don't work or can be misinterpreted. With practice, you'll avoid the Old Body Language mind-reading mistakes and learn what *really* counts.

Step 5: The Interrogation

Now is the time to roll up your sleeves and finish them off. Law enforcement officers, polygraphers, your mom—all are well versed in interrogation techniques that bring home the desired results. What is the proper sequence of an effective "breaking" technique? What's the nervous system got to do with it? You will learn dozens of questions and tricks that ratchet up the liar's cognitive load—the mental demands that give the liar nowhere to run or hide. Hey, if the feds can use these techniques to bring down terrorists and international criminals, surely you can get what you need out of your daughter, sister, or spouse.

POST MORTEM: THE SELF-EXAM

You've completed the interrogation—you have your answer. Maybe you've just been lied to; maybe you suspected an innocent person. In either case, you have resolution. You got the information you needed from your BS Barometer.

Once you're done, you might be tempted to go on with your life and forget it ever happened. But I want you to double down and master this situation—really soak it into your DNA, so you'll make the right decisions more accurately next time.

In this step, you'll do a brief self-exam, to check in and reflect on what transpired. Maybe you finally mastered a technique, and you're jazzed by how effective it was. Maybe you got someone—a person you'd suspected for months, or years—to fess up.

By all means, relish that feeling. You trusted your gut—and you were right. But then . . . what if you weren't?

What if you find that you suspected someone for months, but there was a perfectly innocent explanation for her behavior? What if you believed one thing that kept you in knots for weeks, only to find out you'd totally misinterpreted someone's innocent slip of the tongue? What if it is not the first time this has happened to you—or the second, or even the twentieth?

No better time than right now to give some good thought to why—why are you so suspicious? I give you some very hard questions to ask yourself that can help you get to the bottom of your . . . I don't want to call it paranoia. Let's say, hypervigilance.

But perhaps the most telling outcome of a self-exam is the moment when we realize we're being lied to *a lot*. If you find that you frequently encounter deception, I'll help you answer these important questions:

- What mistakes are you making that are attracting deception?

- Why are cheating partners, lying bosses, and "frenemies" even on your radar? Why are you permitting them to be a part of your story?

- If people are drawn to those most like themselves, what does their poisonous behavior say about you?

This final step of the BS Barometer plan completes the package—once you learn it, you'll have all the tools you need to heal yourself and cure the dishonesty, both from others and from within yourself.

Throughout the book, I share stories of my former students who have used the BS Barometer to make big changes in their lives. In September 2011, I gathered a small group of willing students, whom I dubbed the "Detecting Deception Power Team," for a one-week boot camp in BS Barometer training. Together, the group did an intensive study of the exercises in this book, sharing their own stories with me and with each other along the way. In each chapter, you'll meet one of these brave souls, and his or her inspiring transformational story will help reveal all the ways in which this program has helped that person quickly grow, both in skills and confidence. Reading their stories in their own words is a great time to consider your own story: Have you had some of those same kinds of experiences with lying and manipulation? How do you think this program will help you?

Before You Begin: What Is at Stake?

As we move forward, I urge you to read through the entire program first, one chapter per day, to get a sense of the method and how the stages progress. It will clearly show you why you need to move through *all* the steps. But before you start in on your training, it's important that you understand the most critical part of detecting deception: both parties—both the liar *and* you—*must* have something at stake.

The question isn't just, "What are they trying to get from me?" The more important one to ask is, "Why do I want to know? How will knowing the truth help me?"

Put plainly: "What is at stake for me, right here, right now?"

POWER Team TURNaROUND

Name: Anja Linder

Age: 39

Occupation: International development consultant

(Baron Thrower II)

What was stopping you from spotting master manipulators and liars?

As a consultant, I often work with people I do not know or have not previously worked with. The "stranger factor" can sometimes be a problem—you have to be able to trust that all the people involved will do their part of the work. Generally, I have been lucky, but last year I got burned by a consultant who did not deliver an important assignment, putting my reputation at risk with my clients.

In my childhood and adolescence, some experiences made me suspicious of people's true intentions and feelings. The resulting insecurity has held me back a lot in life. I know my body language gives off unintended signs of weakness or insincerity. I sometimes have trouble trusting people's sincere interest in me as a person, so I developed deceptive or "fake" habits in terms of body language in order to hide the real me and—consciously or subconsciously—be someone who I am not. This "hiding" has always held me back, on a personal as well as a professional level.

How have you changed?

Before I learned to use my BS Barometer, I didn't open my eyes enough, didn't look for the signs and didn't necessarily know what to look for. I thought I was good at spotting liars and relied a lot on my intuition. But that approach failed me in the past, especially in situations where I had some sort of emotional investment. I was clouded by naiveté, insecurity, and a desire that a particular person would be honest.

The tools of deception detection that are most empowering are how to put pressure on people ("Is there any reason why . . . ?" "Really . . . ?"), and the recurring lesson about observing the details and detecting patterns and deviations from norms. I've also learned how difficult it is, and how many

(continued)

observations need to be done, to apply these tools responsibly. I now have the skills to make quick important decisions about working with a specific person or handling job interviews.

If I had taken this course a decade ago, I would have dealt with insecurities and negative thinking that have held me back in my personal and, especially, professional life. It would have been easier for me to create and maintain meaningful relationships; it would have allowed me to approach life with more confidence. But the most important lesson that I learned is about the importance of being myself.

The BS Barometer program helped me to confront life with more faith in my abilities to read people and situations, whether to detect something that might be troubling a friend or to weed out dishonest people from my life. The program taught me a valuable lesson about authenticity, honesty, and openness with those who are close to me. Since taking this program, I am a much better wife, and a better friend.

When people take my classes, they often think that if they learn to spot a nonverbal hot spot or two, they've got it made. They get cocky. And then they get stupid. Their ability to detect deception plummets.

For the BS Barometer to work for you, you have to take it seriously. Here's a look at the breakdown of each factor's importance in getting to the truth:

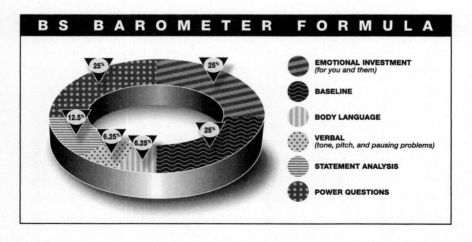

BS BAROMETER FORMULA

- **EMOTIONAL INVESTMENT** *(for you and them)*
- **BASELINE**
- **BODY LANGUAGE**
- **VERBAL** *(tone, pitch, and pausing problems)*
- **STATEMENT ANALYSIS**
- **POWER QUESTIONS**

25% · 25% · 12.5% · 6.25% · 6.25% · 25%

Are you surprised? Many people are. Most are shocked to see how very little import body language can have in the whole. And many are surprised to see that questions play such a large part. But what nearly everyone is stunned to discover is that a full quarter of the whole enchilada is just one piece: the emotional investment. What do we both have to lose?

Multiple studies have shown that liars get away with a lie more easily when they don't have as much to lose. Why? A simple lack of anxiety: they look calmer, so we believe them.

And the inverse is true for us—we're more likely to spot a lie when the outcome means *more* to us. Who cares if the waiter *really* likes the lunch special he's recommending today? But you can bet your bottom that you care whether your nanny has a history of hitting kids.

That's why I want you to always begin the process first with asking yourself, "Why do I care if they are lying? What is at stake?" Imagine the very worst-case scenario for getting this encounter wrong:

> You're a member of the school board. One day a disgruntled husband of a laid-off teacher walks into your meeting with gun in hand, asks all the women to leave, and within minutes, begins shooting. (Which is exactly what happened in a Panama City, Florida, school board meeting on December 15, 2010, when Clay Duke tormented school board members, then shot at a security guard before killing himself; see footage at www.youcantlietome.com. Now ask yourself, how likely is the last man you hired, or the last woman you fired, to snap and go on a murderous rampage?

> Your fifteen-year-old daughter lies about the party being alcohol-free and gets into a car with someone who's been drinking. Now, remember: the leading cause of death for people fifteen to twenty is teenage drunk driving. The average age a boy has his first drink is eleven; a girl, thirteen. And someone dies in an alcohol-related accident every twenty-two minutes. Now, ask yourself: Can you account for your teenager's whereabouts within a twenty-two-minute chunk of time? How would your life be different by falling for one simple little lie?

Sound extreme? Good. These questions get you right in the gut, and they make you take the process seriously—which is the only way it will work. Emotional investment is essential for accurate deception detection; it's the biggest predictor of your success. You must have as much skin in the game as the liar does to have a prayer of catching him or her out.

If you are continually mindful of what's at stake, you'll be fully invested (and, therefore, much more accurate) at the right time—instead of when it's too late. Think of it:

- You'll act quickly and stop your husband's potential affair at the very beginning of those flirty texts and overly casual lunches—*before* the actual cheating and *before* your marriage is irreparable.

- You'll protect your aging parents' well-being *before* they lose their life's savings to a greedy cousin or, even worse, *before* they are neglected for weeks on end at their home in the community for elderly living.

- You'll find out if everything is on the up-and-up *before* you sign the $25,000 check to the charismatic contractor for your new dream kitchen.

- You'll determine if your child's teacher is holding something back *before* you get that last report card.

You'll be successful because you will no longer live in the denial that allows you, and all other innocent people, to be taken advantage of by master manipulators. You will take your safety and security—and that of your loved ones—as seriously as you do your need to be polite and well mannered. You will stay ahead of any future problems brought on by dishonesty, because your entire person will project a quiet confidence that says, "You can't lie to me."

But before we get there, we need to consider what brought us to this place. What are the signs of toxic liars? When will you know it's time to fire up the BS Barometer? Let's turn to chapter 3 to find out.

JUST REMEMBER . . .

- *We are all born liars.* And that's a good thing. The trick is to develop your ability to determine when the lie is good or bad for the world.

- *We are all born lovers, too.* Keep your innate sense of Baby Justice alive— your own empathy will make you a better judge of character.

- *Always ask yourself, "What's at stake?" Why* you want to know is just as important as what you want to know.

WHEN TO USE THE BS BAROMETER

There are a lot of people who lie and get away with it, and that's just a fact.

—DONALD RUMSFELD

WHEN HE WAS TWELVE YEARS OLD, Daniel Kovarbasich saw a cute dog being walked outside of his school. He walked up and petted the dog, and the owner asked if he wanted to take the puppy for a walk. Daniel knew he shouldn't talk to strangers, so he refused. The man shrugged and walked away.

A few days later, the dog and his owner, Duane Hurley, returned. This time he asked Daniel to watch his dog for a second while he ran a quick errand. When he got back, he paid Daniel $30. Pretty great payday for a twelve-year-old!

Daniel went home and told his parents, who were rightfully suspicious. They became even more suspicious when Hurley showed up again, asking if Daniel could do some odd jobs for him. Who was this guy and why was he so interested in their son?

His mom looked up Hurley online, and she was relieved to see he didn't have a record as a sexual offender. Still, his parents kept their guard up—his mom would go with him to Hurley's house, where Daniel would do small odd jobs for money. Eventually, she softened. He seemed so nice! Once when she confessed that she was short cash until payday, Hurley went out and bought her some laundry detergent, a thoughtful move that touched her deeply. She started doing work for him, too, to earn some extra cash. Hurley became like one of the family.

Little did she know that while this was happening, Hurley had begun to slowly isolate her son, creating a web of secrets and shame. After many months of methodical preparation and groundwork, Hurley started to molest Daniel. When Daniel resisted, Hurley threatened to tell his family—and Daniel, too young or innocent or ashamed to know otherwise, blamed himself.

Blinded by shame, Daniel believed he was at fault because he'd let it happen; the abuse continued but, "in exchange," Hurley was now giving him money for sexual favors. This went on for years until one day Daniel talked with Hurley about needing more money to celebrate a coming anniversary with his girlfriend. Hurley asked him how much he needed, and Daniel said, "Eighty bucks." Hurley looked at him and said, "You know this stuff isn't free, right?"

After years of sexual abuse and secrets, blinded by rage and shame, Daniel said he just "snapped"—and he murdered his abuser, smashing him over the head with a giant, deli-size pickle jar and stabbing him fifty-five times.

IS IT TIME FOR a TRUTH CHECK?

Could this tragedy have been avoided? Could Daniel have turned this creep in rather than kill him? Could Daniel's mother have spotted the telltale signs earlier? Yes, yes, and yes. They just lacked the proper awareness and the tools.

Thankfully, most of us will never find ourselves in a situation with such a despicable lowlife. But we may be unlucky enough to fall into another liar's trap. How do we know *when* it's time to check our BS Barometer?

While there are, of course, no surefire signals that someone is lying to you, we can point to a few indicators that might prompt you to dig a bit deeper. Some of these signals are logical—but some may shock you.

You Hear Answers That Seem a Bit "Off"

Recently I returned from visiting one of the most beautiful places on the face of this planet, Scotland. It is a country brimming with Harry Potter–style castles, the world's most haunted underground vaults, and gripping storytellers belting out mysterious folklore and gruesome tales of death and torture. My family took a trip to Edinburgh to celebrate life and my mom's retirement.

Each year I travel more than 100,000 miles to conduct sales training to Fortune 500 companies around the globe, so I've seen my share of airports and their security. But it was my first time in Scotland, and I must admit that I was extremely impressed with Scotland's airport security and the questions their customs agents threw my way. Both when arriving in Glasgow and leaving from Edinburgh, I was interviewed robustly with questions that were intrusive and sometimes laser-specific. Quite frankly, all that prying made me feel safe flying from their airports.

When flying in the States, we're all used to hearing, "Did you pack your own bags today?" and "Has anyone given you anything to hold, carry, or watch for them today?" and "Have you left your luggage unattended today?" We respond with a quick "Yes" or "No."

However, in Scotland travelers are asked, "Tell me about the person who packed your bags." And "Describe the person who asked you to watch their bag or carry something for them today." And "Tell me what happened when you left your luggage out of your sight today." These assumption-based questions imply we have already bent the rules, and they require longer answers, which immediately open up a lengthier dialogue with the airlines, airport security, and Customs.

Since truthful people expect to be believed, my explanation that I'd packed my own bags, had not watched or carried anything for anyone, and that I've kept my bags with me at all times, was said with ease. Because liars need to work, however, at being believed, if I had had something to hide, I might have had an increase in stress and anxiety and oversold my answers and leaked signs of nonverbal deception.

Make sense? Wouldn't you agree that it's much easier to lie when answering the United States's questions with a simple "Yes" or "No" than with a longer explanation when answering an open-ended question?

Thankfully, from this day forward, when you receive an "off" answer, it will be a dead giveaway that you need to break out your BS Barometer. You'll be prepared to act fast. You'll know it's time when:

- Your teen tells you that she's sleeping over Becky's house and you don't know why, but you feel she's not being straight.

- Your boss shrugs, looks over your head, and changes the subject when you ask him about rumored layoffs.

- Your hubby who normally avoids business meals like the plague has had several mysterious "working dinners" with the same client, and when you ask about them, he gets testy.

- Your new employee brushes off your questions about the petty cash reconciliation, saying, "I'll get to it—have the receipts around here somewhere."

Please remember, as a generally trusting person, you are a great gauge of dishonesty. You just have to give yourself permission to listen to those whiffs of suspicion and to investigate further. If it sounds "off," it probably is.

You Feel Off-Balance After Talking with the Person

Practiced liars are uniquely able to distort reality and make us feel like the floor is shifting underneath us, that something odd is afoot, but we just can't put our finger on it. This particular type of manipulation is called "gaslighting."

Gaslighting is a kind of psychological abuse used to keep you feeling off-kilter and at a manipulator's mercy. The term originated from the 1944 movie *Gaslight,* in which an abusive husband steadily messes with his wife's mind, trying to convince her that she's gone crazy—partly by flickering the gaslights while pretending to be a ghost—in order to find some hidden jewels. Eventually she triumphs! But not before being almost convinced of her own insanity.

A gaslighter spouts false information as if it is fact with such conviction that it makes the victim start to question her own recollections of the same incidents or even her own sanity. Gaslighting victims sometimes get to the end of a conversation and experience a sensation of "Hey, wait a second—what just happened?"

Standard gaslighter lines include, "I never said that—stop making things up," "How come you are always accusing me of horrible things?," and "Wow, what is wrong with you? You are so paranoid." These tactics often result in the victims apologizing to the abusers for their own horrible treatment. Gaslighters make you question yourself and reality as they slowly drive you crazy.

Your Gut Tells You There's Something to Fear

In his brilliant book, *The Gift of Fear,* Gavin de Becker talks about zeroing in on our instinct of fear, learning to recognize it, and allowing it to come to the forefront of our conscious awareness. When you're walking by an alley and you have a bad gut feeling, it may not be because you're a Nervous Nelly—it may be because your subconscious picked up on something odd. Maybe you sensed a car left running with no one in it—or a person in a car that's *not* running.

7-SECOND FIX

THE PICKUP ARTIST

(Baron Thrower II)

(Baron Thrower II)

The Problem: You're at a house party and Romeo, sitting off to your side, begins to work his magic by reading your palm. But you're smart, and you know this is a commonly used manipulation tool of pickup artists. If you don't make a quick move, within seconds Romeo will lightly tickle your arm all the way up to your heart—and before you know it you'll be breathing heavy, have goose bumps, and want to be touched some more! Act quickly to get away from this Casanova's hold on you.

The Fix: Use this embedded command: "Whether you [pause] leave me alone or don't [pause] leave me alone, I'm not interested." Maximize your getaway by turning your feet and your belly button away from the palm-reading player and toward safety. I call this move "navel intelligence": we face our belly button in the direction we want to head and toward people we like, admire, and trust.

The Result: Turning away from him may intrigue him more, but after a couple of minutes of the "cold shoulder," he'll be off to find a more gullible victim.

Whatever causes that prickle on the back of your neck, trust it—your brain has likely registered something potentially dangerous that maybe your conscious mind just can't "see" yet.

Researchers talk about this phenomenon as "thin slices"—our brain's ability to notice details much more quickly than our conscious awareness is capable of doing, sometimes in as little as one-twenty-fifth of a second, literally the blink of an eye. In one study, students watched thirty seconds of a silent video clip of a new professor and were able to accurately predict how positive the teacher's global evaluations would be at the end of the semester. What's more fascinating is that when the researchers cut these video clips down to ten seconds, then five seconds, then two seconds, the results were just as accurate.

Another study found that when people's brains were scanned as they looked at pictures of chief executive officers' faces, the faces that caused a greater response in the left amygdala (a site of fear in the brain) were later judged by the subjects to be better leaders. Perhaps we're hard-wired to believe that leaders have to be scary. And how about this? *Those CEOs' companies were later proven to be the most profitable.*[1]

We have access to a wealth of information in these "thin slices" of behavior[2]—we just have to learn to trust ourselves. If you get a gut sense that someone is lying to you, there's a chance you are right. But remember Ronald Reagan's maxim: "Trust, but verify." By all means, trust your gut—then follow it up with the BS Barometer process to know for sure.

You Really, Really Like Someone

You might be surprised by this one! Have you ever felt an instant magical connection with someone—the guy you couldn't wait to hang out with, the new colleague you wanted to take out to lunch the first day? Something about them is like catnip to you—you can't get enough, they're just irresistible.

But when you have the "This person just gets me" feeling right away, be warned. The most effective liars are charismatic and downright charming—but, at their root, they are manipulators. The story about Daniel Kovarbasich, the young teen who killed the man who molested him, provides a textbook illustration of a "groomer" in action. *Grooming* is the deliberate and planned actions that sexual predators use on children with the aim of establishing a connection by either lowering the child's inhibitions or increasing her fear. Once the predator has tricked the child through using one of the Pedophile's Four F's—fantasy, fear, friendship, and force—the predator will touch the child under the guise of being slightly overly friendly to test the waters. His goal is to see how the child may respond to his sexual advances and if the child tells his or her parents.

Groomers are not just pedophiles, however. Your groomer might be the neighbor who, out of nowhere, shovels your walk or brings you fresh brownies "just because." True, she may be the best neighbor in the whole world—or she may be laying the groundwork to have an affair with your husband, sell drugs to your kids, or social-climb over you to get to your prominent boss or best friend.

Sound crazy?

PROFILE OF a PREDaTOR

The child abuse scandal involving former Penn State coach Jerry Sandusky shocked the world, primarily because Sandusky was seen as a pillar of the community. Child predators often disguise themselves behind a guise of civic involvement and commitment to downtrodden children. One self-report study of 377 nonincarcerated pedophiles found they abused an average of 150 children and committed 281 acts *each*. Consider some of the common characteristics of sexual predators:

- Often an adult male
- Usually married
- May seek employment or volunteer with programs involving children of the age of his preference
- Photographs his victims and collects child pornography
- May give narcotics to victims to lower inhibitions
- Intelligent; recognizes his crime but rationalizes it by emphasizing the "good" he does in the child's life
- Often was a child molestation victim and seeks out children of the same age he was when he was abused
- Often a respected community member ("pillar of the community")
- May seek out single mothers with sole aim of gaining access to their children

Oprah once did an entire show on groomers. She talked about Daniel Kovarbasich's tragic case, just as I had on TruTV. Dr. Michael Welner, the psychologist who testified at Daniel's trial, appeared on Oprah's show and identified six stages of grooming. While this process appears often in cases of child molestation, grooming can happen in any situation when one person attempts to manipulate and use another person. As you read about the process, think about how this might apply to areas of your own life.

Stage 1. The master manipulator identifies his victim—usually someone vulnerable, needy, or underconfident in some way. He makes contact in a very low-stress, unsuspicious way.

Stage 2. The master manipulator slowly gets to know as much as possible about the victim (and any responsible parties nearby, like parents or guardians)—what he wants and needs, what he likes most, his fears and weaknesses.

Stage 3. The master manipulator starts to become "everything" in that person's life—he's the "great guy!" who is always around, doing favors, making wishes come true: paying for soccer camp, buying new clothes, always picking up the check at dinner.

Stage 4. The master manipulator starts to isolate the victim—weekends away, time with "just us," heavy-duty conversations ("You're the only one who understands me," "We're in this together").

Stage 5. The master manipulator creates situations that allow the door to the desired goal to open. Welner talks about pedophiles taking advantage of kids' curiosity and tapping into their burgeoning sexuality to make them "part of the secret." Or a sneaky coworker might share some confidential information that could help you but would also implicate both of you if revealed.

Stage 6. The master manipulator now takes freely—whether sex or money or ideas—using shame and threats to reveal secrets as the means to keep the victim quiet. The victim believes the lies and thinks the humiliation of going public will cost him even more friendships—so he keeps quiet.

Now, not all charmers are manipulators. (For instance, I'm pretty damn charming! It's not my fault! I have my mom's personality!) So how can you keep your guard up but not become paranoid that every nice person you know is a raving lunatic?

Here's how: follow the money. Take a cold hard look at potential motives. Instead of saying, "Wow, he's so charming!," make it your first instinct to ask, "*Why* is this person trying to charm me?"

CHUNK IT DOWN / CHUNK IT UP

When people groom us, they study us and figure out our needs and beliefs and devise ways to make themselves useful, sometimes almost irresistible to us. This same process might be used for innocent ends—a potential suitor is trying to make himself as appealing as possible, or a networker is trying to get a business

THE BS BAROMETER READING

AT THE FILM SCREENING

During the promotion of the movie *Mr. and Mrs. Smith,* Brad Pitt was still officially Mr. Jennifer Aniston. Enter Hollywood sex goddess Angelina Jolie and we have a whole new ball game. Study this picture from the 2005 premiere. Is there any indication that they've been playing house?

BS Barometer Reading: Full of It

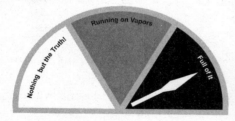

Angelina Jolie and Brad Pitt at the Paris Hotel in Las Vegas, Nevada, March 17, 2005. **(Gregg DeGuire/WireImage)**

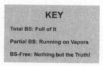

KEY

Total BS: Full of It

Partial BS: Running on Vapors

BS-Free: Nothing but the Truth!

The photograph shows us a few things that point to a level of intimacy uncharacteristic for two individuals *not* engaged in a romantic relationship.

Hot Spot 1. Do you see the dramatic angular distance between Angelina Jolie and Brad Pitt's shoulders and upper body? These two normally friendly and flirty actors are usually much more openly playful with their co-stars, so this shoulder distancing is a deviation in both their "norms." This simply indicates that there might be more to the story here.

Hot Spot 2. Now, what do you notice about their feet? The stances are mirroring each other, at least on the ground. In the arena of detecting deception, we have a shorthand for this type of incongruent behavior: "Convince versus Convey." Liars try to "convince" us of something, whereas truthful people simply "convey" information.　*(continued)*

By distancing themselves so markedly from one another, perhaps they were trying their darnedest to convince us nothing was going on. And sure enough, despite an endless stream of tabloid photos and nonstop speculation, the "sly" superstars did not confirm they were a couple until January 2006. At which point Angie was several months pregnant with Brad's baby. (Hmmm, I think they were together a bit before January—don't you?!)

Hot Spot 3. The most definitive Statement Analysis "clue" came later, in 2010, when Angelina divulged during an interview that she and Brad loved talking about *Mr. and Mrs. Smith* with their extensive brood. After all, "it was when Mommy and Daddy fell in love." Pretty sweet, huh? Yeah, until you realize that they had adamantly denied that there was *anything* going on back then. Whoops. Guess you let the cat out of the bag there!

connection. But some groomers take this process to an extreme, and their aims can be very dangerous.

Finding a charismatic groomer's motives can sometimes be tricky, because she's so darn charming! How could anyone that nice be up to no good? Your best defense is always to start with the question: What does this person want? One trick I learned when I became a certified NLP Life Coach was to "chunk" people's motives.

Chunking Down

Chunking down is a way of breaking down big goals (items, ideas, or thoughts) into smaller steps, of breaking bigger actions into smaller *hows*. The essential "chunking down" question is, "What smaller steps lead to the bigger action or goal?"

For example, let's say you told me you wanted to have another baby.

I'd say, "Great—why?"

Well, because I always wanted a boy. My daughters would be the older sisters, and they'd have a little brother.

"Great—what would that get you?"

Well, that would get me a bigger family. It would get them a little sibling. I want another baby.

"Great. And if you have another baby, and they have a sibling, what does that really get you?"

A loud house? More madness in my life . . . but more love, too.

This questioning is always about that second layer. So in a nutshell: chunking down is all about breaking the main goal into its smaller elements. *I woke up and went to work.* Well, what did you really do? *I rolled out of bed, made it, brushed my teeth, took a shower, then I put the clothes in the hamper.* That's chunking down.

Chunking Up

The essential "chunking up" question is, "Where do these small steps or actions lead?"

Now I'm going to show you how to use this skill to help your all-too-persuadable nice side be more rational, follow the money, and spot groomers who are out for you. Let's look at a sample scenario of their day-to-day behavior and chunk it up to get us to their real motivation.

Why do I always see that woman, my great aunt's neighbor, over at her house? *Because she's spending time with Aunt Susie.* Why? *Because she's her friend.* When did she become her friend? *When she came home from the hospital.* Why was my aunt in the hospital? *Because she had wandered off in the cold and caught pneumonia.* Why did she wander off? *Because she was recently diagnosed with Alzheimer's.* What happens when you're diagnosed with Alzheimer's? *You start to forget and get bad judgment.* So why would her neighbor become her friend at that point? *Because she's kind and concerned?* Is it kindness and concern that makes a person ask about an advance directive? Or is there another possible explanation?

Now, armed with these two tools, make a list of the most charming people in your life. And do a little digging, a little research on them. What are they trying to get from you? Is it benign or potentially harmful?

Chunking is a very versatile life skill that works in both directions—from the big to the small, and the small to the big. You can certainly use chunking to sniff out the bigger motives behind a groomer's charming ways ("chunking up"). Please remember that you can use this same skill to help you figure out how to break down the steps that will lead you to your own best "motives"—you "chunking down" your dreams!

POWER TEAM TURNAROUND

Name: Tim Smith

Age: 33

Occupation: Carpenter / foreman / realtor

(Baron Thrower II)

What was stopping you from spotting master manipulators and liars?

Even though my dad died when I was fourteen, he was a very big part of who I am today. He said, "Always be giving to others," and it stuck! I enjoy helping others, but I can get taken in very easily. I've had bosses lie to shift blame; I've had coworkers cheat on their wives. A good friend swore up and down that he wasn't cheating on his wife anymore, but he was—and it's put a strain in our relationship to this day.

I think I can tell when my five daughters are trying to get away with something. But, overall, I think people can lie to me pretty easily because I want to see and believe in the good in everyone.

How have you changed?

Had I completed this program ten years ago, my life would have been very different. Being able to spot the people who had been lying to me would have made a dramatic difference in the career choices I made, for sure!

Prior to the course, I didn't know what to look for in the body language and verbal statements of a liar. Now I'll be looking for hot spots even before I test the consistency of their stories. Doing Statement Analysis and asking powerful questions were the most valuable lessons for me. I learned to look for things like verb tense in statements to separate fact from fiction. Through using Janine's secrets in this program, I've increased my salary by over 25 percent.

I started using the powerful tool of silence, and I've already applied the things I've learned to keep my daughters in check and spot deception. It will be especially helpful as they get older and I need to spot it in their boyfriends! *(continued)*

I will also be teaching my children how not to be deceived by liars. And I'll apply my new skills when interviewing new employees and vendors or when meeting new clients. Now I'll be able to feel out the clients' true intentions, which will be very useful.

I also learned perfection doesn't happen overnight—practice, practice, practice! In a short time, I have been given the ability to look at life through a different filter. Janine's reminder—that what I say to someone could be the last thing they hear, so I need to make it count—has left a real impression on me.

Practice Like You Play

When I was in high school I played basketball—number 22, that was me! (Go Waltham Hawks!) It was a lot of goofing off and fun until my junior year, when I was placed on the varsity team as a second-string power forward. I had a new coach, Bob Connors. Coach was funny, smart, and creative, but he was serious about teaching us much more than just how to play the game of basketball—he taught us about life. I'll never forget one time at a practice when the ball went out of bounds, and I didn't dive for it—I just jogged over to grab it and throw it back inbounds again. Coach blew the whistle and called me over.

"Janine, why didn't you dive for that ball? You were right there."

I shrugged. "Well, I didn't want to get hurt. The game's tomorrow."

He looked at me dead in the eye, silent. Then he shrugged and turned his head to watch my teammates, who were working on a play. "Well, tomorrow you're on the bench."

"What? Why?" I was pissed.

He turned around and looked at me again. "You've got to practice like you play." He grabbed a ball and held it out. "The ball's there and it's going out of bounds. If you don't dive for it here in practice, you're not going to dive for it during the game. You need to program your muscles and your brain that you *dive* for a ball when you're near it. So you're out of the game tomorrow."

It was a valuable lesson, for sure. And little did I know, it was also a life or death lesson.

Years later, when I was at ATF, we were doing self-defense training called "escape and evade" that teaches you what to do if a person is attacking you with their fists or a gun. We learned that if you target a nerve motor point, the person will drop to the ground as if you broke their neck or their leg. Training makes these moves automatic, so if you're caught in a dangerous situation, you do them almost without thinking. We trained with heavily weighted plastic guns that look and feel real—except you can't pull the trigger.

The key to this training was repetition: we had to practice each of the steps a hundred times, over and over and over, to hard-wire them into our motor neurons. The reason was, when you're in a fight-or-flight situation, and all the blood is rushing out of your organs into your hands and feet, you need to act quickly and switch to autopilot. Let your muscles do the thinking for you. Otherwise, you might freeze up.

Six hours a day, for over a week. Do the movements, get the gun, mimic the hit. Again and again.

Four years after I'd first been trained, I went to get re-certified. They showed us a video of a Customs special agent who had had the same training. He was stationed at the border, with a video camera on his car.

The video shows a man approaching him who pulls a gun. And you see the agent do the whole pattern. He gets the gun—then he hands it right back to the bad guy.

You *need* to practice like you play. In those moments, you're going to do exactly what you did in practice. Exactly.

This incident caused the federal law enforcement agencies to rethink their training methods. Watching the video, it's clear the criminal didn't even realize what had happened. Thankfully, the agent thought quickly and did the whole entire series of movements again and got the gun away.

When you choose to do the exercises in this book, and you do 80 percent of them, that's great—but you may only hit about 80 percent accuracy, too. You've got to practice like you're going to play, with your coworkers, your loved ones, your kids. Although just reading this book is going to be helpful and give you information, really *doing* the program will allow you to soon surround yourself with people you can trust 100 percent of the time. And remember to use all the tools at hand: visit www.youcantlietome.com and look at the video clips; listen to Oscar's Instant Replays; test yourself. Make these exercises work for *you*.

Promise?

Okay, now get to work!

THE BS BaROMETER—On YOUR PHONE!

For those smartphone fanatics out there, be sure to point your phone's camera on the *You Can't Lie to Me* Quick Response (QR) Code (same code on the back of this book's jacket) and get your own exclusive interactive BS Barometer for free!

Scan with RedLaser

EXERCISING YOUR BS BAROMETER: GEARING UP FOR THE PROGRAM

Study in a Room with a View

Would you be surprised to learn that by changing the location of where you read and practice the techniques in my book (or any book), you can improve your ability to retain the information in your long-term memory? In one study, participants were divided into two groups; one studied a list of words in a room with windows and the other group in a room without windows. The results? The group in the room with a view did much better on the test than the students who studied in the room without windows.[3] The researchers believe that varying the context in which you study can strengthen the staying power of the information in your brain because the setting "enriches" the information with more neural connections to each fact. Stow this book in your bag and read it in a variety of settings—and strengthen your BS Barometer from the very first moment you "turn it on."

Improve Your Working Memory—with a Book

Using the following technique will help you enhance your working memory and keep you focused when you're learning new material. It will improve your attention so you can make more accurate observations during your baselining and throughout the five steps of the BS Barometer.

Step 1. Prime your brain by reviewing my "Just Remember" bullets at the end of a chapter prior to reading the chapter.

Step 2. Once you begin reading the chapter, jot down a couple of key questions from the first paragraph in each section to make a mind map. For instance, if the page begins with how Einstein discovered relativity, scribble on a piece of paper the following, "Who is Einstein? Why do I care what he's done? How will knowing this information help me reach my goals in life?"

Psst. Pass It On!

Wouldn't it be great if you could skyrocket your ability to separate fact from fiction while working this program? Here's how you can make it happen. Educators and psychologists have discovered that when we teach new concepts to others, it boosts our own ability to understand, absorb, and recall the information.

Enhance your ability and recall of the BS Barometer techniques by teaching the lessons you've learned to a friend or study partner. Take turns reading the information out loud to each other, or create an mp3 file with a handheld recorder, so you can save it to your iPhone or computer. Research suggests that reading new material out loud significantly improves memory of the material. Use as many different methods as possible to absorb any new, important information—you're creating a broader neural network of memories.

Become More Mindful of Manipulation

One way to help your brain recharge is to zone out intentionally with mindfulness meditation. According to Marsha Lucas, a neuropsychologist in Washington, D.C., two weeks spent with mindfulness exercises will help you integrate your emotional responses and help improve your ability to read other people's body language. Practicing mindfulness has been proven to help increase focus, decrease stress, relieve chronic pain and high blood pressure, and heighten immune system response. People who meditate regularly also may prevent age-related cognitive decline. One study on college students found that twenty minutes of mindfulness meditation daily relieved their symptoms of anxiety in just three days.[4]

Start small—just five minutes a day can make a big difference. Sit in a quiet spot, breathe in and out slowly, and focus on your breath. Notice when you get distracted, and just bring your thoughts back to your breath. That's all it takes! Now you're meditating.

JUST REMEMBER...

- *Thinking "Huh?" does not make you a dummy.* Far from it—it makes you a very smart cookie. You are aware enough to know you may just have been gaslighted.

- *Your gut is a reliable indicator of trouble.* While I'd never say that your gut can tell you someone is lying or not—you need to use the five steps of the BS Barometer for that!—your gut is an exceptional first responder for *potentially* dangerous situations. Always give that remarkable gift of fear of yours your undivided attention.

- *The most charming people can be the most dangerous.* If you're thinking, "Where did this incredible creature come from?," keep your antennae up—there's a good chance you're right to be suspicious. Follow the money.

PART 2

MASTERING THE BS BAROMETER PROCESS

STEP 1:
GATHERING INTEL

Suit the action to the word, the word to the action.
—SHAKESPEARE, *HAMLET*

RECENTLY, a producer from Anderson Cooper's new hit daytime syndicated show invited me back to participate in a segment called "My Husband Is a Murderer and How to Spot a Liar." Just before I walked onstage to reveal how to spot a crooked mechanic, secrets to busting anyone in a lie, and how to use your body language to always appear confident so you send the message "you can't lie to me," I met a kindhearted gentle spirit named Mildred. Had you seen that segment, you would've discovered that Mildred was one of the women who was married to a murderer —although she didn't know it until a couple of ATF special agents knocked on her front door in her Maryland home. "Do you know where your ex-husband John is?," asked the special agent dressed in navy blue with giant yellow letters ATF on the back. "No," she responded. "Well, ma'am, we're here to inform you that your ex-husband John was planning on killing you—next."

In October 2002, the Beltway sniper attacks took place during a three-week period around Washington, D.C. (in various locations throughout the Baltimore-Washington Metropolitan Area and along Interstate 95 in Virginia).

Montgomery County Police Chief Charles Moose with picture of white van officials had been seeking in connection with the sniper attacks. **(Associated Press)**

Ten people were killed and three others critically injured during the terrorizing shooting spree. At the time, I was working for the ATF in Washington, D.C., and lived in northern Virginia, less than four miles from several of the shootings. Buying gasoline was terrifying. Waiting at a bus stop was terrifying. Leaving my house or the confines of ATF headquarters was terrifying.

Yes, Mildred's ex-husband was John Allen Mohammed, one of the D.C. snipers. Mildred was a battered-women survivor and John threatened that if she ever left him with the kids, he would "kill her." Despite her changing her name and moving three thousand miles from their former home, John planned to make good on that promise. When the special agent asked Mildred if she was surprised that her ex was going to be named the D.C. sniper, Mildred was immediately transported back to years earlier, when she and John were watching a

The vehicle used during the D.C. Sniper shootings. **(Associated Press)**

Rambo-type of movie in their West Coast home. Evidentially, John bragged to his then wife about the sniper skills he had gained through being in the military. "I could take a whole community by siege and no one would ever know it was me," John told her. The ATF special agent explained to Mildred that John and his murdering sidekick killed all those innocent people so that when he killed her, it would look like she was a random victim.

Witnesses at one of the shootings said they saw a white male in a white van or box truck leaving the scene—so the manhunt centered almost exclusively on white guys in white vans for several weeks. Anytime I saw a white van on the highway or in my neighborhood, I would act fast and write down the license plate number and get a good look at the person behind the wheel. Police eventually learned, however, that the shooting storm was perpetrated by two men who didn't own or drive a white van or a white box truck. The shootings took place out of the trunk of their blue Chevrolet Caprice. The car was equipped with four doors and a special trunk platform that allowed someone to lie inside and fire a rifle. And they were not even the race that the "eyewitnesses" had described— they were African American.

On October 12, the same day investigators released a wanted poster of a white truck, Washington, D.C., Police Chief Charles H. Ramsey said investigators were also looking for a Chevrolet Caprice that had been seen leaving the fatal shooting of seventy-two-year-old Pascal Charlot. While initially believed to be a separate incident, the Charlot shooting later proved to be done by the D.C. Snipers as well. Montgomery County Police Chief Charles Moose, who led the sniper investigation, was also asked about the car, but he dismissed the question. And, sadly, the Baltimore police found Muhammad and Malvo sleeping in that car one day before a thirteen-year-old boy was fatally wounded and became victim number eight. The car was not searched, and it is believed that they were simply told to move on.

How might this story have changed if the police and the media had remained open to other theories? If they explored all their intel and didn't fall so deeply into the rabbit hole? We'll never know.

Unfortunately, even the pros occasionally sniff out one or two simmering hot spots and turn around and say, "I don't need to do any more digging—this guy is so guilty." But nothing will kill your accuracy—and your relationships!—more quickly than jumping to conclusions.

In this chapter, we dig into the first of the five steps, "gathering intel," or, as I like to call it, "baselining" or "norming." Baselining is a very short stage in which you establish rapport with the "suspect" and then ask a short series of open-ended questions while you study him closely to get a quick take on his normal behavior. While this stage might seem tedious or unglamorous—maybe you're thinking, *Let's get to busting some liars so I can find my genuine "girl next door" or my knight in shining armor!*—baselining is the foundation of the entire BS Barometer. If you don't get a baseline, everything you do from that moment on is simply guesswork.

Baselining is the skill that separates the pros from the wannabes. In my previous book, *You Say More Than You Think,* I talked about how, when I'm baselining, I imagine myself as a host on Mutual of Omaha's *Wild Kingdom:* "We're in the subject's natural habitat, studying his body movements, speech patterns, and behavior under stress, looking for his baseline behavior so we'll recognize the signals when he's about to lie."

Can't you just hear my murmur over the tall grass of the Sahara? Putting it this way might sound silly, but my studying-wildlife-in-its-natural-habitat approach has won me the respect of many influential members of the federal law enforcement community.

In fact, one of the proudest moments of my career happened during a government training session, and at the time I didn't even know it was happening!

A good friend of mine had just been chosen by the State Department to be the American guy who carries the so-called briefcase filled with U.S. secrets over to Germany. While being trained for this highly classified position, the instructor began to slam the world of "body language." He kept saying, "Everything we had taught for years about detecting deception through spotting crossed arms, nose scratches, and mouth touches was all a load of bull." The well-respected instructor tore the entire field of body language analysis to shreds. My friend said he thought of me and cringed a little.

Then, in the middle of his anti–body language tirade, the instructor stopped and said, "Now, if you want to find out the real truth about body language,

ARE YOU a NaTURaL?

Three specific groups of people have been shown to have more accurate lie detection abilities than the average person.

Kids raised in unstable households. When the familial ground shakes beneath them, kids learn to be continually on guard. This perpetual vigilance makes them better at detecting deception than people raised in stable, happy homes.[1] Research from the University of California found that among highly accurate "truth wizards"—people with an almost supernatural ability to detect lies—20 to 30 percent of them had traumatic childhoods involving alcoholic or unstable parents or emotional, physical, or sexual abuse.[2]

Stroke victims. According to the BBC, another group with an extraordinary ability to detect deceit are those who suffer from a specific subcategory of aphasia,[3] a condition often caused by stroke. While the broader condition is defined as an inability to speak, this specific subcategory prevents people from even *understanding* speech. Without other input, they have no choice but to use nonverbal clues. And, indeed, they're likely much more keyed into the microexpressions that flit so quickly across our faces, even when liars try like hell to disguise them.

Secret Service agents. Taught to scan crowds for specific "tells" of abnormal behavior, Secret Service agents develop supercharged pattern recognition skills that help them filter through thousands of individuals to find that *one* person who might have evil intent. And talk about high stakes! Being the last defense between the public and the president comes with some pretty serious consequences if you fail.

---

there's only one book that gets it right—*You Say More Than You Think*, by Janine Driver."

I'm not going to lie—that instructor's praise meant the world to me. And while repeating this moment of tremendous pride here could also be seen as a shameless plug—*damn right!*—it's a great lesson for all of us.

Why did that State Department instructor, a person whose job it is to teach people how to protect our country, respect my book so much? Baselining. While most body language books spend only a few paragraphs on this essential foundation to any deception detection program, I had a whole chapter on it.

As we know from exploring body language myths in the first chapter, there are no 100 percent surefire signs of deception. So if you do not take the time to baseline someone, you will never see the changes in their behavior, and there will be *no way* to use your BS Barometer. It's that simple. Before you can take even the tiniest step forward, you must get a person's baseline, their normal nonverbal and verbal habits, behaviors, and idiosyncrasies. Any "findings" or conclusions made without this core level of knowledge will be based on total fantasy.

GETTING TO FIRST BASE

Everyone has a "norm"—a basic pattern of behavior under normal amounts of stress. Everything from how often they blink to which way they cross their legs (or don't!) to what words they tend to use with their friends. Someone might jiggle his legs under the table or sit still as a statue—either one of these signs has been pegged as a tip-off of deception, but that might honestly just be the way he holds himself. Others might never mention their husband's first name, instead your neighbor might say, "My husband": "My husband said the cutest thing the other day. . . ." "My husband and I are thinking about visiting Denmark in October." Or you might witness the exact opposite; your BFF always updates her Facebook posts by mentioning her husband by name: "Charlie said the funniest thing the other day. . . ." "Charlie and I are thinking of visiting Dublin in October."

And just like everyone has a norm, everyone has a tic, a "tell," a signal that they are uncomfortable. You've seen these in your kids or your husband—that little smirk or quick scowl when you say something they don't like or ask them to do something they don't want to do. Again, even if you see a "tell," keep looking—you won't know what the person is "telling" you until you learn how to ask powerful questions, which is the fifth step. (You'll read about it in chapter 8.)

For now, getting to know her baseline will help you determine three key elements:

1. How does she normally speak and act?

2. What words does she use and how does she act under stress?

3. When do I see the most dramatic differences between those two instances?

Let's see how you can find the baseline for anyone in just minutes.

POWER TEAM TURNAROUND

Name: Caroline Girgis

Age: 41

Occupation: Managing director of a wealth counseling firm

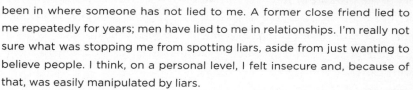

(Baron Thrower II)

What was stopping you from spotting master manipulators and liars?

I don't know of a personal relationship that I have been in where someone has not lied to me. A former close friend lied to me repeatedly for years; men have lied to me in relationships. I'm really not sure what was stopping me from spotting liars, aside from just wanting to believe people. I think, on a personal level, I felt insecure and, because of that, was easily manipulated by liars.

I am accomplished and confident professionally, but I don't feel that way personally. I was looking for that same sense of accomplishment in my personal life for so long, that I think I just saw what I wanted to see, ignoring my gut instincts.

I look back now and can't believe I let someone lie to me repeatedly and I always believed him when he said it wouldn't happen again. Now I can see that I had been giving him permission—he was like a child who pushes the envelope to see what they can get away with. I had been letting plenty of people get away with it!

How have you changed?

The key to deception detection is being acutely observant. Before this program, I was not very observant. Had I learned these skills years ago, I believe I would be in a healthy, honest relationship and not have wasted so much time convincing myself that the deception would change.

The most valuable lesson the program taught me is to get a complete picture of the situation *before* I make any judgment. You have to dig deeper and ask powerful questions to know for sure.

This program opened my eyes to the world and helped me come out of my shell. I'm more observant and am leading a much healthier, more

(continued)

confiident personal life. I listen to my instincts, but I'm not quick to judge! Going forward, I will go into relationships without blinders on. I am too good of a person to allow deception into my life and let it be repeated. The beauty is, now I can be more open, and let sincerity and honesty in.

FIRST THINGS FIRST: ESTABLISH RAPPORT

When my mentor and dear friend, J.J. Newberry, a retired ATF agent and president of the Institute of Analytic Interviewing, once interviewed a possible suspect in a bombing case, even he was surprised at how smoothly he was able to get a confession. When J.J. asked the man, "Joe, what would you say if I told you your fingerprints were on the bomb?" Joe responded, "J.J., you wouldn't because I wore gloves."

True story!

How, in less than an hour, was J.J. able to build up enough comfort, and ultimately trust, with this suspect to get to the truth faster than Chelsea Handler can say vodka? *Rapport.*

Your best chance at getting an unguarded assessment of any person is to establish rapport. Rapport helps you establish a person's comfortable, relaxed baseline so that you can spot lies later on. Being in rapport with someone—having them feel warm and trusting toward you—increases the likelihood that they will be honest with you. People tell more lies in situations where they feel uncomfortable or less connected with others.[4]

Building this rapport convinces people that you are trustworthy and makes them want to help you. One study[5] found that when employees developed rapport with their superiors by mirroring their voice patterns and activity level, and by being conversationally engaging, they received nearly 30 percent better terms during employment negotiation. People in rapport with each other are predisposed to cooperation. Let's learn a few ways to establish the rapport that's essential for gathering an accurate baseline.

Set your intention and your body language will follow suit. More than anything, you want your body language to be open and welcoming. Aim for steady (but not oppressive) eye contact. (In Western cultures, this means maintaining eye contact about 60 percent of the time; in Eastern cultures, much less.) Uncurl your arms or legs—keep all your zones "open" when you're establishing rapport.

Angle your belly button directly toward her, even if the rest of your body is pointed away.

Next, lead with empathy. To detect deception, you *must* learn to think in someone else's shoes. When you are confronting your teen, think like a teen. If your goal is to outwit a sneaky salesman, put yourself into his head. What do you want out of this encounter? You need to see how they view you from their perspective—what are your triggers? What are the things you want to hear? How might he be molding his message to you?

Listen to their stories. Hostage negotiators know that the first thing you do in a high-stress situation is to let the person tell his story. As James Cavanaugh, a retired ATF special agent in charge of Nashville, taught me years ago, it's up to us to determine "What's different today than yesterday?" Yesterday, that guy wasn't standing there pointing a gun—what happened? What pushed him over the edge? Get *him* talking, so he can get everything off his chest, so he can begin to think straight again.

Now, chances are good you're not using your BS Barometer with a guy on a bloodthirsty vendetta. But until the shooter, the liar, or other bad person can get their story heard in a high-stress situation, they won't be able to get back to homeostasis. They need to regain their equilibrium—for you to get to the truth.

Mirror their movements—but very *subtly.* You can mirror someone's posture, but be extremely cautious—obvious mirroring can turn the other person off and backfire in a huge way (that is, the other person might believe that you are not an honest person and clam up right away).

Carefully study the way he holds his arms or the way she is sitting: Are her legs crossed? Are her legs firmly down on the floor, evenly spaced? You can mirror someone's arm or hand movements. If someone is jiggling his feet at a certain speed, you can very subtly shift in your chair at exactly the same rhythm. Matched rhythms literally put you in sync with one another.

Allow transparency to create an atmosphere of trust. In the winter of 2005, during an ATF training workshop in New York City, my good friend and ATF investigator Wayne Bettencourt called my room and inquired, "Hey buddy, I'm going to a party at Carson Kressley's—want to join me?" Being a big fan of *Queer Eye for the Straight Guy* (and of Carson), I jumped at the opportunity. In person, Carson was just as charming, playful, and energetic as he was on *Queer Eye.* After some small talk, Carson asked the small group if we'd like to stroll over to check out the new co-op he had recently purchased—it was in the process of getting remodeled.

While we made our way out of his current building, Carson shared with us a story about how he had barely made it on time for his interview with the board of his new co-op. As he had sprinted out of his current home, his sleeve got stuck on the door and ripped a gaping hole in the shirt.

With no time to run back upstairs and change, Carson simply turned lemons into lemonade. During his interview, Carson said something along the lines of, "My old building was trying to stop me from making it here today. It values me as a tenant and it wants me to stay put!" The board laughed, and Carson was approved to join the co-op.

"Confess" to something that might be slightly embarrassing and see what happens. By appearing more human, you're simultaneously less threatening, which immediately lowers others' guard around you.

The first impression you give determines how much another person will trust you—if you breach that trust at the beginning, you won't be able to get an unbiased baseline because he or she will be guarded and looking at you suspiciously.[6]

Always err on the side of their relaxation. Your mantra for obtaining a baseline is, "How do I lower the stress in this situation?" Because how you confront any situation can change the outcome.

Instead of . . .	Do this . . .
Having the conversation in a formal place (from behind a desk, or in the "principal's office")	Talk in a well-lit, casual setting (on a couch; at the person's house; in a lawn chair in the backyard)
Launching right into the topic at hand	Start off with some small talk
Making it high stakes ("This could cost you your job!"; "Don't lie to me, young lady—or you'll be grounded!")	Keep things very low pressure ("I just want to ask your opinion about something that I'm a little confused about"; "I'm curious what your thoughts are.")
Talking about embarrassing information (grades from high school, SAT scores, salary)	Talk about neutral info (what classes did they take, where did they go to college, what do they like about their job?)
Getting into a heated debate (religion, politics)	Keep things light (weather, summer plans)[7]

ASK OPEN-ENDED QUESTIONS

The real secret behind detecting deception is asking questions. But you're not out to win the Pulitzer in this interview—you just want to get an accurate read on the person. For right now, your primary objective is to get them talking.

A SPY'S GUIDE TO a COVERT BASELINE

It was a humid summer Saturday afternoon in Washington, D.C. He and I ate at a small sandwich shop named Cosi. He sat opposite me—sizing me up, I'm sure. We weren't alone; I brought a couple of instructors from the Body Language Institute to join the meeting. My lunch companion wasn't as tall as I expected. He was about five-foot-seven—maybe five-foot-eight. He had dirty-blond hair, was clean shaven, and had a deep, resonant voice. This handsome stranger had a mysterious charm about him and a warm gentle smile; yet I knew that he knew more about me than my BLI team did—he and I think alike.

This modern-day James Bond is one guy whom, when you meet him, you wish you had a pen and a pad of paper with you to take notes—or, better yet, a tape recorder. His name? Brian O'Shea. Though he never told me exactly where he had worked or where he worked now, it was clear that Brian works in the intelligence field and is an adorable badass. Brian did let me know that he is a private contractor for various individuals, private companies, and (I assume) the government.

Brian could teach anyone how to get everyone to tell you exactly what you want to know. With Brian's permission, here are some of his (and now my) favorite go-to strategies to get a target to open up and talk.

Be convincing. When Brian has to lie while on the job, he'll keep the lie as close to the truth as possible. One time while in a local D.C. bar with a group of young government staff people who didn't know him, a woman asked him, "So, what do you do, Brian?"

"I'm a government contractor." He was close to the truth—and government contracting in the D.C. area is so common that he knew by saying that, it wouldn't pique her interest.

And be boring. When Brian wants to get a target to talk, he will intentionally dumb himself down and make himself as boring as possible. That helps keep the target's guard down. "Most people really don't care what you're saying," explains Brian. "They're just waiting for their turn to tell you about themselves."

If the person asks specifically what he does, he'll break out some really dry technical jargon. "If she says, 'Where do you work?,' I'll say, 'I primarily

(continued)

work in the field of network architecture.'" Note that she had asked which organization he worked for, but he told her what field he works in—adding in some hum-drum details, about service views and unique visitors, to really bore her. "And then soon enough, she can't wait for the conversation to get back to her."

And be funny! Brian recommends humor (which is, of course, my go-to as a former stand-up comedian!). The same woman asked him, "So, do you support an agency or anything?"

"Yeah, I support one of the three-letter agencies. . . ." He paused dramatically while she leaned in close: "the DMV."

And she cracked up. "I can tell you all about it," he said, "but, honestly, you'd fall asleep in your beer. So what do you do?"

And now he was off and running, drawing her out, listening to her story. And they never come back to the topic of him again.

Believe it or not, you can baseline people with just one or two very simple open-ended questions. The trick is to keep it light. Bring yourself into the conversation in a way that disarms the subject and takes the focus off of them.

- "I'm so excited to get home this afternoon—I'm buying my little five-year-old his first bike. Man, that brings back memories, huh? Tell me about the first bike you had as a kid?"

- [Check iPhone or BlackBerry, then put it away] "My best friend from when I was a kid just friended me on Facebook. I couldn't believe it! It has been twenty years since I heard her name. She's one of those friends that I always wondered what happened to them, you know? Tell me about your best friend when you were a kid?"

- [Putting wallet away] "I just remembered I have to go and get my driver's license renewed. I hope I don't have to retake the test. Man, I almost flunked it when I was seventeen! You, too? Tell me about the day you got your driver's license?"

The key to crafting these sentences is to share a bit about yourself, then pose an open-ended question about personal information they'd have no reason to fabricate. Most everyone had a first bike, a first best friend. Everyone remembers getting their driver's license (or in my case, embarrassingly flunking the first test after missing that damn three-point turn). And nothing about those experiences could possibly implicate them in this current situation, so they'll be relieved to have a nonthreatening conversational topic to talk about—the perfect time for you to run through the baseline checklist.

FOLLOW THE BASELINE CHECKLIST

In my first book, I talked about the baseline as essentially the same process laid out by the children's song: head, shoulders, knees, and toes. (You're singing it, aren't you?)

Body language is where I typically start with my baseline, simply because I am extremely visual, and as a body language expert, I'm always putting my visual information channel to the test. In fact, research suggests that our nonverbal baseline is way more stable over time than our verbal one. One study found that medical residents' body language norms remained consistent over two years—through their training and into an entirely new phase of their lives. Contrasted to this were their verbal norms, which fluctuated almost immediately after the start of their program.[8] That makes the body language baseline information extremely helpful because those hot spots—those points of deviation—really stand out once you have a nonverbal baseline. We get into more nitty-gritty details about each communication channel in the subsequent steps, but this list gives you a quick start.

This list works equally well when you encounter strangers for the first time—car salesmen, other parents on the playground, new doctors—or people you've known forever but whom you've just started to suspect of lying.

As you go through this checklist, keep in mind two baseline rules to live by:

1. Keep your communication simple—we often get lost in smoke and mirrors.

2. Sometimes what's *not* there is the most important clue.

Is He a Space Invader?

First you'll determine how "big" the person is—and I'm not talking body mass index. I mean, how much space does this person take up, both while he's stationary and while he's moving? Is he becoming as large or as small as he possibly can be? Is he a big target or a little target?

(*Left*) Vince Vaughn poses on the red carpet with the definition of a wide open stance. **(Getty Images).**
(*Right*) Coldplay at a press conference in Madrid, all with average open stances with their feet, but disappearing stances with their hands! **(Getty Images)**

Wide open stance. Are the person's hand gestures outside the frame of her body, beyond her shoulders? Does he hook his elbow over the back of the chair? Or is he sitting in a figure four? With his leg outstretched in front of him, as if marking his territory?

Average open stance. Are his feet flat on the ground? Are her hands on her desk or doing a steeple? Are his gestures usually around his midsection, hovering near his belly button?

Disappearing stance. Are her ankles crossed? Does she always cross her legs—maybe her hands are folded on her lap? Are his gestures very soft and subtle, happening below the waist?

We are looking for the baseline, so we'll notice when we see a change. He might still be making a hand gesture, but now all of a sudden instead of being up at shoulder height his gestures are really low. Why? What's going on here?

What Is His Face Factor?

We talk about universal emotions and microexpressions more explicitly in step 2, but for now, we're talking broad strokes—let's look at the face as a whole rather than at the individual features or expressions.

Chin position. What's his chin positioning? Does he tend to have his chin pulled in, level headed, or is his chin up? President Barack Obama loves his chin held high in the air. Is her chin pulled down in the Princess Diana pose?

Head position. Is her head generally straight or is it tilted? Tilted right or left? When you tilt your head to your right, you appear more attractive. When you tilt your head to your left, you appear more intelligent. We're looking for a baseline because we want to see the shift. (If I ask you, "Did you cheat on me?," and you suddenly change your head tilt the other way, why the change in tilt?)

Morgan Freeman and Sidney Poitier backstage at the Thirty-Ninth AFI Life Achievement Award honoring Morgan Freeman. Morgan's chin is level, whereas Poitier's is pulled in. **(Getty Images)**

Facial touches. Does he typically touch his face? How often is he touching his face? Does she have an itchy nose? When he's thinking, does he put his hand

Neil Patrick Harris tilts his head ever so slightly to the right. His thumbs are out, pointing to his naughty bits, which tends to be a signal of confidence. **(Eugene Gologursky/WireImage)**

over his mouth? Does she put her hand on her chin? Does she play with her earrings? Does she always push her hair back behind her ears?

How High Is His Fidget Factor?

When a person talks to you, does he turn his belly button toward you or turn it away? Does he cross and uncross his legs, continually changing the direction of the belly button? Is she sitting on her legs, or is she sitting still and facing forward?

Relaxed and calm: This person can sit still for hours on end, the perfect student sitting at a wooden desk.

WHICH CANDLE ARE YOU?

(Baron Thrower II)

These two best friends sharing coffee have completely different baselines. The woman on the left has a wide foot stance, what I've dubbed, "the short fat candle"—if you walk by and bump a table, the short fat candle will stay put and won't be knocked off the table by accident. Her hands are open and relaxed. Her friend on the right has her ankles crossed and pulled dramatically under her chair—she's a "tall skinny candle." (If someone bumps her table, boy, she's going to fly!) Also, both of her hands are holding her coffee up, which creates a block in between her and her friend. What are the baselines for the people in your life?

Slightly fidgety: Every five minutes or so, she changes positioning.

Constantly fidgety: Can't stop moving, his foot is bouncing, his leg or legs are constantly bouncing. He's sitting on his leg, he's facing you, he's facing away—he is full-on twitchy.

What Is His Voice Saying?

Nonverbal vocal changes are among the best indicators of emotion—*if* you have the person's baseline. A bonus: as we get older, our ability to detect deception via other channels dips dramatically—but tonal changes remain one of the factors we can still pick up just as easily as when we're younger.

Our voices are a kind of music, and because differences in vocal tone are almost impossible to describe in words, please take a listen to the clips on my website. Where does your target's baseline fit into this spectrum?

Tonal Differences

- **Soft talker:** You might have to lean in to hear—his voice sounds almost like a whisper. (Example: Michael Jackson)

- **Medium talker:** You can hold a normal conversation without straining to hear his words. (Example: Matt Lauer)

- **Loud talker:** You have the feeling you might have to lean back or get bowled over by her voice. (Example: Suze Orman)

Pitch Differences

- **Low pitch:** Like a deep down bass drum. (Example: Don Imus)

- **Medium pitch:** Average, everyday voice, like the strum of a guitar. (Example: Simon Cowell)

- **High pitch:** Starting to get a little like a piccolo. (Example: Kelly Ripa)

Speed Differences

- **Slow talker:** People from the South tend to speak slower than folks from other regions. Speed is where you can see some interesting combinations with tone and pitch. Speak slowly and quietly, and you might be putting a child to sleep; speak slowly and loudly, and a person might come across as a raging idiot. (Example: Will Ferrell in *Talladega Nights*)

- **Medium talker:** Average speeds of talking will be 150 words per minute. (Example: Ann Curry)

- **Fast talker:** People from the Northeast, especially the D.C., New York, and Boston areas, have incredibly fast speech. (Example: Me!)

What Are His Words Saying?

Statement Analysis is an incredibly useful tool—once you start to notice the little language idiosyncrasies, you'll be amazed at how much information you'll get from them. We cover more about this in steps 2 and 5, but for now, there are a few global questions to ask yourself.

Is she using pronouns? Dropping pronouns is one of the few language faux pas that's been definitively tied to deception—*if* you already have a baseline for the person. Some people never use pronouns; some use them without fault. You have to know which is normal for them. "I got up this morning, I called my mother, took a shower, went and got a bite to eat." The person used two pronouns up front and then dropped them afterward—why? What's happening there? Pay attention to politician's speeches—you'll hear this a lot.

Is she using verbal fillers? Many people clutter their chatter with a lot of *um, ah, er.* This tendency is extremely handy to recognize because once the lies start flowing, you're bound to see a change in the number of these—if people use them normally, they may disappear, but if they don't normally use them, any appearance of verbal clutter is a hot spot.

Is she using absolutes? I always do that, I never do that, I swear to God. I always shut the front door when I leave. Some people say, "I swear to God, I would never do that." Really? Sounds like you're overselling me. But only if it's not their baseline. A lot of people speak this way normally: "I swear to God, when I was at the grocery store, this woman in front of me was the most obnoxious person I'd ever heard in my entire life."

That's it! If you run through this checklist and make these observations, you will have a very serviceable baseline. For now, absorb what you can about their norm. Soon you'll discover how to spot the changes in their baseline, and you'll also find out *why* they might be changing—that comes in later steps.

MASTER CLASS: HOW TO MAKE YOUR BASELINE EVEN MORE ACCURATE

Once you've mastered rapport building and you're becoming more confident in your baselining skills, you can up your game by keeping these helpful suggestions in mind.

Whenever possible, remain calm and in the same position. Whenever you exert yourself, your memory and your powers of observation are greatly hampered.

One study found that when officers had to exert themselves in pursuit of a suspect, their memories of the situation and the suspect were faulty and incomplete. The officers made greater recall errors and had less accurate recollections of visual and auditory information when compared with officers who merely observed (but didn't pursue) the suspects. During the test, 90 percent of the officers who observed remembered at least one detail about a random guy standing off to the side—but 30 percent of the running officers *didn't even notice he was there.*[9] Exertion will hamper your powers of observation.

This is one of the reasons that science is starting to prove that "eyewitness testimony" is a lot less bankable than good old-fashioned evidence. While more than 75,000 witness identifications are made every year, recent science indicates that only one-third of them may be legit. Since its introduction, DNA evidence has overturned hundreds of convictions.[10]

Make inattentive blindness work for you. Inattentive blindness can make you miss some key details—but it can also help you observe a target while he or she is totally oblivious.

Move over Loretta Lynn and Patsy Cline, I'd like to introduce the world to my former BLI student and now friend Marti Miller, who is a ridiculously well-mannered, super-southern private investigator in Memphis (and author of *Kid Raising That Works: Learn Your Child's Body Language and Keep That Critter Safe*). Marti specializes in following people to see whether they are breaking their agreements, whether a prenup, an employment contract, or a nondisclosure agreement. She hires mostly women, because she believes that women can go anywhere—they're seen as less threatening and, as they get older, even as wallpaper.

As maddening as that last sentence is, being "invisible" is a huge asset to anyone getting a baseline. When Marti gets into an elevator with a target, she'll go out of her way to talk to him in her sweet-as-pie southern drawl. "That's a really nice shirt. Gee, it's getting warm out, isn't it?" So when she heads to court, she can positively identify him, because she actually spoke to him.

Most targets won't think anything of it—she's just a little country woman in an elevator. If you're upfront and your body language is open, you're perceived as no threat. But if you remain stealthy and pretend to ignore them, you close up your body language—you're instantly suspect.

Seems counterintuitive, right? But imagine you're in a restaurant and somebody comes walking in with their shoulders rolled over, hands shoved in their pockets. They're looking around from one corner to the other, kind of shifty. These are the same tells of a shoplifter. When we spot this posturing and behavior, it feels dangerous to us. Now imagine that *you* have something to hide, and *you* see somebody in a public setting like that, you would be on high alert, right? Hell yeah; you'll pay close attention to that person's every move. You'll spot that man or woman before you'll see the woman over to the side laughing or the person who walks by and accidentally brushes against you and says, "Oh, excuse me, I'm sorry."

Get a variety of baselines. A baseline will tell you who that person is under one circumstance: being with you. We all wear a variety of hats in our lives, though, and although our personalities and some idiosyncrasies may remain stable, our reactions will differ depending on the audience and the circumstance. What's essential in detecting deception, and what makes the BS Barometer different than straight body language reading, is that you must also get a baseline when your target is with you *and* with people other than you.

Just think of how you would react to an off-color joke in front of your girlfriend, your dad, or your boss's boss—you'd likely have three different reactions. To be really thorough, you need to baseline a person with three other people.

This approach works with anyone: you want to see how a person reacts with more than one person. This same strategy is behind the first interview / second interview approach to applicant screening—every interaction with a new person is another opportunity to learn about the potential new hire. You gather intelligence and build your dossier with every conversation.

Look for patterns. Wait until you have a pattern of activity before you confront the person. You want to be sure he can't just claim it was a one-time deal if it isn't—and your ultimate goal is to keep your relationships healthy, authentic, and strong, right? How long does it take to establish a pattern? You never truly know. The shortest amount of time it ever took Marti to fully bust someone was when a woman cheated on her husband twice in three days. Had she only photographed the wife coming out of her boyfriend's apartment one morning, the wife could have said, "Hey, I went to a party and got too drunk to drive, so I crashed on the couch." But once Marti caught her twice, the wife had nowhere to hide. Busted!

Make it thorough. When possible, it's great to norm someone for several minutes—but it's not always possible. Sometimes, an ATF arson investigator will only have two minutes with potential witnesses to do everything: establish rapport, read them, adjust her own body language (if necessary), *and* get the witnesses' versions of the event. The longer the amount of time you have with someone the better—but it is possible to do this in a short period of time, just a couple of minutes, especially with the BS Barometer tools.

EXERCISING YOUR BS BAROMETER: GATHERING INTEL

The five-step program to strengthen your BS Barometer is designed to be flexible, depending on how much time you have. If you have five hours a day, great! Do everything. But if you're a busy person, look over the following list and see which one of the exercises appeals to you, and do that one. You can customize your complete plan to the time available in your life.

Assessing Your Inattentive Blindness

Throughout the book, you'll find exercises that train your brain to pay close attention. This is one of my favorites—I have given it to thousands of my students and clients.

Consider this bus exercise, as it's the perfect illustration of why we sometimes miss the lie. In repeated testing, 90 percent of elementary students get this brainteaser right. Yet, when I test law enforcement (chiefs, detectives, special agents, lawyers, and so on), fewer than 1 percent do. That gels with what researchers uncovered in a study about empathy and inattentive blindness. Adults and children were both asked to look at a picture and answer the same question. While almost all the students got the answer correct, the adults most often failed. Let's see how you measure up!

The picture is similar to the one used in the study. Notice the A at the bottom left of the picture and the B on the bottom right. Left of the bus is a school; to

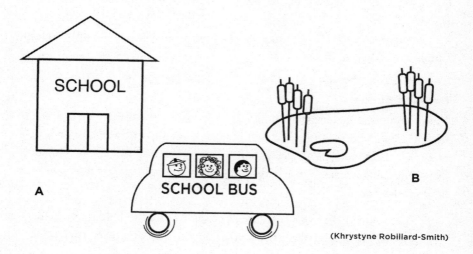

(Khrystyne Robillard-Smith)

the right is a pond in a park. In my keynote presentations, I ask the audience whether this bus is going toward A or B, and why. Inevitably, almost everyone becomes a mind reader:

- It's going away from the school because the kids are smiling.

- The bigger kids are in the back, so it's headed toward the school.

- The bus tips slightly down to the back, because it's heavier. That means the motor's in the front, so it's going away from the school.

- It's heading toward you.

- It must be heading left, otherwise the words would be written backward. (To which I say, "It's a school bus—not an ambulance!")

For twenty minutes, they go on and on. Out of five hundred people, I'm lucky if I get three people who know the answer. What's your guess?

The answer is, the bus is heading toward A, toward the school, because we don't see the door—it's on the opposite side of the bus.

When I showed this to the director of education at the Body Language Institute (BLI), my mom, Lorraine Driver, she replied, "It's going toward A because the door is on the other side. I don't get it. Is there some trick?"

Prior to accepting her position at BLI, Mom retired as a nurse. At Mt. Auburn Hospital in Cambridge, where she worked for decades, she would park her car in an employee lot a half-mile from work and take a hospital shuttle to her building. Just like all the kids knew the correct answer because getting on and off of buses was part of their world, getting on and off a bus was part of my mom's world.

The biggest lesson for us? Put yourself in someone else's shoes and you'll see things you didn't see at first!

Baseline Builder

I have done this exercise with hundreds of people—the results are as close to foolproof as any exercise I've devised. I've even used it with my husband, Leif! Now, you'll obviously never get a chance to use this exact exercise on your subject—but doing it teaches you, with your own eyes, just how stark deviations can be from their norm.

1. Stand directly in front of another person. Ask him to hold up his arms, shoulder height, toward you. You're going to look at how he stands and

where he holds his arms: Does one wrist turn in? Does one hand go higher than the other? Is his thumb inside his fist or is it outside? Is one hand closer to you or farther away? This is all about paying attention to details. Once you learn how to do this as a habit, it will help you get a quick baseline.

2. Take a coin and ask him to put it in one of his hands without showing you which one. You'll guess which one it's in, and then he will reveal it. As it's being revealed, you're going to look for subtle signs—is he quickly glancing at either hand? Based on your first impression of the way he held out his arms, has something changed? Is one hand further out than the other? That person might hold the coin closer to his body or thrust it away—you don't know which—but the key is, there has been a change in behavior.

When I did this exercise with Leif, every time he held his hands out, he unconsciously tilted his head toward the side with the quarter. I figured this out by comparing it to his baseline, which was his head in a central, neutral position. The final time, he held his head up straight, and the hand I guessed was empty when he opened up his palm. It wasn't until several months later that he confessed that the final time, he had stuck the quarter in his back pocket. Dope!

Are You Ready to See the Doctor Now?

Visit www.youtube.com and search "Derren Brown Change Blindness" (www .youcantlietome.com). Watch this five-minute video and find out just how often we don't see what is right in front of our eyes. What tricks can you glean from watching this YouTube clip? Now put your own observation skills to the test:

- Describe what the last person you saw was wearing, without looking at him or her again. What shirt does she have on? What pants is he wearing? Describe his belt or her accessories.

- Ask yourself how many people in your office have blue eyes. How many have brown eyes?

- Recall the tallest person in your office. How about the shortest? Can you remember who prefers to stand with hands in their pants pockets or with arms crossed?

Were you surprised by how difficult this exercise was? Our brains conserve energy by discarding "meaningless" information—but you never know when you might need to call upon this info.

When you interact with the people in your life, what goes on inside your head? Are you having an internal dialogue? What's your brain saying? How can you focus and pay more attention to the person standing right in front of you?

These regular mental workouts will help strengthen your observational muscles and train you to start paying better attention to small details in your environment.

For fun, ask your husband what color your eyes, your children's, or his mother's eyes are. . . . His answer might shock you!

Try It On

A study of forty-eight men and women published in the *Journal of Experimental Psychology*[11] found that the people who could best identify which camera angles corresponded with the position of LEGO figurines within a display—in other words, those who could imagine themselves in the position of the little dolls—were also the most socially adept. We know that empathy is a key skill in detecting deception; this study shows that the people who have the best spatial awareness are also the most empathetic; they literally have the ability to think from another person's perspective.

To help develop this sense of "perspective-taking," complete this exercise. Go to a pool, a mall, or another public place (a park, a bar, a restaurant). Taking one person at a time, study their place in the pool and imagine yourself looking at the world through their eyes—physically. If her right shoulder rolls forward, roll your right shoulder forward. If he has his chin tilted slightly higher than everyone else, get your tilt on. If she is biting her lip while looking to the ground to her left, do the same, Chief. Physically become as much like them as possible. What does the physical space around her look like, from her position, right now? What has caught his eye? What's his breathing rate like? How do you feel being in her posture, stance, and facial expressions?

A Penny for Your Thoughts

We have held pennies in our hands so many times. We leave them all over the place, suck them up in the vacuum cleaner, dig for them at the bottom of a purse. We *know* pennies. Or do we?

I decided to do this test from Dr. Richard Wiseman, author of *Quirk-*

ology, during a January 2011 seminar with the Federal Aviation Administration (FAA). The results were surprising—even for me!

I gave each individual this prompt: "Visualize a penny standing on its side [as in the image shown]. Using your memory of the thickness of pennies, estimate how many pennies you would need to stack up to reach the top."

Participants wrote down their answers. Check out the results from my guinea pigs at the FAA:

(Megan O'Neil)

Number of Pennies	Total Attendees Who Guessed That Number
5	28
6	5
7	30
8	4
9	3
10	5
11	1
12	1
13	3
15	9
17	3
21	2
38	1
39	1
40	2
42	1
49	1
51	1

Actual number of pennies it takes: thirteen.

I offer this test because it's an excellent reminder about how fallible we can be when we take the accuracy of our own perception for granted. In my FAA trial, only 3 percent of the people in the audience got it right. Now, I'm not saying 97 percent of the people don't have accurate perception—but we all do need to check our assumptions regularly.

JUST REMEMBER...

- *Dial down the anxiety and put the person at ease.* The best way to get a baseline for a person's normal behavior is to have the person as relaxed as possible. Start out with positive intent. Use welcoming gestures and mirroring body language.

- *Ask low-stress questions.* Using questions like "Tell me about where you grew up again?" or "What are you guys up to this summer?" can help you get a gauge of what people's baseline honest responses look like when they're not worried about being believed.

- *Trust your gut—but not exclusively.* Our brains are sophisticated deception detection tools, but many intervening factors have muddled their accuracy. Remember, a quick read can be dangerous. Getting the baseline is only the first of the five essential steps. Keep in mind: trust your gut, but verify, verify, verify.

STEP 2:
THE WIRETAP

Speech is the shadow of action.
—DEMOCRITUS

AFTER YEARS OF RESPECTING, trusting, and even calling him a friend, imagine confronting your ten-year-old son's assistant football coach or your thirteen-year-old daughter's swimming, gymnastics, or basketball coach to ask him if he was sodomizing *your* baby—and this is the response you get:

> In terms of—my relationship with so many, many young people. I would—I would guess that there are many young people who would come forward. Many more young people who would come forward and say that my methods and—and what I had done for them made a very positive impact on their life. *And I didn't go around seeking out every young person for sexual needs that I've helped. There are many that I didn't have—I hardly had any contact with who I have helped in many, many ways.*[1]

Wouldn't you get suspicious? Maybe even pissed? Of course you would! At what part during Penn State's retired assistant football coach and accused child molester, Jerry Sandusky's, November 2011 televised interview with Bob Costas, noted above, would you have wanted to smash his face in? I've put in italics the screaming hot spot that most likely already had you pulling in your top lip in anger or curling up that top lip of yours in disgust. These little puppies are called start-stop sentences and they're kind of like pre–Freudian slips—the person is *just about* to tell the truth but is able to catch herself before she reveals it. These midsentence course corrections can be very revealing and we'll discuss them again later in this chapter. Start-stop sentences are one type of the many verbal faux pas that liars unconsciously leak for us, allowing us to take action immediately and bust them in a lie.

Although I am often recognized as a body language expert, my first training was in detecting deception. So in this chapter, you're going to "hear" more about the verbal side of dishonesty—signs to listen for in people's speech, especially in the words people choose to explain themselves.

Why focus on the verbal so much? With so much of our communication taking place over the Internet or by phone these days, you may not have the benefit of a person's body language to help you determine their guilt or innocence. Also, as you get older, your ability to detect deception reduces because your overall ability to "read" emotions visually declines. But your ability to "hear" a lie remains strong.[2] If you are getting up there in years (and who isn't?), instead of "I'll believe it when I see it," your new credo should be, "I'll believe it when I hear it."

I share many tricks on how to capitalize on your keen auditory soothsayer sense. No matter whether you are turning on your BS Barometer at a distance or in person, you'll be able to hear the verbal indicators of deception in the words people choose and in the changes in their speech rates, volume, and pitch that naturally occur in most deceptive statements. Let's learn about the dangerously deceptive verbal flags that should make you sit up, pay attention, and take action fast.

The Voice as BS Barometer

The tone of a person's voice has an amazing effect on us. Think of how different it sounds when you sing-song a request to your kids—"Come down for dinner, please!"—or when you shout it out in an exasperated voice. This variation has a direct effect on our trust level. One Harvard study of surgeons' voices found that, once all other factors were stripped away, those whose vocal tones were rated as more dominant and less concerned were actually two and a half times more likely to be sued by their patients for malpractice than those with gentler delivery.[3]

Vocal tone is a powerful indicator of emotion. Research has shown that a person's vocal tone will waiver from baseline in up to 95 percent of all deceptive

TRUTH TELLERS SIGN HERE

External factors can make a big difference in how honest people are. Some situations tempt us to tip the scales a bit more than others. One interesting study found that people are more likely to be dishonest and cheat more when lighting is low, possibly because they feel more anonymous.[4] A related study found that people acted more selfishly when they wore sunglasses![5] But making very simple changes, such as requiring a signature at the top of a form rather than the bottom, can affect how truthful and forthcoming people are.

Researchers at Harvard Business School found that when people sign a form *before* rather than after they've had the opportunity to "cheat"—as in an employment application or on a tax form—they're more likely to consider ethics and morality, which leads to a significant reduction in dishonesty.[6] The researchers believe that the practice helps "bring one's moral standards into focus," which promotes honesty and discourages cheating. Another study found that simply reading an honor code—not even signing anything—made people less likely to cheat.

statements—it's one of the most reliable indicators of deception. Whether it goes up or down depends on the emotions involved.

Vocal tone rises when we're angry or excited. You might see this in liars who are trying to convince you of something. (See "Convincing-Not-Conveying" on page 106.) Imagine you're a security guard who's confronting the person with the extra pair of jeans in her bag, and the person yells back, "You know what? You're just doing this because I'm a woman. You're just doing this because you don't like women." A typical innocent person wouldn't raise her voice and wouldn't get instantly angry. She would simply say, "I don't know what you're talking about—I didn't do anything."

If your friend denies that she has the hots for your husband, listen for her tone of voice when she talks with him. An article in the *Journal of Evolutionary Psychology* found that the pitch of women's voices will shoot up when they are speaking to a man they find attractive.[7]

Vocal tone lowers with sadness and shame. When a person's voice gets lower, pay close attention. We saw this with Britney Spears when she was being interviewed about divorce rumors, insisting everything was great in her marriage to Kevin Federline—you couldn't even hear the words coming out of her mouth.

Now that we've learned about the deception you'll hear in the sound of their voice, let's consider the meaning of the words themselves—they usually say more than you think.

THE STORY BEHIND YOUR WORDS: STATEMENT ANALYSIS

One of the most powerful BS Barometer tools we have is our own education! All the years of learning our ABCs and our verbs and nouns come into play when we use the "Wiretap." Mastering the art of detecting deceptive speech is best learned from a process called Statement Analysis. Created by former Secret Service agent and U.S. Marshal Mark McClish, Statement Analysis is a system of analyzing the grammar and logic of words that come out of our mouths. Often our brains will pick up inconsistencies in people's stories based almost entirely upon shifts in tense or word choice. Statement Analysis is a way of making these unconscious tip-offs more conscious, so you can start to get very precise about hot spots within a conversation. Experts such as McClish have been studying these verbal and grammatical inconsistencies for years, and there are hundreds of them! But at their root level, they follow a few basic patterns that have everything to do with your target, her personality, and how she tends to handle stress.

TAKING CARE OF BUSINESS: TEETER-TOTTERING, CONVINCING-NOT-CONVEYING, AND BACKSLIDING

I want you to get this mental picture in your mind: Liars are all tightrope walkers. They want to get from where they are now, talking to you, all the way across the canyon of your skepticism and doubt, to the other side—freedom, the moment at which you've been convinced of their lie. Their task is to remain upright and make steady progress through the lie and not fall off the rope before they get to their destination.

Now, as we've discussed, their brains are carrying an awful lot of weight on this journey:

- The truth: the facts about what really happened

- The "facts" in their own lie: the whole story they're trying to convince you of

- What they've already told you in every conversation up until now

- The new information they may not yet know—but once they learn, will have to instantly assimilate without slipping up

- Your reaction to their tale, whether positive or negative

- And, last but not least, their own visible and audible reactions to the stress of telling the lie

That's an awful lot of weight to be toting across a tightrope!

Now, for many liars, all that extra baggage is going to keep them off balance. The stress triggers their fight-or-flight instincts. And if you concentrate and know what to listen for, you might hear three different categories of signals that can reveal their stress response or lying strategy and suggest there's more to the story.

Teeter-Tottering. You know how a kid on a balance beam might suddenly throw a leg out to one side to compensate for a weight shift on the other side? You'll often hear this same kind of "teeter-tottering" when people are lying. Their speech wobbles around, deviating from its normal baseline patterns, suddenly shifting in odd, uncharacteristic ways.

Convincing-Not-Conveying. For some liars, the stress of the tightrope spurs them to fight! They charge ahead, full blast, and try to overwhelm you with the brute force of their lie. They puff their language up with lots of absolutes and extreme language and rush at you full speed, playing their "role" to the hilt—anything to avoid teeter-tottering.

Backsliding. For other liars, the stress of all this wobbling is almost too much. All they want to do is run and hide. While teeter-totterers tend to steadily make it through the lie, willing themselves not to fall, backsliders are a bit more reticent and subconsciously minimize themselves, trying to hide the truth or retreat from the conversation to make themselves seem smaller.

Now let's consider what kinds of individual signals you'll hear within each of these categories.

TeeTeR-TOTTeRiNG

A teeter-totterer will leak inconsistencies in many of her statements or will try to make everything seem like "sunshine and roses." Her language is garbled and she may even blurt out clues midsentence—all signs of an off-balance, klutzy liar. As long as it's a deviation from her baseline, it's cause for a closer listen.

Sunshine and Roses

Liars don't like to talk in the negative. A study from Stanford Business School found that deceptive chief executive officers tended to use more extreme positive emotional words and fewer extreme negative emotions.[8] I've busted some of that pie-eyed lying myself: the night ten years ago I caught my boyfriend cheating on me with his ex-girlfriend, it was one of the coldest nights of the year—but you'd have never known it from his story.

March in D.C. can be bitter cold, and my boyfriend claimed to have been walking around in Georgetown in his business jacket (without a winter coat on), supposedly "thinking about us." Well, I knew it was freezing because I had walked from Chinatown over to Dupont Circle, which is about a mile, with a winter coat, hat, scarf, and gloves—and I was still super-cold. And he's telling me he's walking around Georgetown in a sport jacket, thinking about the future of our relationship. Hot. Spot.

"I left work around six and then just walked around all night," he said.

"You must have frozen your ass off!" I said.

"Nah, as long as you kept moving, it wasn't that bad." BS Barometer through the ceiling. It was about 5 degrees below!

The man was not outside—he was inside, very warm, having sex with a married woman!

Mixed-Up Tenses

When a person recounts a story, pay close attention to the tenses that he or she uses. Sometimes they'll switch tenses in the middle of their story, which is a great marker for a hot spot. At a press conference following his arrest, John Mark Carr, the man who falsely claimed to have killed child pageant star JonBenét Ramsey, said, "I was with her when she died—[shoulder shrug]—I love Jon-Benét." Present tense! Total fantasy (and lunacy). It should have been, "I loved JonBenét."

Seem like a small distinction? Well, think about it this way: I loved my nana up to the sky and down to the pipes and I miss her every day of my life. But I don't say, "I love my nana." She's been gone for several years. So the present tense doesn't fit with Carr.

Double Talk / Details That Don't Add Up

Sometimes the mixed tenses get jumbled together with a bunch of dependent clauses, until you feel like you're being led down a rabbit hole. When famed

THE DRAMA OF THE WORD "LEFT"

My dear Marine friend and master instructor Frank Marsh, who now works for the National Drug Enforcement Center, always cautions the students at the Body Language Institute's elite deception courses about the unrelenting power of the word *left*.

I left my wife.

I left the kids.

There's always drama behind the word *left*—perhaps they were stuck in traffic, or they got in a fight with their neighbor about their dog peeing on their lawn, or maybe they killed someone by mistake. When Casey Anthony was first questioned about her missing daughter, she repeatedly said the word: "I left work around 5 P.M., and went back to the apartment to pick up my daughter," she said. "Two hours passed, and around 7 P.M., I left the apartment, and headed to familiar places that Zenaida would go with Caylee."

When people are just doing their everyday life, they'll talk about where they're going, not what they left behind. Take this word as a probing point: "What did you leave there? What was going on there?"

baseball player Roger Clemens was being questioned about steroid use at a hearing on Capitol Hill, he was pressed on the testimony of his former friend, Andy Pettitte. Pettitte had testified that Roger knew he was using human growth hormone.

CONGRESSMAN: . . . . You said your conversation with Mr. Pettitte never happened. If that was true, why would Laura Pettitte remember Andy telling her about the conversation?

CLEMENS: Once again, I think he misremembers the conversation that we had. He and I had a relationship close enough to know that if I would have known that he was [pause] had done HGH, which I now know [pause] if he was knowingly knowing that I had taken HGH, we would have talked about something for me to ask him about.[9]

Huh?

Clemens was indicted by a federal grand jury on six felony counts for perjury, false statements, and obstruction of Congress. Eventually, after several delays, the whole affair ended in a mistrial. We'll never know for certain if Clemens was lying, but I think you can guess where I stand on the issue.

Remember, our default is to always tell the truth. Our brain doesn't want us to lie, so we teeter-totter and say things in a weird way.

Entering the Twilight Zone

Sometimes liars will get the details of time and space incorrect. While listening to their story, you might be thinking, "Hey, hang on a second—that store is on the next block, not on Elm Street, . . ." or "That show isn't on Wednesday night, it's on Monday night. . . ." Bingo—that's a hot spot.

Another aspect of the twilight zone is what I call "yadda yadda syndrome." When the liar gets to the sticky part of the story, he'll often gloss over the details, like pressing fast-forward on a cassette deck. "I went to the club and met Steve, then yadda yadda, and we came home." That yadda yadda is where all the interesting details are hiding. Other yadda yadda variations include "a bit later," "one thing led to another," or "some time after that."[10]

The Sorta, Kinda Disorder

Sometimes it's the squishiness of the language itself that's the tip-off. The details of the Mark Zuckerberg versus Winklevoss twins' whose-idea-was-Facebook debate can truly be known only by the parties involved, but one thing that cannot be denied is the digital trace of their electronic communication at the time. While no one disputes the claim that the Winklevoss twins hired Zuckerberg to create a website for them, there was a question of timing—did Zuckerberg "stall" in creating his version in order to get a jump on his supposed clients? *Business Insider* published some emails that Zuckerberg sent to the Winklevoss twins during the time he was supposed to be creating their site. I've highlighted Zuckerberg's squishy language:

> *December 4:* "Sorry I was unreachable tonight. I **just** got **about three** of your missed calls. I was working on a problem set."

> *December 10:* "The week has been **pretty** busy thus far, so I haven't gotten a chance to do **much** work on the site or **even** think about it **really,** so I think it's **probably** best to postpone meeting until we have more to discuss. I'm also **really** busy tomorrow so **I don't think** I'd be able to meet then **anyway.**"

A week later: "Sorry I have not been reachable for the past **few** days. I've **basically** been in the lab the whole time working on a cs problem set which I'm **still** not finished with."[11]

Freudian slips. Freudian slips are named for famed psychiatrist Sigmund Freud, father of modern psychotherapy, who believed that when people repress their true feelings and beliefs, they'll come out in odd ways—kind of the definition of teeter-tottering. To Freud, brutally honest verbal slips were a great indication of what is *really* on your mind.

Classic example: John Allen Muhammad, one of the D.C. Snipers, represented himself on trial, waiving the right to counsel. Standing before the judge and jury, he said, "By the grace of God, when you find me guilty . . . I mean innocent." That's what I call a Freudian slip!

Too Much Pausing

When there's a dramatic pause at an inappropriate moment, the person's brain may be thinking of the real word their brain *wants* to say and then gathering the fake word to say instead. We saw this in Drew Peterson, the police sergeant who was indicted by a grand jury, charged with killing his third wife, and held on a $20 million bond while his fourth wife, Stacy Peterson, was (and is) still missing. Before Peterson was sent to prison in Joliet, Illinois, to await trial, he spoke about Stacy to Matt Lauer on *Today*.

Focus on the pause at *missing*. What word do you think he was trying not to say? (My guess is the word *alive.*)

MATT LAUER: Why haven't you participated? We've seen images of people out in the area where you live searching for Stacy. Right. Have you ever taken part in the search for Stacy?

DREW PETERSON: Well [pause] there's two things: one thing is like, I'm such a media sensation right now, if I go out and search, I think the search would be hampered by number one: all the media attention I'd be getting. And two: why would I look for somebody who I don't believe is [pause] missing? She's just gone. She is where she wants to be.

Not Enough Pausing

Pausing too much can be an indicator, but as I mentioned in chapter 1, so can pausing too little. Let's say you asked me what I ate for lunch last Thursday, and, without missing a beat, I say, "Tuna on rye." Why would I remember that so quickly? Raking through your memory banks to dredge up the truth takes time. When a person is trying to recollect something that happened years, months, or even weeks ago, if the answer is right on the tip of her tongue, there's either a legit reason why she remembers that detail—such as Thursday is always "deli day" in the cafeteria, and that's your go-to sandwich—or it's a hot spot.

Start-Stop Sentences

You'll see start-stop sentences when a person realizes he's about to tell you something he doesn't want to tell you—*Oh, no, this will get me in trouble*—but the cat is already halfway out of the bag. Then you'll see an abrupt about-face, like in Sandusky's explanation about his relationships with young boys at the beginning of this chapter. In midsentence, Sandusky abruptly stops and takes us in a different direction. It's almost as if he's changing the channel on the television—it's noticeable and makes us want to scream, "Cut the shit already!"

Varied Speech Rate Within a Sentence

You may have heard of liars as "fast talkers," but actually, the speed of their speech varies as much as an honest person's. As a corporate and association keynote speaker, I use dramatic pauses and change my tone of voice to keep things interesting. But although honest people may vary their speech rates within a whole conversation, liars will alter their speech rates within a single sentence. Typically, a liar might begin to speak slowly, because he's trying to figure out his lie—but once it comes into his head, he tries to spit it out as fast as possible.

Now that we've learned all about the off-balance teeter-totterers, let's hear about a more aggressive, in-your-face type of liar: the convince-not-conveyer.

CONVINCING-NOT-CONVEYING

Honest people convey information. Liars, on the other hand, try to *convince* us that their story is the truth. While a truthful person expects that you believe them, a liar will fight to be believed. Convince-not-convey signals are all about "puffing up" the liar and his story—throwing their friends in the mix with "character testimony," backing themselves up with absolutes, extreme language, and unnecessary adjectives, and even getting angry. These liars and louses really, really, *really* want you to believe them!

THE BS BAROMETER READING

AT THE PRESS CONFERENCE

COLUMBIA, SC—
JUNE 26: South
Carolina Governor
Mark Sanford fields
questions from
the media outside
the South Carolina
statehouse.
(Getty Images)

South Carolina Governor Mark Sanford disappeared for five days in June 2009, after he told staff he was taking a solo hiking trip along the Appalachian Trail. In reality, he had hopped a plane to Argentina—to visit his mistress. Upon his return, he held a press conference at which he uttered his confession: "I have been unfaithful to my wife." End of story? Not so fast!

When subsequently asked a question from a reporter, he revealed more than he intended to. He was asked if he had previous extramarital affairs, any relationships outside of his marriage with any other woman besides his South American sweetie. *Before* the reporter even finished asking the question, Sanford had already replied, "No." He swiftly looked away and took another reporter's question, effectively "changing the subject."

BS Barometer Reading: Partial BS

KEY

Total BS: Full of It

Partial BS: Running on Vapors

BS-Free: Nothing but the Truth!

Although preemptively answering a question does not guarantee deception, it is to be considered an abnormal behavior in general conversation. Therefore, it should be viewed as a hot spot. *(continued)*

After Sanford's initial press conference (in which he denied other affairs), the Associated Press contacted me for my analysis. At that time, although I couldn't be entirely positive there was deception in his statement, I felt there was definitely more to his story. Fast-forward a few days, and Sanford spills his guts once again. Sure enough, he *had* in fact participated in other inappropriate behavior with women.

Character Testimony

"Just ask my friends—they'll tell you." Character testimony is one of the most common convince-not-convey tactics. The liar is dragging other people into the conversation for support because he's not sure you're going to buy his story. Other variations include "I swear on my mother's grave" or "As God is my witness." If God is your witness, my friend, you're in a heck of a lot more trouble with Him than with me!

Never-Never Land!

In 1995, when President Bill Clinton addressed the nation about "not having sex with 'that' woman, Monica Lewinsky," he made matters worse when he gave an over-the-top denial: "And I never told anyone to lie. Never. Not a single time, never! These allegations are false and I'm going back to work for the American people." Umm, yeah, Bill, I think the expression goes something like, "Methinks thou doth protest too much!"

When it comes to the word *never* we should all be instantly suspicious. For those naysayers and nonbelievers out there, go ahead and answer these questions: "Did you hit and run over a dog on your way to work yesterday?" "Did you kill President John F. Kennedy?" "Have you been stalking Susan Boyle?"

Remember, these are not hard and fast rules. Not everyone who says, "I would never take drugs" is a liar and a dope fiend. But you're always looking for that definitive sister statement to go with it: "No, I do not take drugs."

The Shoulda, Coulda, Woulda Syndrome

Saying "I would never do that" is also not the same as saying "I didn't do that." "Would never" indicates intent for the future—it does not talk about the past. I once had an assistant who stayed in my house while I was on vacation. When we arrived home, I noticed that my bed had been slept in, despite my request that

EIGHT PHRASES LIARS LOVE

1. What kind of a person do you think I am?

2. I'd have to be stupid to do something like that.

3. Just ask my friends—they'll tell you I would never do anything like that.

4. I swear to God.

5. My word is my bond.

6. I knew this was going to happen to me.

7. Why don't you question the person down the street?

8. You think I'm lying to you?

she sleep in the guest room. When I confronted her, she said, "I would never do that. . . . It is not who I am. I never slept in my parents' bed. You're my boss. I would never sleep in your bed."

I believe her that she didn't sleep in her parents' bed. But I knew she slept in mine, and I was right—she confessed. It might seem like a small distinction, but a truthful person would say, "I didn't sleep in my parents' bed, and I didn't sleep in your bed. I would never do that." Again, it's okay to say I would never do that. But you have to get the "I didn't do it" in there, too.

Overuse of Adjectives

All we really need to communicate are nouns and verbs. All the other stuff— adverbs, adjectives, conjunctions, prepositions, and so on—is either just window dressing or very handy directional signals that help us learn more about the person who is trying to sell you his story.[12] Pay special attention to the use of adverbs and adjectives in the story—they tell you about the person and what the person wants you to believe.

The girl looked at me.

The mean girl looked at me nastily.

Why did I add *mean* and *nastily*? Why is that important? Why am I telling you that? This person is putting their twist on the story.

PSYCHOPATHS: THE ULTIMATE "CONVINCERS"

One study published in the journal *Legal and Criminological Psychology* compared the statements of fourteen psychopathic male murderers with thirty-eight non-psychopathic murderers. Both groups were asked to talk about their crimes. Compared to the non-psychopaths, the psychopaths used more language that "justified" the crime, such as "because," "since," or "so that." They also talked more often about food, sex, and money—they even talked about what they had to eat the day they committed murder! In contrast, the non-psychopaths talked about their families, or their spiritual beliefs.[13]

The psychopaths also talked about the crime in the past tense, as if they were "over it," and they used more "ums" and "uhs" in their speech. The researchers believed this may have been because the psychopaths were trying so hard to make a favorable impression that they used more mental effort; the non-psychopaths were perhaps more contrite and not so intent on convincing others of the justified nature of their attacks.

Escalation to Anger

Inappropriate anger is a telltale sign of the convince-not-conveyer. Often, when a liar is found out, he is backed into a corner, and he becomes like a cornered animal that lashes out. In the Gwyneth Paltrow movie *Sliding Doors,* Paltrow plays a woman who very nonchalantly asks her boyfriend what a brandy glass was doing in the laundry basket. At first, the boyfriend denies knowing, and then spins into a whole tizzy, blaming his own insomnia, her head injury, one of her "mad" friends. And then, he immediately escalates to anger, saying, "Women never ask—they insinuate." He tops it off with a nice, "Thank you—thanks a lot!" and then "No wonder you got sacked!" for good measure. And she's left thinking, "What the hell just happened?"

I'll tell you what happened—she needs a new boyfriend.

Classic gaslighting. Bad guys do the same thing to the cops. "This is ridiculous. I've answered the same five questions ten times! Don't you people ever look at notes? Why am I repeating this sentence?" We assume the person is angry, but in a deceptive person, that anger is masking fear—he's afraid you're onto him, so he tries to bully you into backing down. Some FBI investigators recommend that if you see genuine anger, contempt, or disgust when confronting a possible liar, it might be time to use another tactic. (You'll learn to spot these distinctive facial cues in the next chapter, "The Stakeout.") But this kind of fake anger is simply a way of distracting you from the truth.

Flip the Script

This classic gaslighting move can come quickly on the heels of fake anger. The liar turns the whole question back on you: "I can't even believe you're asking me if I cheated on you. You are so insecure. You have no friends. The only person you ever talk to is your mother. And your mother puts these sick ideas in your head. No wonder why she has three failed marriages." Simmer down, Francis.

Now that you have a better understanding of what to look out for when it comes to convincing-not-conveying, and the importance of calling the bluff of those who seek to overpower you with their deception, now let's decode the verbal cues of those who try to hide from you: the "backsliders."

BaCKSLIDING

Backsliders' primary mission is to shrink or back up on that tightrope—anything to get away from being found out. The backslider is a master of obscurity and camouflage, usually using many ways to distract you or distance himself from the lie. Whether with sneaky statements or overwhelming politeness and

BUT IS HE REALLY HAPPY?

An interesting inverse of convince-not-convey's fake anger is fake happiness. We all know people who've smiled through their tears—"No, really, I'm doing great!" But if someone in your life suddenly starts drawing smiley faces on their notes to you, dig deeper. Federal law enforcement officer at the National Drug Intelligence Center Frank Marsh contends that when people draw smiley faces on handwritten notes, they are very often depressed. Even O.J. Simpson's suicide note in 1994, written while America watched the police chase O.J.'s white Ford Bronco down Interstate 405 in California, ended with a smiley face, drawn right into the "O" of his name.

7-SECOND FIX

THE BLURTER

(Baron Thrower II)

(Baron Thrower II)

The Problem: Someone keeps interrupting your conversation and you need to act quickly to take control of the situation.

The Fix: Simple! . . . Stop talking. Put your index finger, or if you're at a conference table or in an office, a pen will do, over your mouth in the *Shh* position without saying "Shh!" and get the results you want fast.

The Result: Years of conditioning from mothers and librarians have given the finger-over-the-mouth move the power to change behavior instantly, even if the person doesn't consciously realize you're doing it.

---

self-deprecation, the backslider would love nothing more than for you to forget the entire incident ever happened.

Being Overly Polite

Here you go, sir. Here's my license, sir. It's like a little kid syndrome, like they're in trouble and going to the principal's office. Customs agents are often trained to keep an eye out for people who say too many *sirs* or *ma'ams* and to spot exactly when they switch over to that overly polite backsliding speech.

Where are you headed? *United States.*

What do you do there? *I'm going to my sister's wedding.*

Do you have anything in the trunk of your car? *No, ma'am.*

When the *ma'am* comes out of nowhere, that's likely a sign of stress—so now they'll politely ask you to pull over so they can take a look in the trunk of your car.

Self-Deprecation

A good way liars "minimize" themselves as a threat is to put themselves down. Sometimes, it even borders on pathetic. We saw this with the Anthony Weiner sexting scandal. When the news first broke, Weiner denies that the picture of the penis is his, but then as it becomes more apparent that it is him, he cracks a joke (another tactic of liars). A reporter asks him why he isn't fessing up, and Weiner says that he's embarrassed because of something comedian Jon Stewart said about the size of his penis. Basically, he's telling the whole world that this picture couldn't be him, because he's much smaller.

I'm sorry, but what self-respecting guy does that? "I'm sorry that I have a small penis" is not a sentence you'd expect someone to say to millions of television viewers, unless the alternative truth—that it *was* him, and it would cost him his job—is even worse.

The Missing "I"

One of the ways the backsliders hide is to literally hide themselves from the conversation. Truthful people use more pronouns, especially *I,* when making statements.[14] Backsliders avoid "I" statements at all costs. Deceptive businesspeople use significantly fewer self-references and choose more third-person plural *(they, their, them)* and impersonal pronouns *(it).*[15]

Distancing Language

The missing "I" is only one type of distancing language. Backsliders might also heavily employ words like *that* (which pushes away further than *this*). Or they might say, "They went to *the* house" instead of "They went to *my* house." Anything to push the language—and the crime—away from themselves.

When Dick Cheney accidentally shot his friend Harry Whittington on a quail hunt, you might assume you'd hear Cheney say, "I shot Whittington." After all, there was no doubt what happened—everyone knew. But listen to what he said instead: "Ultimately, I'm the guy who pulled the trigger that fired the round that hit Harry."

A lot had to happen before those bullets hit his pal, huh?

Smokescreening

Some backsliders who shower us with information or details can easily distract us from the truth, especially in unexpected situations. This "inattentive blindness"—which we talked about in chapter 4, when we fail to see something right in front of us while focusing on something else—is the result of lower working memory capacity, a measure of how much information people can process at any given time.

Master manipulators and liars know we all have a limited amount of attention, so they play with that and use it to their favor. That's why I include so many exercises that develop your attention—learning how to maintain focus and spot unexpected discrepancies, while not being distracted by them, is the main driver of your BS Barometer. We want our brains to be flexible enough to notice all the details of the situation, not just the ones the target *wants* us to see.

Sometimes, the smokescreen is just blatantly obvious.

WEINER: This [tweeted picture of a penis] was a prank that I've now been talking about for a couple of days. I'm not going to allow it to decide what I talk about for the next week or the next two weeks, and so I'm not going to be giving anything more about that today. I think I've been pretty responsive to you in the past.

REPORTER: You're here, which we appreciate, but you're not answering the questions. Can you just say why you haven't asked law enforcement to investigate what you are alleging is a crime?

WEINER: If I were giving a speech to 45,000 people and someone in the back of the room threw a pie or yelled out an insult, would I spend the next two hours responding to that? No. I would get back—I would get back—

REPORTER 2: This is not that situation though. You—

WEINER: Why don't you—do you want to do the briefing?

REPORTER 2: You sent—

WEINER: Do you want to do the briefing, sir?

REPORTER 2: You sent—a lewd photograph was sent to a college student. Answer the question, was it from you or not?

WEINER: Sir, permit me—do you want me to finish my answer?

REPORTER 2: Yes, this answer: Did you send it or not?

WEINER: If I were giving a speech to 45,000 people and someone in the back of the room threw a pie or yelled out an insult, I would not spend the next two hours of my speech responding to that pie or that insult. I would return to the things that I want to talk about to the audience that I want to talk about.

REPORTER 2: All you have to do is say no to the question. Say no to the question.

REPORTER: Let me try this question. The woman who allegedly got this tweet or was directed to, twenty-one-year-old college student in Seattle, she released a statement to the *New York Daily News* yesterday saying you follow her on Twitter. Is that true? Did you follow her on Twitter and, if so, how did you find her? What was the reason?

WEINER: You know, I have, I think said this a couple ways and will say it again. I am not going to permit myself to be distracted by this issue any longer.[16]

Most of the time, smokescreening is more subtle than this. Like a magician, the liar wanting to create a smokescreen draws attention to his right hand so he can pull something out of his pocket with his left. That's the moment to say, "Hey, hey. Let's go back. What were you going to say a second ago?"

Repeating the Question (and Other Verbal Fillers)

Verbal fillers can be anything from *umms, errs*, and other such nonwords to full sentences: *Are you asking me if I killed my wife? What kind of person do you think I am? I'd have to be stupid to do something like that. Are you asking me if I'm a liar? Are you calling me a liar? You think I killed my wife?* Anything to throw a couple of hundred words in between you and the truth. Here's another instance where disgraced former Penn State coach Jerry Sandusky showed a hot spot. Making a surprise appearance on NBC's *Rock Center* to be interviewed by Bob Costas, Sandusky insisted on his complete innocence of all of the forty charges against him. Costas showed tremendous grit in his questions:

COSTAS: Are you sexually attracted to young boys, to underage boys?

SANDUSKY: Am I sexually attracted to underage boys?

COSTAS: Yes.

SANDUSKY: Sexually attracted, you know, I—I enjoy young people. I—I love to be around them. I—I—but, no, I'm not sexually attracted to young boys."[17]

If someone walked up to you and said, "Are you attracted to ten-year-olds?" what would you say? What would any rational person say? "No! Ugh, God! That's disgusting! How can you ask me that?" An innocent person would not carefully consider the question with a thoughtful, "Hmm . . . let's see. *Am* I sexually attracted to young boys? *Sexually* attracted?"

Minimizing Language

While phrases like *by the way* or words like *incidentally* are often used by liars, detectives can also watch out for minimizing language. When the police came to the home of convicted murderer Scott Peterson with a second search warrant, after they found the dead bodies of his wife, Laci, and their unborn baby, they brought Laci's sister along to see if there was anything out of place. Scott Peterson allegedly said to Laci's sister, "Hey, by the way, if they happen to find any blood stains here, it's just because I cut my hand while I was out on the boat."

Another version is *obvious:* Nothing's ever obvious. When someone says that, it's not obvious—they're likely downplaying something that's interesting and important.

Or *just so you know:* "Hey, just so you know, I haven't seen my cousin in like six years." You're giving us an alibi before we even get there.

These minimizers are all verbal highlighters—pay attention when they're said, because they're the most important part of the story.

Watch Your Big Buts

Backsliders can also downplay their lies with the word *but.* On CNBC, live on air, as part of a detecting deception exercise to test my fine-tuned BS Barometer skills, I asked television personality and advertising superstar hottie Donny Deutsch, "Tell me the nicest thing your father ever said to you." And he said, "I know this is going to sound strange, but my father told me I remind him of his father." Busted! Why would that be strange? That's the opposite of strange—that's probably pretty typical of what people would say. (And, being a good sport, Donny fessed up to the fib right away.)

"I know you're not going to believe this, but . . ."

"I know you're going to think I'm making this up, but . . ."

"I know this is going to sound strange, but . . ."

"This is not going to make sense, but . . ."

We're watching your Big Buts, liars.

Dumbing Down the Crime

Even while he's denying his crime, the liar will try to lessen the severity, plead it down to a misdemeanor instead of a felony.

Did you steal money from me? *I didn't take any money from your purse.*

Did you rape her? *I didn't hurt her.*

Did you hit your brother? *I didn't hurt him.*

Are you lying? *I'm not holding anything back.*

Did you have sex with her? *I never slept with her.*

Or, my personal favorite:

Did you gossip about me? *I didn't say anything bad about you. I didn't say anything that wasn't true. I didn't say anything that I wouldn't say to your face.*

Just the Facts, Jack

Liars don't like to talk about feelings of others—some pathological or compulsive liars can't even feel them themselves. Listen closely for frank assessments of emotions, words like *angry, scared, hurt, hilarious, anxious, worried.* Liars won't stop to think about the mental state of the other person—they're just focused on getting the objective details down.

Some backsliders simply say as little as possible, just the "bare bones" of the story.[18] They focus on just the simple action words *(walk, go)* rather than words that describe anyone's thoughts *(think, believe).*[19] Social psychologists from the University of Texas–Austin have found that some people who lie also tend to avoid complex language such as conjunctions *(and, but, because, although)* and prepositions *(at, before, on, to, for).* All that pesky grammar just pins them down![20]

Despite this study, I know from twenty years of experience that some liars definitely go overboard with the details. Especially when they're attempting to distract us with a smokescreen. That's why we always have to start with the baseline. If someone is usually terse, then turns into Chatty Cathy, that's a hot spot. And, likewise, if someone normally chews your ear off but now won't squeeze out one superfluous detail, know there's more to the story there.

Percentage Violation

These detail variations show up even within the storyline itself. Whenever a truthful person tells a story, you can expect to hear approximately 20 percent of what happened before the time in question, 60 percent of what happened in the middle of the story, and 20 percent after the crux of the story. People will set up the story with details ("I was just watching the security cameras and nothing was happening, until—*bam!*—I saw this punk steal a pair of gloves. That's

POWER TEAM TURNAROUND

Name: Blanca Jimenez Cobb

Age: 41

Occupation: Stay-at-home mom / T-shirt designer / founder of sprish.com / BLI instructor

(Baron Thrower II)

What was stopping you from spotting master manipulators and liars?

Unfortunately, deception bled deep into my personal life as a young girl, teenager, and now into my adulthood. In high school, I had a controlling and mentally abusive boyfriend who isolated me from my friends. I stayed with him until several months after graduation because I thought it was better to have at least one friend—however horrible—than none at all.

I tried to proceed in life as a trusting person, but with my childhood history of victimization, it is difficult for me to trust people. I want to believe the best in people, but it isn't easy. It takes a while to develop trust and open up and share intimate details of my life. There were times when being able to spot deception would've helped me.

How have you changed?

With the techniques learned in Janine's program, I'm better able to determine whom I can trust, as well as discern who has abused my trust, from my colleagues and business partners to my husband and kids. Intuition is a gut feeling that tells you something isn't quite right—but it can't distinguish fact from fiction. Powerful questions cut through the BS to get to the truth.

I will empower my children with these techniques. As much as my childhood victimization was painful, it is well worth the suffering if I can help children to not fall victims to manipulators and abusers.

when I ran out to chase him"). If the person then skips immediately to what happened afterward, you have an issue. That's the moment you want to hear about: How did you catch the guy? "I didn't realize it at the time, but later, after I got home, I realized that I had a pretty bad bruise and it was starting to swell. So I drove myself to the hospital." Ugh, what happened there? When the events before or after the moment in question are spelled out in greater detail than the linchpin moment itself, that's a hot spot.

Now that you're armed with your full arsenal of wiretap tools, it's time to move on to the stakeout. You'll learn the secret signals of truth that are written all over the face.

LIARS IN PRINT

It's time to put down your iPads, iPhones, BlackBerries, and laptops and dust the cobwebs off a good old-fashioned pad of paper and a pen. The way a person dots his *i*'s, crosses his *t*'s, and signs his name all create a person's unique trademark. (You should see the lovely dots on the top of my *i*'s!).

Michelle Dresbold (www.michelledresbold.com), author of *Sex, Lies, and Handwriting,* is one of the elite few handwriting experts who attended the U.S. Secret Service's Advanced Document Examination training program. Michelle consults private attorneys, police departments, and prosecutors throughout the United States; she is considered one of the top experts in the nation on handwriting identification. Michelle shared some of the hand-written hot spots that we should be most careful of. Three that stuck with me are ambiguous letters or numbers, the "Bee Stinger," and the "Felon's Claw." (Note: just as in all aspects of the BS Barometer, no one handwriting signal means only one thing.)

1. Ambiguous Letters or Numbers

3/27/08

(Michelle Dresbold)

(continued)

The Tell: Numbers and letters can be interpreted as other letters or numbers. For example, my tour guide, on a recent business trip, had the last name Glasgow, but his *w* looked like a large tipped-on-its-side 8.

The Tale: Your new financial advisor writes down some estimates for you of some current stock that's exceeding everyone's expectations and you can barely understand what he's written. Run. Run fast. These people can be found backstabbing, blackmailing, and bank scamming. Bernie Madoff was known to use ambiguous letters and numbers.

2. The Bee Stinger

(Michelle Dresbold)

The Tell: A sharp piercing stroke inside the letters *a, c, d,* or *o.*

The Tale: If your new lover writes with Bee Stingers, he is up for a challenge and he most likely likes to play games, but he will be the first to say without being asked, "I'm not a player." Your new bed buddy will either have some crazy fun sex with you, or he'll suddenly become bored with you and is no longer interested.

3. The Felon's Claw

(Michelle Dresbold)

The Tell: A straight lower loop that forms a fishing hook lure (check out the letter *G* to find the "Felon's Claw").

The Tale: Your wedding planner sends you a handwritten thank-you note acknowledging you as a new client. You immediately spot the Felon's Claw, and you know that deep down he is most likely feeling shame and embarrassment over something. He feels like he doesn't deserve anything good to happen to him, so after he builds you (and himself) up and trust is in place, he will do something disastrous to prove himself right—he can't be trusted.

In 1987, I suddenly changed my uppercase *J*'s and lowercase *y*'s to what I now know is a Felon's Claw. But why? At the time, I was a junior in high school and I had lost my virginity (Shh! Don't tell my mom!) to my high school sweetheart in the camper parked next to my parents' house—and they were home. I've since discovered I'm not alone; many recently deflowered teens feel guilty for a short period of time and the Felon's Claw makes its temporary appearance. Have you checked your teen's swing on the letters *b, d, f, g, j, l, n,* or *y* lately?

EXERCISING YOUR BS BAROMETER: THE WIRETAP

Again, I offer exercises to help you strengthen your BS Barometer in the time you have available. I've given you three assignments, but the most important one is the TCB Statement Analysis Test. If you can start to see the patterns here, you are in good shape. But no cheating! We're honest folk around here.

The TCB Statement Analysis Test

In the five sentences following the box, identify all of the variations of the TCB indicators for Statement Analysis with its corresponding symbol:

Teeter-Tottering: The suspect leaks inconsistencies in her statements. (I've indicated these with a zigzag underline.)

Convince-Not-Convey: The suspect tries to "puff up" and sidetrack you with miscellaneous details that are irrelevant or misleading. (I've indicated these with (parentheses).)

Backsliding: The suspect is attempting to disappear, either separating herself from the story or falling short in her statements. (I've indicated these with a straight underline.)

Questions

1. All I can say is I didn't see that girl at work that day. I woke up at 7 A.M., I ate breakfast. Around 7:30 A.M., I took Angus to school. By 9 A.M., was at my office. Then throughout the day, I did the same thing I do every day. And obviously, I was back home by 6:00 P.M. I swear to God. I hope you don't think I'm lying.

2. Are you talking about my pistol? I know you're not going to believe me, but the last time I saw that gun it was in the locked safe in my garage, just ask my mom, she'll tell you what I just told you.

3. I'm trying to be honest with you about what happened when I went to the beach with my friends. I don't know for sure how Marcy got separate from the group.

4. Obviously, Beth and I walked into the store together. I went to the pharmacy while she went to the video section. I told her that I would meet him, I mean her, at the register.

5. To tell you the truth, I have no idea why my neighbor would say that I would hurt her dog. I work in an animal shelter for goodness sakes. Just ask my friends, they'll tell you I love animals. I would never hurt any animal.

Answers

1. (All I can say is) I didn't see that girl (at work) that day. I woke up at 7 A.M., I ate breakfast. Around 7:30 A.M., I took Angus to school. By 9 A.M., X was at my office. Then throughout the day, I did the same thing I do every day. And (obviously,) I was back home by 6:00 P.M. (I swear to God.) I hope you don't think (I'm lying).

Probing Point	Type of Hot Spot	Explanation
(All I can say is)	Convincing-Not-Conveying	*Suspicious Words or Phrases*: If this is all they can "say," then what else does this person actually know? A more truthful response would have been "This is all I know."
that girl	Backsliding	*Distancing Language:* Why is he trying to separate himself from his statement? He knows her name, but he avoids using it, perhaps to act like she's no one important to him.

Probing Point	Type of Hot Spot	Explanation
that day	Backsliding	*Distancing Language:* Hmm . . . "that day." Is he indirectly implying that he does see her on other days? And why not mention the actual day, for example, Monday, Tuesday, Wednesday? Why use distancing language?
By 9 A.M., X was	Teeter-Tottering	*Inconsistent Pronouns:* Here the pronoun "I" was dropped; however, this person used pronouns in all his other statements. Why the deviation from his norm?
I did the same thing I do every day.	Teeter-Tottering	*Deceptive Time Variations:* Fast-Forwarding: Perhaps every day, he has sex with her in her car in the garage or at a hotel or maybe they meet for lunch and flirt? What is it that he does "every day"?
(obviously)	Convincing-Not-Conveying	*Suspicious Words or Phrases:* Why is it "obvious" that he was back at home? Were we also home at that time and that's why it's "obvious"? Or is it an obscure "obviously"? When people use the word *obviously* about an action they took, a place they were, or a time, and we weren't there, then it's anything but "obvious." *Caution:* My intern, Janine, uses the word *obviously* almost every time she tells a story; therefore, it's simply her baseline and has no meaning for her.
(I swear to God)	Convincing-Not-Conveying	*Suspicious Words or Phrases:* If a person does not normally use this expression and it suddenly appears in a statement, it's a hot spot. Why is he trying to overly convince us? He's "selling" versus "sharing." Truthful people share; liars try to sell us.
think (I'm lying)	Convincing-Not-Conveying	*Suspicious Words or Phrases:* Here he literally tells us, "I'm lying." So, believe him! Always be on the lookout for people who unconsciously tell you exactly who they are or what they've done or what they are capable of doing. A truthful person would be more likely to say something like, "I don't know why you don't believe I'm telling the truth!"

2. Are you talking about my pistol? (I know you're not going to believe me but,) the last time I saw that gun it was in the locked safe in my garage, (just) (ask my mom, she'll tell you what I just told you.)

Probing Point	Type of Hot Spot	Explanation
My pistol	Teeter-Tottering	*Inconsistent Language:* Which is it? A "pistol" or a "gun"? We would need a longer statement to determine which word is a deviation in this person's norm. When someone's language for an item, a person, or a place suddenly changes, this is a definite probing point. It doesn't mean she's lying to you, but there is certainly some type of stressor at that point in the story.
that gun	Backsliding	*Distancing Language:* Why is this person separating herself from the gun? Is there another gun she has seen or used lately, or did she in fact have the gun in question? Or is there some other stressor that is causing her to leak a probing point?
(just)	Convincing-Not-Conveying	*Suspicious Words:* The word *just* tries to downplay what came either before or after that word.
(ask my mom,	Convincing-Not-Conveying	*Character Testimony:* There's no need to bring up "Mom" here. This person is trying to "sell" us.
she'll tell you what I just told you.)	Convincing-Not-Conveying	*Suspicious Words or Phrases:* If Mom tells you the same story, it doesn't mean it's the truth. Always listen closely to what people say to you, and be cautious to not add meaning to their statements; instead ask clarifying questions.

3. (I'm trying to be honest) with you about what happened when I went to the beach with my friends. I (don't know for sure) how Marcy got separate from the group.

Probing Point	Type of Hot Spot	Explanation
(I'm trying to be honest)	Convincing-Not-Conveying	*Suspicious Words or Phrases:* When people use the word *trying,* use extreme caution. "Trying" means to fail. If someone asks you to "try" to catch the ball, if you caught it, then you failed that exercise. You were instructed to "try to catch it!" Liars tend to use the word *trying* a lot.
(don't know for sure)	Convincing-Not-Conveying	*Suspicious Words or Phrases:* Perhaps this person is 100 percent sure, but they most likely have additional details that they aren't sharing. A truthful person would simply say, "I don't know."
separate	Teeter-Tottering	*Inconsistent Past and Present Verbs:* "Separate" should be past tense and therefore it should have a "d" at the end. Why the change in tense here?

4. (Obviously,) Beth and I walked into the store together. I went to the pharmacy while she went to the video section. I told her that I would meet him, I mean her, at the register.

Probing Point	Type of Hot Spot	Explanation
(Obviously,)	Convincing-Not-Conveying	*Suspicious Words or Phrases:* Why is it "obvious" that he and Beth walked into the store together?
him, I mean her,	Teeter-Tottering	*Freudian Slip:* Always pay close attention to when someone leaks a word that they immediately change to something else.

5. (To tell you the truth,) I have no idea why my neighbor would say that I would hurt her dog. I work in an animal shelter (for goodness sakes). (Just ask my friends,) they'll tell you I love animals. I would never hurt any animal.

Probing Point	Type of Hot Spot	Explanation
(To tell you the truth,)	Convincing-Not-Conveying	*Suspicious Words or Phrases:* Ask yourself, was he not telling the truth earlier? Or is he about to try to "sell" us instead of "share" the real truth? It's your job to figure out why this hot spot is here.
(for goodness sakes)	Convincing-Not-Conveying	*Suspicious Words or Phrases:* This expression is similar to "I swear to God," and it attempts to push us away from finding the truth. Also keep in mind, often when people get defensive immediately and show what you think is anger it could actually be *fear*, because you are getting closer to uncovering the truth.
(Just ask my friends,)	Convincing-Not-Conveying	*Character Testimony:* Here we spot the speaker attempting to persuade us that he is telling us the truth by bringing his friends into the story. This is evidence that we haven't asked for yet, so why is he so quick to offer up witnesses?
would	Teeter-Tottering	*Inconsistent Past and Present Verbs:* This person did not answer the question and with "would" spoke about the future, not the past. A more honest answer would be, "I did not hurt my neighbor's dog and I've never hurt any animal and I would never hurt an animal."

Ask for Some Truth!

Simply asking someone to be honest makes them more honest—so we have to get into the habit of asking for the truth. The trick here is to set the expectation before the encounter rather than wait until the end—the reminder is what keeps people honest. Otherwise, you'll only encourage "cover-ups"—no one wants to admit that they've already lied. As soon as you set foot on the car lot, and the salesperson approaches you, set the expectation: "You seem like a really honest guy. Thank you—I really appreciate you being straight with me."

The Grocery List Handwriting Challenge

Let's review *your* handwriting for any troubling signs. Review your old grocery lists or other handwritten notes. Do you have any of the dangerous three from the "Liars in Print" sidebar starting on page 119? Is the analysis accurate? Next, make a list of three to five people in your life who seem too good to be true or might be hiding something. Ask each person to jot down a short grocery list that contains the items noted by bullets below. Last, see if you can spot any of the dangerous three in each person's writing. Here's a possible list; feel free to add additional items. (Make sure each person uses numerals.)

- 10 cans of Chef Boyardee, 6-pack of Miller Lite, and 2 gallon jugs of water—and 1 bottle of aspirin (ambiguous letters that could easily look like numbers)

- Potatoes, oranges, oatmeal (they have *o*'s and *a*'s to check for the Bee Stinger)

- Mayo, jam, yogurt (Can you spot a Felon's Claw?)

FEELING GUILTY MUCH?

Study the following two sentences—can you tell from the handwriting whom the writer is feeling guilty about?

(Janine Driver)

Answers:
1. Jill
2. George

When someone feels guilty about a particular person, a task, or a moment in time, they may unconsciously use the Felon's Claw to indicate specific words that reflect that guilt, as seen in the image above.

JUST REMEMBER...

- *Liars are on a tightrope.* Your liar just wants to get to the other side as fast as possible. He'll use teeter-tottering, convincing-not-conveying, and backsliding tactics to do so—but you will be prepared to take care of business!

- *Listen to changes in vocal tone.* Unlike almost any other signal, vocal tone is a consistent source of accurate information—95 percent of people change their speech rates, volume, and pitch when lying.

- *Remember your baseline.* Any possible deceptive (or honest!) signal here could very easily be part of the person's normal baseline. You must have that to compare with to get an accurate reading—be patient!

STEP 3:
THE STAKEOUT

The face is the index of the mind.
—LATIN SAYING

OOPS, SHE DID IT AGAIN! The summer of 2006 had been a rough one for pop star Britney Spears. She'd been photographed driving her black SUV down Pacific Coast Highway with her four-month-old baby boy on her lap. She'd been filmed in New York City walking with a full drinking glass in one hand and her baby in the other, then stumbling and nearly dropping him on his head on the sidewalk. The tabloids were screaming that her marriage to Kevin Federline was down the tubes, that he was living in the basement. Hounded by paparazzi every time she left her home, Britney felt cornered, nearly imprisoned. To set the record straight, she agreed to have a sit-down interview with Matt Lauer for *Dateline*.

The two superstars sat across from each other in what appeared to be slightly uncomfortable beige chairs with brown wooden armrests in the Princess of Pop's multimillion-dollar home. Matt went in for the kill pretty early on when he asked the future mom of two how it felt to think that Kevin had left the mother of his first two kids when she was six months pregnant, and now Britney herself was six months pregnant—and the same kinds of rumors were flying.

"I didn't know they were together," she said as her eyebrows momentarily scrunched together and her hands ran halfway down her leg.

"Britney, do you believe in karma?"

"No, no!" she said, leaning back, swaying side to side, her eyes roaming around the room, chewing her gum like a fourteen-year-old girl waiting outside the principal's office. "I didn't know that until a couple of months later!" While her face faked surprise, the distressed femme fatale took her right and left hands and rubbed down her whole entire leg, down to her ankle, and all the way back up. The mother lode of all self-touches.

"So," Matt said. "When the magazine says, on the cover, 'Pregnant and Divorcing' . . . ," and he paused.

Britney's mouth flipped into a perfect upside-down U of sadness, her lips scrunched together. She almost looked like she was going to cry. "Oh, no," she whispered, almost inaudibly. "None of that is true," as she nodded her head faintly, "Yes."

Britney filed for divorce six months later.

If you had only read a transcript of that *Dateline* conversation, you might have thought that Britney and Kevin had been deeply misunderstood and really they had a storybook romance. But when you watch the video, the body language, especially Brit's facial faux pas, make it plain to see that there is much more to the story here. In retrospect, with the benefit of time, we see a vulnerable young woman desperately trying to mask her obvious anxiety and sadness, which sadly sprang a facial leak that revealed a soon-to-be doomed marriage. Spotting emotional leakage in the face can be one of the most powerful ways to sense that the message someone is *trying* to share is not necessarily the truth.

Now that you have gathered your intel and have your subject's baseline squared away and you've conducted your wiretap, it's time to focus on the stakeout, where you'll learn how to decode the facial signs that are likely indicators of deceptive hot spots. Wouldn't you feel empowered if you knew what the lightning-fast changes to facial expressions and forehead tension were telling you? Although facial findings won't give you all the information you're looking for—for example, whether or not the person is actually lying—spotting them gives you potential areas to later probe.

PREPARING FOR THE STAKEOUT

Our expressions affect each other *dramatically*—we need to continually be aware what effect our nonverbal communication makes on other people, and how their nonverbal messages may be coloring our impressions of them. One Harvard study found that the patients of physical therapists who used more distant non-verbal communication—by not making eye contact and not smiling—took a turn for the worse in the short term (during the hospital stay and at discharge), and this negative effect lasted up to three months afterward. In contrast, the health of patients of physical therapists with more open, caring nonverbal communication—with more smiles, nods, and frowns—improved immediately and over the long haul.[1] Remember: how you approach any situation changes the outcome of that situation. If you approach the stakeout with calm ease, you will keep your target at ease as well.

Scale back on the mirroring. When other people look nervous and uncomfortable, we feel nervous and uncomfortable. When people appear angry, we get angry. Moods are somewhat contagious. And when people try to convince us of something, they often will expend energy trying to change the way we feel about a situation: smiling more, touching more, yelling more.

One way to sidestep these efforts is to consciously stop mirroring. While mirroring is an excellent way to establish rapport, once you get to this stage in the process, you want to stop because it might interfere with your ability to detect deception. One Dutch study asked a group of forty-six students to have a conversation with someone and try to tell whether their conversational partner was fibbing about a charitable donation. The students who were told *not* to mirror—versus the ones who were told to mirror, or told nothing at all—scored significantly better at detecting the lie.[2]

When we mirror others' expressions, the mirror neurons in our brains stimulate the same kinds of emotional responses as the person with whom we're talking. We are wired to connect! So, if you find you've been drawn in by this person's charm before, you'll have to consciously force yourself to step back, switch on your BS Barometer, and not get drawn into his or her web of deceit.

Remember that baseline! Remember the golden rule: always start with the baseline. Everyone has his or her own "normal" way of interacting with the world. Her idiosyncrasies could be mentioned within this chapter as "potentially deceptive signs"—but she could have been doing those things every day since she was six months old! You have no idea until you've collected her personal intel from the beginning.

Beware of nonverbal wild cards. Before you get started looking for nonverbal hot spots, ask yourself if the person you're about to do the stakeout on is in one of the following wild card categories. Margo Bennett, captain of the University of California at Berkeley's police department, identified a few things that might make suspects' nonverbal behavior an untrustworthy source of information. These factors include:

Their intelligence. The smarter the suspect, the more likely his or her body language "makes sense" and mirrors his or her thinking. But when people are not the sharpest tools in the shed, their body language might reflect confusion or misinterpretation of the questions instead of anxiety about lying.

Their emotions. When people are unstable, so are their body language signals. You can never know where the emotions are coming from or what they relate to.

Their age. Kids and teens may not have matured enough to appreciate the consequences of their actions—so they may not feel fear, even when they should!

Their culture. Some cultures consider the direct eye contact favored by Caucasians to be rude—so a person's averted eyes would be a sign of respect rather than disrespect or guilt. (This is especially true among African American, Middle Eastern, Asian, or Native American people.)[3]

Their partying status. Drinking and taking drugs dramatically alters behavior. Don't look at a drunk person and think you can gauge his *real* baseline—he's far from it.[4]

Trust yourself. Above all, with this process, you have to trust your eyes. Your BS Barometer is helping your brain absorb and process more than you can ever consciously know. One study published in the journal *Psychological Science* found that people can recall specific faces, even just from blurry photographs, up to two years later. All it took was to look at the image several times over the course of a couple of days—then it was committed to memory.[5] This "perceptual learning" is a form of pattern recognition, and it sticks with us even though we might see thousands of faces in between. Your brain is like an FBI database, filled up with all the images you took the time to study even years ago.

Okay, now it's time to act fast and take care of business—let's break down how to spot nonverbal indicators of deception.

TaKING CaRE OF BUSINESS IN THE STaKEOUT

Remember, pretenders and phonies are all tightrope walkers, and their primary objective is to not fall off the rope while threading their web of deceit. If you

POWER TEAM TURNAROUND

Name: Edward Ashak

Age: 33

Occupation: Software developer

(Baron Thrower II)

What was stopping you from spotting master manipulators and liars?

Because I am new to this country, there are a few different nuances in body language that I am not completely familiar with. When I first started at my current job, the guy that I was supposed to work with explained that there is no "actual" boss over me. Later on he started assuming himself to be the boss even when we were supposed to be working together as a team. It felt like a stab in the back to me, especially because my experience in the job is far greater than his. That led to a lot of friction at work that later on started affecting my life even after work.

How have you changed?

I think I've been deceived in the past mainly because I didn't look at the whole picture and didn't listen with my eyes. I also never paid attention to the changes in the body language of the speaker that would indicate a hot spot. I now listen with my eyes as well as my ears. I consider myself a good listener, but now I have better skills to not only listen to what people have to say but *how* they say it—and how their body says it.

The BS Barometer has helped improve my communication with others, especially with computer geeks such as myself, where communication usually is very awkward. The training also helps me when I'm talking to people in the office about deadlines and when I must obtain some information that they are not willing to share. I know it will help me better negotiate my job and advance my career.

concentrate and know what to look for, you'll *see* the same three categories of signals in their body language that expose the possibility that there's something they're not telling you with their words.

We humans have long believed that "the body never lies." In ancient China, people who were suspected of lying were forced to chew rice powder, then to spit it out. If the rice powder was wet, the person was judged as honest; dry, the person was branded a liar and punished.[67] We know now that one of the physical signs of *fear* is a dry mouth—but lying has no reliably accurate facial or body language signal. That's why people with the best BS Barometers are the ones who can quickly spot deviations from a person's baseline.

It's time for you to rev your engines because you're about to drive circles around every nervous, teeter-tottering, convincing-not-conveying, and backsliding liar who, without knowing it, has very little control over facial faux pas.

The Teeter-Tottering Face

We spend our entire lives gathering information from other people's faces, so we don't have to work that hard to get the basics down. The special motor neurons in our brains called "mirror neurons" react immediately to subtle signs of true emotion on others' faces—a flash of a genuine smile or a tiny hint of sorrow can trigger that same emotion within us.

Nearly fifty years ago, nonverbal communication researcher Dr. Paul Ekman discovered that all humans share seven universal emotions: happiness, sadness, disgust, fear, surprise, anger, and contempt. These can be seen in microexpressions that are universally hard-wired into us primates and have been studied in human populations from the United States to Japan to Papua New Guinea. These automatic expressions are the same whether you are male or female, black or white, young or old. If you are surprised, you make the same expressions.

These microexpressions may only leak out for one-fifteenth of a second—literally a flutter of your lashes. While these micromovements can be a challenge to spot, learning to see these fleeting emotions is incredibly useful because each of these emotions registers with very distinct patterns that are almost impossible to fake. Consciously moving one of the more than forty intricate muscles in our face is hard to do, hard to manipulate, hard to disguise—for everyone. All of these reasons make spotting microexpressions about the closest thing we have to mind reading. Now, mind you—we still can't know for sure what the catalyst was that sparked the wobbly leakage on the tightrope of those emotions (she says she's sad, but we spot happiness; he tells us he's happy, but we decode disgust and surprise). But if we see the microexpression, the person is *definitely* feeling that emotion—which, for a liar, makes these moments of emotional leakage the face's version of teeter-tottering.

The good news is that, even before we study them to enhance our BS Barometer, our brains are already innately keyed into these microexpressions. One study found that people could determine the winner of an unfamiliar race for governor simply by watching ten-second silent video clips of a debate. Their predictions got *worse* when they added in the sound (but, considering how disingenuous and deceptive many politicians' normal debate language is, that's hardly surprising!).[8] Spending time learning the traits of each universal emotion's microexpression will greatly bolster the diagnostic capability of your BS Barometer. Studies have found that FBI agents trained in spotting microexpressions can increase their detecting deception accuracy to 70 percent, and, in some cases, to more than 90 percent. (Coast Guard investigators—who do a fair bit of intercepting smuggled drugs with non-native English speakers and often have to use more body language to communicate—also score well, at 80 percent.[9]) Now it's your turn!

Leaked Happiness

(Jordan Strauss/WireImage)

(Janine Driver)

Two of my favorite women: (*Left*) Comedian, TV host, and actress Ellen DeGeneres splashes a genuine smile when she arrives at COVERGIRL Cosmetics' Fiftieth Anniversary Party. (*Right*) My beautiful and loving mom with Vice President Joe Biden at the Susan G. Komen Race for the Cure barbecue at the vice president's house on June 10, 2011 (my forty-first birthday).

A person's genuine smile is pulled up toward the ears, not back toward the jaw, and you will see crow's feet around the eyes. A real, honest smile has a powerful and immediate effect on its viewer. For example, even though we know that almost every line that a politician utters is manufactured, the genuineness of their smiles still can have a big impact on us. One study found that politicians got bigger laughs for jokes that were delivered with genuine smiles—involving that "eye crinkle"—than those delivered with less sincere smiles.[10]

Leaked Sadness

A flash of sadness is almost impossible to manufacture. When someone is truly feeling sad, his bottom lip will pout, but his inner eyebrows will pull together and curl up. That inner eyebrow is the hardest muscle to move on your face. That's why you can tell babies are sad even when they have pacifiers in their mouths. You can't see their mouths, but you can see that inner eyebrow curving up, and you know they're about to cry.

Tiny expressions of sadness are hard to fake. If you fake a pout, your bottom lip will stay there for a while, but the forehead won't be touched. See if you can spot the true sadness in the next photos.

Susan Smith was pleading for the safe return of her two sons, who'd

(Associated Press)

Toyota CEO Akio Toyoda chokes up and leaks genuine sadness and remorse with pulled-together eyebrows, wrinkled forehead, lip pout with corners of lips pulled down, and wrinkled chin, at the National Press Club after testifying on Capitol Hill about the car manufacturer's massive recalls and numerous safety problems.

(Associated Press)

(Karl Larsen/FilmMagic)

(*Left*) Susan Smith confessing to the murder of her two sons after insisting nine days earlier that they had been kidnapped. (*Right*) Paris Hilton rides home after her sentencing for a driving under the influence (DUI) violation in 2007.

THE BS BAROMETER READING

AT THE MEA CULPA PRESS CONFERENCE

At Tiger Woods's infamous press conference, when he issued his official apology to his wife, his family, his fans, and his sponsors, everyone was expecting a serious mea culpa, hoping for a show of sincerity and contrition that would help them remember why they loved Tiger to begin with.

Tiger knew the stakes were high. "I know I have bitterly disappointed all of you," he said. "I have made you question who I am and how I could have done the things I did. I am embarrassed that I have put you in this position. For all that I have done, I am so sorry." But was he really sorry?

Golfer Tiger Woods speaks during a press conference at the headquarters of the PGA Tour, his first public appearance since admitting to marital infidelity. **(Getty Images)**

BS Barometer Reading: Running on Vapors

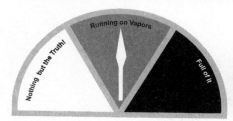

KEY

Total BS: Full of It

Partial BS: Running on Vapors

BS-Free: Nothing but the Truth!

Not! If Tiger were truly "so sorry," we would see more sadness—his eyebrows would pull together and slightly lift up. His lip would pout out at the bottom, and he wouldn't be doing the zombie death stare. Instead, what we see is nothing—no activity on the forehead at all, staring straight ahead, stock still. He also did a couple of chest touches that followed his words, indicating he'd been highly coached on body language. The whole press conference is like watching a really bad actor impersonating a person who is apologizing.

been missing for over a week and whose bodies were found strapped into their car seats, in their mom's car, at the bottom of a lake. Smith confessed to the murders a day after this photo was taken. Look at this classic teeter-totterer's eyebrows—they betray no sadness at all. Then look at Paris Hilton, who is trying to cover up her true feelings after being sentenced to forty-five days in jail for her DUI conviction in 2007. (She eventually served twenty-two days.) She covers her mouth with her hand and most of her face with her huge sunglasses—but, like a crying baby with a pacifier, she just can't escape those telltale eyebrows.

Leaked Disgust

Disgust is a visceral response—*eww!* Your upper lip pulls up, your nose wrinkles, and your brow pulls down. You might also see this with the upper lip drawn up but without any involvement of the brows or nose.

We look at the mouth more than any other place on a person's face. We tend to think we're looking people "in the eye," but we actually look at people's mouths and tongues more. You may be surprised to learn that when a person is

Oakland Athletics' outfielder Jose Canseco grimaces in disgust after tasting Japanese sake as his wife looks on during a reception for the U.S. All-Star baseball team at a Tokyo hotel, Friday, October 31, 1986. **(Associated Press)**

HeaD-SHaKING NOS OR YeSeS

GIRL: "I had a great time tonight."

GUY: "Me, too! I'd love to get together again soon."

GIRL: "Absolutely [shakes head from left to right]. Let's do it again!"

This incongruence between the verbal and the nonverbal is often spotted in televised liars, such as when President Bill Clinton nodded his head "Yes" as he proclaimed, "I did not have sexual relations with that woman." Or when baseball's infamous ladies' man Alex Rodriguez nodded his head "Yes" when he told Katie Couric that he never took steroids. Your gut reaction to your date's head shake might be to think that you're never going to hear from her again. But simmer down, that might not be the case!

In moments like these, you need to give yourself permission to attract authentic and real people in your life by *avoiding* the trap of being a mind reader. After all, by not probing deeper into your date mate's uncertainty, you might be stupidly walking away from a second date with your future wife! Perhaps your gal pal shook her head "No" while saying "Yes," because she's not sure when she's getting back from her month-long summer vacation, or because she suddenly remembered that she told her mother she'd call her back hours ago, and in the hustle and bustle, she forgot. Or maybe she is, in fact, lying, and she wants nothing to do with you. You won't know what that shrug is all about until you probe further. Yes, it's up to *you* to do your own due diligence.

being deceptive, he is more likely to keep his mouth closed: either he is semi-consciously trying to avoid allowing the truth to slip from his lips, or he is simply trying to keep a tight rein on his body language. It's true! So although disgust is not the most lovable expression, it could be worse. Wait until you see the mouths of some of the most infamous lips-sealed liars!

Leaked Fear

In fear, the mouth opens and is taut, as are the jaw muscles. Eyebrows may rise and go straight across. The eyes get huge, and you can often see the whites of the eyes all around the iris. Also, when we are terrified or shocked, we may put

On Tuesday, September 11, 2001, people in front of New York's St. Patrick's Cathedral react as they look down Fifth Avenue toward the World Trade Center after two airliners crashed into the twin 110-story buildings. **(Associated Press)**

our hands in front of our mouths, almost as if to say, "I can't take any more in." We tend to touch our faces as our mouths hang open—as in this picture. This is genuine fear combined with shock.

Leaked Surprise

When you see surprise, the mouth opens and is relaxed. The eyebrows go up but remain curled like rainbows. Surprise is the only microexpression that is always a catalyst to another emotion. So you have a surprise party—the guest of honor could leak surprise and then burst out crying. Or leak surprise and burst out smiling. But if you're in a haunted house, that microexpression is likely to start as surprise and then quickly turn into fear, like in the next images.

The man in glasses on the right is startled and demonstrates surprise with his mouth hanging open wide. His jaw is relaxed, not taut, and his bottom lip is loose. His eyebrows are up and curved (in fear they go up and go straight across). However, we clearly witness fear within the whites of his eyes, and his hand pops up to protect his throat. The woman in the middle is also demonstrating surprise, but less dramatically than her friend. (My fave is the guy on the far left, who is scared to death, curled up in a standing fetal position.)

In the other picture, you can't help but wonder what the heck just shocked and terrified these strong young men? Other than the man on the far left (who shows disgust with his pulled-up upper lip and wrinkled nose), the other three

Patrons at the Nightmares Fear Factory in Niagara Falls show signs of surprise and fear. **(Nightmares Fear Factory)**

are 110 percent surprised with a splash of fear. Surprise itself only lasts less than three seconds and is always a catalyst to another emotion—in this case, likely pants-wetting terror.

If you knock on the door to a suspected cheater's or liar's house to confront the person and you see pure surprise, chances are you are looking an innocent person in the face. But if you see fear, you might be looking at a liar—because he knew it was a matter of time until you knocked on the door. He knows *exactly* why you're there.

Leaked Anger

When angry, our brows come down, our mouth gets tight, and we lose color in our top lip—and that lip becomes one solid line.

In this photo of disgraced teeter-totterer Congressman Anthony Weiner, who was busted sending pictures of his penis to women online and denied it for weeks before finally admitting he did it, you can see his jaw and mouth are extremely tight. He clearly did not like being asked about this subject.

Former New York Congressman Anthony Weiner shows a combination of embarrassment, anger, and arrogance while listening to a reporter's question at a press conference during his Twitter photo scandal. **(Associated Press)**

SPOTTING MIXED EMOTIONS

It's important to understand that in the everyday world, such distinct emotions as those mentioned in the examples are rare. Emotions are not that clear-cut. More often you'll get a combination of emotions. Not just 100 percent fear—you'll see fear and sadness. Or surprise and happiness. Or disgust and anger. The best way to learn microexpressions is simply to study them enough so that you'll be better at spotting them on the fly. Sharpen your new observational skills in a fraction of a second. Visit www.youcant lietome.com and use San Francisco State University psychology professor David Matsumoto's training tools to train your brain to notice the facial expressions of the seven universal emotions.

Leaked Contempt

Contempt is the half-smile, the smirk of superiority. This teeter-tottering expression is one of the most dangerous for relationships—psychologist John Gottman found that this expression is evidence of a doomed marriage. It screams, "I have

Democratic Senate nominee, Illinois State Treasurer Alexi Giannoulias, prepares for his debate with Republican Senate candidate Representative Mark Kirk (R-IL) on October 19, 2010, in Chicago, Illinois. **(Getty Images)**

A SPECIAL KIND OF LIAR'S SMILE: DUPING DELIGHT

While a genuine smile is hard to fake, a certain other kind of smile—equally genuine—is hard to hide. Some liars, especially the sociopathic kind, derive tremendous enjoyment from pulling one over on other people. Despite their ability to snow their victims, their giddiness at their own successful duplicity sometimes leaks out in a genuine smile, a phenomenon that Dr. Paul Ekman has labeled "duper's delight."

Bernard Madoff walks down Lexington Avenue to his apartment in New York City in December 2008. (Getty Images)

Exhibit A: Bernie Madoff strides down a New York City street, hounded by press, after the revelation of the extent of his scams. His smirk leaks not only duper's delight but also contempt, though we'll never know for whom—the reporters? Or his victims? If you ask me, this is clearly *not* the face of a contrite man.

it all figured out, I'm better than you." For cops working in violence prevention, this is a dangerous face to see. You should consider contempt a thinly veiled threat: "I am either going to go around you or *through* you."

We've seen contempt leaked by a lot of alleged bad guys (and gals), such as Scott Peterson, O.J. Simpson, Casey Anthony, and Lindsay Lohan when they were in court. They presented themselves as credible but they leaked that contemptuous, unilateral half-smile, because they think they're better than the people judging them and the people whom they've harmed. (For a particularly horrific example, see "A Special Kind of Liar's Smile: Duping Delight," opposite.)

The Convince-Not-Convey Face

Convince-not-convey shows up on our faces as extreme versions of natural expressions. If you've ever had to grin and bear it through an excruciating violin recital or mask a giggle while you shot a stern look at your child for making an admittedly hilarious joke in church, you've been on the convince-not-convey facial tightrope yourself. Liars are no different—and some are pretty good at it.

Fake Emotions

The big gun for the convincer is consciously faking emotions. They try very hard to convince you just how honest they are. But often they miss very key, subtle differences in the movement of the forehead, eyes, cheeks, and eyebrows—all those microexpressions we talked about earlier. So a great way to bust a liar is to really focus on some key differences between genuine and fake emotions.

Fake sadness. When people "buy" fake sadness, they're often falling for a frown. My son fakes it all the time when he wants to play more of his LEGO Wii game. "Please, Mom! I only have one more level!" And that lip goes upside down and the little bottom lip comes out in a pout—but he doesn't have a sign of sadness in his eyebrows or on his forehead. (Angus, when you get your forehead involved, we can talk.)

Fake anger. True anger could point to someone being outraged at being falsely accused—but "fake" anger could be an attempt to throw you off the scent ("How dare you accuse me?"). We talked about this in the wiretap as being a big one for convincers—they like to bully you into backing down. And most people do back down! But when you're confronting someone on an issue and she gets angry, remember the picture of Anthony Weiner. If you don't see those flat lips or tight jaw, give yourself some credit—it's just bluster, and it's clear you're getting closer and closer to the truth. We talk about this more in

(WireImages)

(Getty Images)

(Getty Images)

chapter 8, "The Interrogation." For now, know that in deception, anger can be used as a disguise.

Fake happiness. Here's the thing: we're all suckers for a nice smile. First of all, when we see a genuine smile—a so-called Duchenne smile, characterized by "crow's feet" wrinkles next to our eyes—our mirror neurons light up and cause us to feel pleasure. We naturally pay more attention to smiling faces, and genuine smiles help people trust each other faster. A naturally occurring genetic mutation also causes some people's brains to respond even more significantly when they see people smiling—so be aware that you may be one of those people who are more drawn to smiles.[11]

As the general public becomes more and more savvy about genuine versus faked body language, sometimes celebrities create new tricks to generate those "genuine" smiles. Sometimes stars like Reese Witherspoon use these tricks to make the most of their already happy faces.

If you study the hundreds of red carpet photos Reese Witherspoon has posed for, it's clear the warm, sweet, and genuinely kind actress has learned that tucking your tongue behind your teeth generates the cheek muscles that most mimic a natural smile. When you tuck your tongue back there, that action forces your cheeks to go up and to get the crinkles on the side of your eyes.

Lightning-Fast Changes in Demeanor

The speed of a switch in emotions is, in itself, a telling sign. I'll say to my son, "Angus, I'm not buying it. It's time to stop the Wii. Let's go read a book." And his "sadness" is just gone—like turning the channel on the TV. If someone can

LET FAUX EYES DO THE WATCHING

Sometimes body language can help you keep people honest even when you're nowhere around. Several studies have found that just a visual representation of eyes may subliminally make people feel like they're being watched. One UCLA study found that when people were playing a computer game, the presence of eye-like shapes in the background caused people to share more resources with others.[12] Another study found that the image of a pair of eyes on a parking fee collection box (versus a picture of some flowers) sparked a 300 percent increase in money collected.[13]

If you are concerned about people snooping in your office after hours, or your kids sneaking candy when you're not around, copy a picture of a person's eyes and create a funny, lighthearted sign: "See Mom Before Sweets!" near the candy jar, or "See Anything Interesting?" in your office. That will certainly make them think twice!

One of my students made this sign to encourage her partner to quit smoking. The French note says, "I want you to love you as much as I love you!" **(Anja Linder)**

go from sad to happy or from fear to anger to happiness in the time it takes to switch the station, that's the big red flag of the convincer.[14]

Changes in Eye Contact

When psychologists at Texas Christian University surveyed more than 2,500 adults in sixty-three countries, they found that more than 70 percent believed liars give less eye contact than truthful people.[15] During each of my keynote presentations, I ask the audience, "Do you think liars are more likely to decrease eye contact or increase eye contact?" What do *you* think? If you didn't guess either answer, then you are on the right track!

The whole amazingly complex, tiny muscle system that allows us to raise and lower our eyelids communicates a ton of emotional information. When study subjects are asked to guess how a person is feeling, they'll be just as likely to get it right whether they see the entire face or they just see their eyes.[16]

People are all over the map with eye contact—some people give you the epic long stare; some people never catch your eye. Neither is necessarily a liar. What you're looking for in the convincer is a *change* in their level of eye contact. In the United States and Canada, having eye contact about 30 to 60 percent of the time is the norm. But if they've been looking at you about 50 percent of the time, and suddenly drop to 20 percent, or shoot up to 80 percent, those are hot spots.

One study from the University of Alabama found that male experts who testify in trials have more credibility with the jury when they make large amounts of eye contact than if they make average or low-level eye contact. Interesting, this didn't change at all for women—their credibility remained constant, regardless of how much eye contact they made.[17]

Changes in Blink Rate

With convincers, look for an increase in blink rate. While newborn babies only blink one to two times a minute, the average blink rate for an adult is between four and fourteen blinks per minute. However, during a recent Body Language Institute certification program, I put my students' blink rate to the test. On the low end was Cory, with two blinks per minute; on the high end was my mom, Lorraine, with forty-two blinks per minute. The difference between two dramatically different base lines could be due to fatigue, disease, or medication. For instance, my mother, who has breast cancer, had received chemo that week. The severely intense medication could have been drying out her eyes, and the additional blinks provided additional lubrication. When detecting deception, your job is to look for an increase or decrease in a person's eye blink baseline. While

BP Chief Executive Tony Hayward testifies before the Oversight and Investigations Subcommittee during a hearing on "The Role of BP in the Deepwater Horizon Explosion and Oil Spill," June 17, 2010, in Washington, D.C. **(Getty Images)**

increased eye blinking is a sign of nervousness—another result of the "drying" phenomenon of fight or flight—a decrease is a sign of increased cognitive load. A person is focused so hard on thinking that his eyes stay quite stationary.[18]

Go ahead, test your blink rate. Ask a friend to time you, or set your timer on your cell phone for one minute, and baseline your blink rate as you share a story about your day today. Are you average, or are you at the extremes like Cory and my mom?

THE BACKSLIDING FACE

The backsliding face just wants to *hide*. By whatever means necessary, the owner of the backsliding face wants to turn tail and run back on that tightrope to keep his or her true emotions from the rest of the world.

Facial Blocking

Facial blocking happens when the backsliders in our life not only want to disappear, they also literally can't look at the danger that's right in front of them. Unconsciously, when you turn up the heat, they'll deviate from their norm and cover their eyes, mouth, or entire face with their hand, arm, a pair of sunglasses, or maybe even a forward-tilted baseball hat, all in a subconscious attempt to disappear. Sometime during your confrontation, you may see the person peek around, to check if you're "buying" his story about why he's been cheating on his wife and how it's not *his* fault. However, if he doesn't like what he sees, facial blocks will pop up again and he'll revert to backsliding.

Hiding in Their Hair

During the first couple weeks of the infamous Casey Anthony trial, Casey was often seen neurotically pulling her mousy brown chin-length bangs in front of her face. This backsliding behavior was such a screaming red flag that both Nancy Grace and CNN's *Headline News (HLN)* invited me on their shows to discuss possible reasons why Casey would be acting so ridiculously odd. Perhaps her lawyers saw the discussion, because for the remainder of the trial, her hair was pulled away from her face.

Yes, liars will often twist, stroke, braid, and play with their hair when they're nervous, but so do people who are nervous on a date. Be sure to put the behavior in perspective. Not every kindergartner playing with the braids in her hair is a lying, cheating manipulator. But when an adult woman suddenly drapes her hair in front of her face, it screams, "Now, you can't see me." (For more of these "pacifiers," see the table in chapter 7 on pages 170–171.)

Lip Locking

Backsliders embroiled in scandals in the public eye often leak strong emotions. Many of these emotions can be seen in the lips. I have a favorite saying: "When we don't like what we see or hear, our lips suddenly disappear." And we certainly saw that rule of thumb with these cheating scandals:

The Cheater	The Transgression	What the Lips Say
	In this December 11, 2010, file photo, former Democratic presidential candidate **John Edwards** is seen in Raleigh, North Carolina. Edwards and federal prosecutors are arguing over whether the money used to cover up his extramarital affair was a campaign contribution or just a gift from his old friends. **(Associated Press)**	The sadness leaked here is totally clear. He did it, he got caught, and now he has to pay the price.
	New York Governor **Eliot Spitzer** addresses the media at his office in New York, March 10, 2008. In this image, Spitzer had apologized to his family for a "private matter" but made no reference to a *New York Times* report that he may have been linked to a prostitution ring. **(Associated Press)**	Governor Spitzer's massive upside-down U is a perfect example of utter embarrassment tinged with a little sadness. He cannot take any more stress.
	Kobe Bryant, seated next to his wife, Vanessa, pauses during a news conference about his arrest for sexual assault of a nineteen-year-old in July 2003. **(Associated Press)**	Just imagine the discomfort here— Bryant is denying the assault but "confessing" to consensual sex with another woman. With his wife sitting two inches away.
	Alex Rodriguez holds a press conference at Yankees Spring Training at George M. Steinbrenner Field to address his steroid use. **(Getty Images)**	These lips are so far gone, I don't think we see *any* lip at all here.
	Former New York Yankees pitcher **Roger Clemens** testifies on Capitol Hill about the illegal use of steroids and other performance-enhancing drugs in baseball. **(Getty Images)**	This perfect upside-down U shows just how sad Clemens is to be in this situation.
	The sixty-two-year-old Socialist politician and former International Monetary Fund chief, **Dominique Strauss-Kahn,** answers questions on September 18, 2011, outside Paris concerning a civil suit from his New York accuser as well as a probe into allegations he tried to rape writer Tristane Banon, an allegation he denies. **(Getty Images)**	Strauss-Kahn is denying the assault and rape and before he's had due process, all his dreams of becoming France's president are sunk.

Involuntary Physiological Reactions

The fight-or-flight response to stress is automatic and can cause a number of real physiological changes that indicate how much stress a liar is undergoing. Next are listed some facial fight-or-flight findings you'll be able to spot with your new, stronger, more powerful BS Barometer.

Breathing more deeply. People might take deep breaths or flare their nostrils to get more oxygen (again, the fight-or-flight response is in effect here).

Going pale in the face (blanching) indicates fear, which is most typical in people who think they're about to get caught.[19]

Going red in the face (blushing) indicates embarrassment, most typical in people who feel guilty (but are not necessarily lying).

Runny nose (or lack thereof!). Our nose, mouth, throat, and eyes are all connected. So when someone is truly heartbroken or devastated, there should be real tears, her nose should get stuffed up and run, she should do deep swallows.

Nose Rubbing

We all have erectile tissue in our noses (same as in our genitals), and when we're being deceptive, our fight-or-flight response forces more blood into our outer extremities—which can make the nose tickle. This physiological response has long been suspected as the basis of the Pinocchio story, and any liar worth their salt knows this—but you might be able to spot this tic in a little kid. Tread carefully with this tip, Sherlock, because according to Dr. Oz, all men and women touch, scratch, or pick their noses approximately five times in an hour.

Now that you've mastered the art of deciphering people's facial flubs and faux pas, the truth is within your grasp. You know how to get your target's baseline; study his words and vocal tone for hot spots; and pinpoint the changes on his face that indicate there's more to the story. Next stop, the full body surveillance. You're about to master the art of observing the moving target.

EXERCISING YOUR BS BAROMETER: THE STAKEOUT

Much of the exercises for this step are about training your attention to fine details, a skill that will help you spot microexpressions as they're happening. Remember: the more practice you have in studying truthful people's emotional expression, the better you will become at spotting liars!

Download Your *Free* Instant Replay for This Chapter

Visit www.youcantlietome.com and listen to my dear friend Oscar Rodriguez, a hypnotherapist in the Washington, D.C., area, as he reviews with you all the tools you learned on your stakeout.

Tube In!

Visit www.youtube.com/user/bsbarometer and watch a person's baseline video first, then two corresponding stories next. Can you spot which one is the lie based on the person's facial expressions alone? Once you've made your guess, click on my video analysis for that person. Good luck!

The Sherlock Holmes Exercise

This exercise helps train your visual-spatial sense and your working memory, both essential brain activities that help you pay attention to small details while still maintaining a big-picture perspective—exactly the skills you need while using your BS Barometer. Set the timer on your phone, watch, or oven. In a second, you'll hit start on the clock and time yourself to see how quickly you can scan the following patterns and find the letter or symbols that are different. Think like an observant Secret Service agent and look for what doesn't belong here! During this exercise, you won't know exactly what you are looking for; the same holds true when you are detecting deception with the liars in your life. Stay focused, be open-minded, and give your eyes permission to find the break in the pattern. Good luck!

xfgxfgxfgxfgxfgxfgxfgxfgxfgxfgxfgxfgxfgxfgxfgxfgxfgxfgxfgxfgxfgxfgxfgxfgxfg
xfgxfgxfgxfgxfgxfgxfgxfgxfgxfgxfgxfgxfgxfgxfgxfgxfgxfgxfgxfgxfgxfgxfgxfgxfg
xfgxfgxfgxfgxfgxfgxfgxfgxfgxfgxfgxfgxfgxfgxfgxfgxfgxfgxfgxfgxfgifgxfgxfgxfg
xfgxfgxfgxfgxfgxfgxfgxfgxfgxfgxfgxfgxfgxfgxfgxfgxfgxfgxfgxfgxfgxfgxfgxfgxfg
xfgxfgxfgxfgxfgxfgxfgxfgxfgxfgxfgxfgxfgxfgxfgxfgxfgxfgxfgxfgxfgxfgxfgxfgxfg

Next,

!@#$%^&*()!@#$%^&*()!@#$%^&*()!@#$%^&*()!@#$%^&*()!@#$
!@#$%^&*()!@#$%^&*()!@#$%^&*()!@#$%^&*()!@#$%^&*()!@#$
!@#$%^&*()!@#$%^&*()!@#$%^&*()!@#$%^&*()!@#$%^&*()!@#$
!@#$%^&*()!@#$%^&*()!@#$%^&*()!@#$%^&*()!@#$%^&*()!@#$
!@#$%^&*()!@#$%;&*()!@#$%^&*()!@#$%^&*()!@#$%^&*()!@#$
!@#$%^&*()!@#$%^&*()!@#$%^&*()!@#$%^&*()!@#$%^&*()!@#$

Next,

```
,",",",",",",",",",",",",",",",",",",",",",",",",",",",",",",",",",",",",",",",",",",",",",",",",",",",",
.",.",.",.",.",.",.",.",.",.",.",.",.",.",.",.",.",.",.",.",.",.",.",.",.",.",.",.",.",.",.",.",.",.",.",.",.",.",
.",",",",",",",",",",",",",",",",",",",",",",",",",",",",",",",",",",",",",",",",",",",",",",",
.",",",",",",",",",",",",",",",",",",",",",",",",",",",",",",",",",",",",",",",",",",",",",
.",.",.",.",.",.",.",.",.",.",.",.",.",.",.",.",.",.",.",.",.",.",.",.",.",.",.",.",.",.",.",.",.",.",.",.",.",.",
.",",",",",",",",",",",",",",",",",",",",",",",",",",",",",",",",",",",",",",",",",",",",",
.",.",.",.",.",.",.",.",.",.",.",.",.",.",.",.",.",.",.",.",.",.",.",.",.",.",.",.",.",.",.",.",.",.",.",.",.",.",
.",",",",",",",",",",",",",",",",",",",",",",",",",",",",",",",",",",",",",",",",",",",",",
.",.",.",.",.",.",.",.",.",.",.",.",.",.",.",.",.",.",.",.",.",.",.",.",.",.",.",.",.",.",.",.",.",.",.",.",.",.",
.",",",",",",",",",",",",",",",",",",",",",",",",",",",",",",",",",",",",",",",",",",",",",
```

Next,

```
-=-=-=-=-=-=-=-=-=-=-=-=-=-=-=-=-=-=-=-=-=-=-=-=-=-=-=-=-=-=-=-=-=-=-=-=-=-=-=
-=-=-=-=-=-=-=-=-=-=-=-=-=-=-=-=-=-=-=-=-=-=-=-=-=-=-=-=-=-=-=-=-=-=-=-=-=-=-=
-=-=-=-=-=-=-=-=-=-=-=-=-=-=-=-=-=-=-=-=-=-=-=-=-=-=-=-=-=-=-=-=-=-=-=-=-=-=-=
-=-=-=-=-=-=-=-=-=-=-=-=-=-=-=-=-=-=-=-=-=-=-=-=-=-=-=-=-=-=-=-=-=-=-=-=-=-=-=
-=-=-=-=-=-=-=-=-=-=-=-=-=-=-=-=-=-=-=-=-=-=-=-=-=-=-=-=-=-=-=-=-=-=-=-=-=-=-=
-=-=-=-=-=-=-=-=-=-=-=-=-=-=-=-=-=-=-=-=-=-=-=-=-=-=-=-=-=-=-=-=-=-=-=-=-=-=-=
-===-=-=-=-=-=-=-=-=-=-=-=-=-=-=-=-=-=-=-=-=-=-=-=-=-=-=-=-=-=-=-=-=-=-=-=-=-=
-=-=-=-=-=-=-=-=-=-=-=-=-=-=-=-=-=-=-=-=-=-=-=-=-=-=-=-=-=-=-=-=-=-=-=-=-=-=-=
```

More Practice Spotting Microexpressions

Humans often have more than one expression on their faces at any given time—
especially when engaged in a possibly intense experience. Check out the flickr
stream of images from the Nightmares Fear Factory in Niagara Falls, Canada.
Of the thousands of people that come year after year, a total of 100,000 people
have been too scared to go in. From these images, I think you can see why.

Take five minutes and scroll through some of the pictures. See if you can spot
the different mixtures of fear, surprise, sadness, and anger. Also notice how, even
though we can spot the same few emotions on everyone's faces, their bodies'
responses to these emotions are all slightly different—some cover their mouths,
others make a fist or create a shield with their arms, others bend down in the fetal
position—and others even lean toward the danger. A fascinating look at genuine
extreme body language! http://www.flickr.com/photos/nightmaresfearfactory/.

A Truth and a Lie

This one is a favorite in all my classes and is a great one to share with a group of friends. You'll need about an hour or so to get the maximum benefit. This exercise will get participants used to asking questions and watching the nonverbal tells in people's faces.

Step 1. Divide people up into groups of three.

Step 2. Have one person tell the stories and one person ask the questions. The interviewer should only take into consideration what is happening on the face and ignore all other nonverbal movements. The third person is a silent observer watching every facial twitch and facial block.

Step 3. The interviewer will ask the storyteller any of the following questions, and the storyteller will tell two different complete stories. One is the truth, the other a bald-faced lie. (Caution: remind the storyteller that his lie cannot be a true story that happened to someone else he knows.) Give him three to five minutes to think of both stories.

- The time you first got your driver's license
- When you found out there was no Santa
- Your first kiss (or the first time you had sex)
- When you bought your first car
- When you bought your first condo or house
- Your first heartache
- The biggest mistake of your life
- The best day of your life
- The nicest thing someone has ever done for you
- The time you've experienced the most fear
- Your most embarrassing moment

Step 4. The observer should be taking notes on what happens with all aspects of the storyteller's face. At what point did the person's forehead move, did their lips disappear or get pulled back? When did their eyebrows move? At what point in their story did they touch a part of their face? And so on.

Step 5. After twenty minutes of questioning, the interviewer will guess which story is the truth and which story is the lie by writing his or her answer down. The silent observer will do the same. The storyteller will share with them the truth.

Step 6. Take turns until everyone has played all three roles.

Step 7. Discuss the results.

JUST REMEMBER...

- *Reading microexpressions is not mind reading.* Although leaked microexpressions will tell you what emotion someone is feeling, they will not tell you why he or she is feeling it—you have to follow through with the entire BS Barometer sequence to find out whether the person is being honest or not.

- *Some people's body language can't be trusted.* Not everyone's body language is a true reflection of their feelings. Children, those who are mentally limited, and drunk people all are nonverbal wild cards. Don't put too much stock into their nonverbal messages.

- *The mouth is the window to the soul.* When in doubt, look for the lips. Because remember: when we don't like what we see or hear, our lips disappear.

STEP 4:
THE FULL BODY SURVEILLANCE

Obviously we're under constant surveillance,
a camera on every phone, a camera in every
home. Wake up people, it's 2011.
—RAPPER BOBBY RAY

EOPLE WITH THE BEST BS BAROMETERS are the ones who can quickly spot deviations from the baseline—like my friend Marti the private investigator, whom we first met in chapter 4.

Marti was hired by a trucking company to investigate who was at fault when a tractor-trailer full of iPods was stolen. The pair of drivers had been instructed that, before they turned in for the night, they were to back their truck up to an electrified fence in order to discourage anyone from swiping their pricey load. Sadly, the team had not backed up the truck, and sure enough, the next morning, the truck was cleaned out.

Marti went down to see them for a little chat. One of the two seemed a little too "savvy," she says. She could tell he was lying by the fifth or sixth question she'd asked him. How could she tell? She started to notice these little hot spots on his left side—he'd hold the corner of his mouth down to create a crease, and he'd roll his left shoulder every time she'd ask him where he was from. Hmm, what was going on here?

He was honest about most other things: he'd immediately handed over his cell phone (which most crooks wouldn't do) and he'd confessed to being too chicken to back up to the electric fence (which had allowed the thieves ready access). So why the crease about something as innocent as where he was born?

"Son," Marti said kindly. "It's going to be a whole lot easier for you to tell me now than for me to find out later." He took a deep breath and put his head down and shook it from left to right, and confessed. "They never found out I got a criminal record for burglary," he said. "And now they're going to find out." He hadn't stolen the iPods—but he had lied to his employers originally on his job application, and those were the deceptive stressors Marti was seeing.

With the information you've gathered from the first three steps—the intel, the wiretap, and the stakeout—in hand, it's time for your training in the rest of nonverbal communication: full body surveillance.

In this chapter, we'll learn how to mine this amazing channel of communication that some experts say contains more than 50 percent of the true message behind our words. This info will give you instant power every time you go on a first date, secure a job interview, or apply for a mortgage—you'll have access to knowledge that no one else knows because you'll see the hidden subtext of those gestures and movements all around you. Your job in this chapter is simply to learn to note the hot spots—not to proclaim guilt or innocence. You have to reserve judgment until all the facts are in, until after you complete the next chapter, called "The Interrogation." Let's start with your own body language.

Be The Change You're Looking For

Bearing in mind that people tend to mirror one another, it's in your best interest to present honest, open body language. This will serve two purposes:

1. Using strong, open, honest body language will help any subject feel more secure with you.

2. Because he'll unconsciously feel like you trust him, he may be more open to telling you the truth.

Because, remember: we're not looking for the lie; we're looking for the *truth*. Anything you can do to help other people be honest will help you, too.

7-SECOND FIX

WITH THE CAR SALESMAN

(Baron Thrower II)

The Problem: You get roped in quickly by a charismatic car salesman's charm and at first you don't pick up on the fact that his right foot is across his left leg, where he's flashing you his "naughty bits," but you soon catch on! You cannot afford to be taken advantage of, so you need to move quickly.

The Fix: Use this embedded command: "Listen to me [pause]. When you [pause and lower voice] do what I say and [pause] accept less, then we'll close the deal."

Once he pulls out the heavy artillery with that "A-Okay" emblem (which in this picture looks 100 percent super-sexual—and inappropriate), you can maximize your power when you take action fast and turn your body away from him, use a palm-down gesture, and get out of the car.

The Result: You are always in the driver's seat!

When you consciously use open, honest, natural body language cues, people around you will subconsciously mirror them.

Honest people tend to:

- Point their toes and body toward you

- Lean forward with casual interest

- Be somewhat casual and at ease, but not artificially, so they shift their body posture fluently, without any nervous tics

- Keep their throat, neck dimple, belly button, and "naughty bits" all open and pointed toward you

- Use a wide, solid, powerful stance ("short fat candle") versus a tight, wobbly stance ("tall skinny candle")

- Uncross arms, keep their hands down at their sides or on their chairs

Taking Care of Business in Full Body Surveillance

By now, you must have the tightrope walker's analogy frozen in your brain! So you probably are not surprised to know that our body's nonverbals walk along that same tightrope, with the same three categories of signals to make your BS Barometer's needle go crazy.

Now let's consider what kinds of individual body signals you'll see within each of these categories.

Teeter-Tottering

The biggest teeter-tottering red flag you might see during your full body surveillance will be obvious physical discomfort or unconscious incongruence of a liar's gestures with what's coming out of his or her mouth.

Ill-Timed Shoulder Shrugs

Shoulder shrugs indicate uncertainty, so when a shrug shows up with a definitive statement, it could indicate deception.

"Have you ever cheated on your husband?"

If you see "No!" partnered with a shoulder shrug, there's definitely more to the story there. Although typically very subtle, and often involving only one side, the shoulder goes up around the ears. That shrug belies the "No"—there's something being held back. But it may not be her infidelity. Perhaps it's the fact that she knows her best friend is cheating on her husband, or she thinks her husband is running around on *her*. Or maybe her father cheated on her mother for years. Or maybe, just maybe, she's lying and she is in fact cheating. But one shrug does not a guilty spouse make. Slow it down there, Speedy Gonzales!

Ill-Timed Hand Shrugs

The often less noticeable hand shrug is very similar to the shoulder shrug. The palms typically stay facing down on the lap or table, and all of a sudden, they face up. The meaning is the same as a shoulder shrug: ambiguity and uncertainty.

Involuntary Bodily Functions

The fight-or-flight response to stress is automatic and can cause a number of real physiological changes that indicate how much stress a teeter-totterer is undergoing. Following is a short list with the description for each involuntary body function that, with your new calibrated BS Barometer, you'll be able to spot.

Excessive sweat. The body produces sweat during stress to keep it from overheating. This effect might show up as just sweaty palms or full-on pit-soaking.

Growling stomach, burping, gas. Some folks have a nervous gut and can start to have all kinds of digestive reactions to stress.[1]

Jittery hands. We lose our dexterity during fight or flight. At ATF, special agents do target practice while being shot at with paint balls—which really hurt!—in order to mimic the stress of a dangerous situation. You may have experienced this effect when you have to stop short suddenly in traffic—when you resume driving, you have to use both hands instead of the one lazy hand you used before the scare.

Convince-Not-Convey

Let's go back to the image of the liar on the tightrope. The teeter-totterer is focused solely on getting to the other side, and in that effort and concentration, often other signs of deception leak out. The reaction of those who seek to convince-not-convey is brute force: they want to bowl you over with their innocence. In the fight-or-flight reaction, this is definitely fight mode. Here are the most important areas to focus on when preparing to bust the overly anxious and arrogant convince-not-convey liar in your life.

Timing of Gestures Is Off

A lot of keynote speakers, trainers, workshop facilitators, athletes, and politicians are coached to touch their chests when they speak—because it's supposedly a sign of honesty. Pardon me, but that's BS.

In 2007, during an interrogation training class in Canada, I worked with an eccentric and fascinating man named Alan Gough, a former movie director and film photographer. Today, Alan's specialty is working with law enforcement agencies to detect deception by monitoring where the gestures appear when compared to the voice. Alan's even created a software program that slows down an interview frame by frame by frame, so he can spot the exact millisecond when someone speaks versus making the corresponding gesture.

Alan clued me in to an interesting distinction with gestures and speech. What he's discovered, and what other researchers have proven, is that when people are being honest, the hand gesture comes a beat before the word. So when

THE BS BAROMETER READING

AT THE AWARD SHOW

Music's most revered country-pop sensation Taylor Swift is often seen clutching her chest. She famously hugs her heart at awards shows when she is lauded. I've noticed another commonality to this seemingly charming embrace: Swift generally goes in to touch her heart about two full beats *before* she says how "touched" she is to be bestowed with (yet another) statue. Is she being genuine—or is it all an act?

LOS ANGELES, CA—JANUARY 5: Taylor Swift attends the 2011 People's Choice Awards at Nokia Theatre in Los Angeles. **(Getty Images)**

BS Barometer Reading: BS-Free

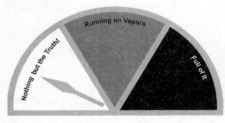

KEY

Total BS: Full of It

Partial BS: Running on Vapors

BS-Free: Nothing but the Truth!

Honest people make an emblem (like A-Okay) or illustrate a gesture (such as touching your hands to your heart) a beat or two prior to their corresponding words. When the gesture comes a beat *after* the corresponding words, that timing indicates insincerity, coaching, or too much forethought in trying to match gestures to words. Honest people don't have to try this hard.

I say, "Hey, Judy, I'll call you later," the gesture of holding the phone comes a half-second before the word.

Think about the opposite: Would you say, "Janine, I'll call you later!," wait a second, and then make the hand signal for the phone, or vice versa? Thought so! That's the difference between a great actor and a not-so-great actor—the great actor's body language gestures come before. You might remember how the cast of *Saturday Night Live* used to make fun of George H. W. Bush because his gestures would always come after his statements. That misstep told us he had been coached on what body language moves he should be making.

Try it: say to someone, "I agree," and then nod. Weird, right? Same thing if a friend tells you his personal views on politics. If he taps his chest before saying "That's what I believe," it seems genuine. If he does it afterward, he seems either dishonest or mentally challenged.

Palm-Down Gestures

A palm facing down at a meeting is almost always an attempt to control and keep a tight reign on the conversation. When convincers use this move while addressing a group from a standing position, it's their attempt to get everyone to back off!

(*Left*) During her weekly news conference in June 2011, House Minority Leader Representative Nancy Pelosi refuses to answer questions about the news that House Representative Anthony Weiner was to resign that day amid a lewd Twitter photograph scandal. (*Right*) Former Illinois Governor Rod Blagojevich leaves the Dirksen U.S. Courthouse on Tuesday, June 7, 2011, after another day in his retrial on federal corruption charges in Chicago, Illinois.

"Convincing" Steepling Gestures

As the awareness of body language grows, so does the artificial use of certain gestures to communicate power—or a lack of power, as you'll see in the next section (which I affectionately call "the naughty bit bonanza"). Both the attempt to

Check out my super-cool and awesome dad, who is a fire department mechanic. He's making a steepling gesture, a power move, next to his work truck. Once Dad had to testify in court as an expert and he was nervous for nearly a year, so on the big day, while testifying, he brought out the big guns—yup, the steeple—to overcompensate for his nerves. **(Janine Driver)**

show power or a lack of power can be used to try to convince us of lies. For instance, when someone genuinely uses a steeple—holding hands in a way so that all fingertips are touching—it communicates power, security, and confidence. But steepling can also appear with liars who are overly confident and trying to nonverbally bully you: "I've got it all figured out; I have a plan. Don't even try to question me." Donald Trump does it; Oprah does it; even Mr. Burns on *The Simpsons* does it.

Crotch Displays

In law enforcement, we see a lot of the bad guys' crotches, or what I've nicknamed "naughty bits"—especially when they're getting defiant. During an interrogation, as we're getting closer and closer to the truth, convincers will suddenly pull their feet underneath their chair. Or they'll wrap their feet around the legs of the chair, spread their knees, and do a crotch display. These movements are not a sign that they're confessing—not even close. We see this when they're being openly defiant. This sign is like saying, "Screw you—you're not getting anything from me."

The openness may also be giving the liars in your life more confidence. Columbia University psychologist Dana Carney says that these open postures

On July 19, 2011, this hooded man holding a gun was demonstrating a confidence crotch display in a neighborhood in the southern outskirts of Guatemala City. He and many other men in hoods were there to prevent an attack from the Mara Salvatrucha gang, who have threatened and extorted members of their community. **(Getty Images)**

stimulate a biochemical response, raising testosterone and lowering cortisol, all in one simple shift of body language.[2] When you see this shift, know that the person is feeling more confident—and the position itself will only help that.

Forward Leans

While liars tend to bring out the big guns, flash their private areas, and lean their upper bodies back, the opposite is usually true of truthful people. They are more likely to bring their groins backward and put their "bits" in lockdown, as they lean the upper body toward people—*I want you to believe me, I'm telling the truth*. In convince-not-convey, liars might use this pose for the exact same reason—trying to lean forward to impress you with their "genuineness."

NONVERBAL SIGNALS OF POWER

Power is more than a state of mind—it's also a nonverbal signal. People associate power with people who:

- Smile less
- Gaze more
- Touch others more
- Gesture more
- Interrupt more often
- Speak in a louder voice

In situations when degrees of power are not immediately known, people will use these nonverbal signals to understand who holds the most power in a room. People who stride across a room, or who move around more often, are seen as having more power because they are perceived by others as having the freedom to determine their own actions.[3] Check out the body language of everyone lined up to see Obama—notice how they all make themselves smaller with self-soothing gestures and body blocking.

President Obama talks with Americans involved in Chilean miner rescue. **(Associated Press)**

Fake Fig Leaves—Keeping the "Bits" in Lockdown

When the fig leaf—holding your hands in front of your naughty bits—is real, it communicates humility, timidity. But when it's not real, it's an attempt to manipulate the other person into believing you're not a threat: *I'm way more innocent than you might think, really!* Case in point: our very distraught Paris Hilton, with her turned-up eyebrows of true sadness, is now skipping down the path out of jail, *very* contrite—can't you just tell?

You would never know she immediately went on *Larry King Live* and lied about not doing drugs. Keep talking, Paris—that will convince everyone.

Paris Hilton, when she was released from jail after two days. **(WireImage)**

BACKSLIDING

Now we come to the category that's among the easiest to spot: backsliding. Whereas convince-not-convey was all about "puffing up" signals, making them more pronounced and in your face, backsliding is exactly the opposite—the suspect is trying to minimize everything about herself: her voice, her movements, even the space she takes up within your vision. She is looking to beat a hasty retreat—but you're not going to let her because you know how to spot the secrets to backsliding.

The Implosion

Think about when you're embarrassed and you screw up. Or, when your little kid comes in from doing something they shouldn't have. They point their right foot in a circle on the ground. *Mom, I broke your vase.* Their shoulders are up, and they're not using hand gestures. They want to disappear.

We get small when we get embarrassed. When I do speaking engagements, I start going toward the audience to get volunteers. You can see the people who are deathly afraid or introverted and don't want to be on stage—just watch their feet. Their feet might be straight in front of them, like underneath the table, and all of a sudden both feet pull underneath the chair, right under their butt. *Please don't pick me.*

When you're norming people for detecting deception, note their stance. If a guy is sitting there with open stance, and then you ask, "Are you in love?," and he crosses his ankles, he's getting smaller—that's backsliding.

If you ask, "Are you married?," and she suddenly covers her neck dimple with her hand, or does a thinking pose with her hand over her mouth or on her chin to cover neck vulnerability, that's a hot spot—she could be lying to you. Or maybe she's telling the truth and there's another story there.

The implosion is all about retreating into yourself—slouching, giving short answers with little detail, hiding hands in pockets or under sweaters, leaning back. It's all about retreat.

Body Blockers

Body blockers are little protective shields people use to feel less exposed. They may hold their coats or their briefcases, or put their pocketbooks across their laps, or suddenly cross their arms. It doesn't mean they are lying, but it does mean there's a sudden increase in anxiety in the room. (Just check out the crossed arms and facial touches in the picture of President Obama's elite team of politicians as they officially heard the news that Osama bin Laden was dead.)

Backsliders will always opt to have a table, a book, a plate, a cup, anything in front of them. That's why it's much better to confront the subject when nothing

President Barack Obama and Vice President Joe Biden, along with members of the national security team, receive an update on the mission against Osama bin Laden in the Situation Room of the White House, May 1, 2011. **(Getty Images)**

is available to block him. For example, if you're headed into Starbucks, go for the couch versus the table—you'll leave him much more exposed.

Women love to cover their chests by folding their arms and literally putting their hands over their breasts. They'll suddenly pick up their purse from the floor and put it across their lap. And they'll begin looking for a pen or something and then keep their purse in their lap. They'll have their coat on the back of the chair, and they'll put it across their lap instead. The naughty bits are officially in lockdown mode.

Other forms of body blocking include putting hands on the mouth, neck, throat—any of the vulnerable areas where most people feel the truth can leak out. A big one is eye blocking. You'll see this when people start to squint.

You say, "Janine, I asked you to pick up the groceries at one o'clock."

"You did? You said one o'clock to pick up the groceries? At one?" And I squint my eyes.

Now, I know damn well you said one o'clock—but I'm trying to block my eyes, to prevent you from seeing the truth.

Eye blocking should be a big red flag when it's done by people who care for the most vulnerable—your child, your aging parents, your pets. When you pick up your kids at school, does the teacher give everyone eye contact but you? What about the principal? The school bus driver? Maybe they always look away. You go to pick up your kid, and they're busy putting the backpack on little Johnny while you're picking up Sara. Always busy so they never look you in the eye. Don't let it go—walk right up and ask how the day went.

Let all who care for your dependents know that you are a family, you stick together, and you see what's going on. Leave the cell phone inside, walk your kid

Navel InteLLIGence

In my last book, I spoke a lot about how the belly button rule (a.k.a., "navel intelligence") shows us that people align their belly buttons with the objects of their interest. So unless someone is incredibly savvy about body language, you can usually tell where they want to be in a conversation. If he started the conversation with his belly button pointed straight at yours, and now his entire body is twisted toward the door, and only his head and neck are turned to you, he is aching to leave—that's a hot spot.

to the school bus, look the bus driver in their face, say their name, tell your kid, "I love you. I'll see you later today." Let the people who surround your family know you pay attention to everything that's happening.

Pacifiers

Self-touch is often used as an unconscious way to relieve tension. If you've ever seen someone bite their nails, twirl their hair, or pick their cuticles, you've seen what nonverbal expert Joe Navarro termed "pacifiers" in action. They're ways that we unconsciously touch our bodies to self-soothe. You may see these in a nervous person, whether she's a backslider—it's her way of dialing down the anxiety of the situation.

Some of the most common pacifiers are listed in the table.

Body Part	Pacifier
Hands	Biting nails
	Cracking knuckles
	Examining nails
	Folding hands or arms across chest
	Hands wrapped up in shirt, scarf
	Picking cuticles
	Picking "dirt" out from under nails
	Rubbing hands together
	Stretching/pulling on fingers
	Squeezing/pinching skin on top of hands
	Tapping fingers
	Wringing hands
Mouth	Chewing on lips
	Chewing gum
	Clearing throat
	Coughing
	Hand over mouth or on top of lips
	Licking lips (dry mouth caused by nerves)
	Requesting to smoke
	Sighing or yawning (need to get extra oxygen!)
	Swallowing

Body Part	Pacifier
Body	Continually crossing and uncrossing legs
	Picking
	Pinching
	Picking lint off clothes
	Pulling threads in clothing, nylons, or leggings
	Scratching
	Smoothing skirt, pants
	Stroking arm, leg, or throat
	Suddenly crossing legs at a critical moment
Ears	Digging in ear canal with finger or object
	Playing with cartilage
	Pulling or pinching earlobes
Hair	Blowing bangs around
	Braiding
	Making ponytail, "up-do"
	Playing with dead ends
	Putting ends in mouth (gross, I know!)
	Smoothing, rubbing, stroking hair
	Twisting and twirling
Face	Hand covering part of face or eyes
	Picking zits
	Scratching
	Tearing up (genuine or feigned)
	Wiping forehead (trying to hide sweat)
Feet	Behind chair legs
	Jiggling
	Swinging legs
	Tucked up under bottom

(all photos: Baron Thrower II)

We all do some of these sometimes. But if someone has been exhibiting confident open body language and then suddenly starts pacifying with one or more of these signals, that's a massive hot spot!

THE FINAL TAKING CARE OF BUSINESS REMINDER: JUST SAY NO TO MIND READING!

I hope by now you know that mind reading is an approach that is destined to trash a lot of your relationships. You simply cannot point to any one body movement or gesture or verbal tic and say, "That's it!" Trust me—hundreds of experts spend millions of dollars a year looking for that Pinocchio sign. It simply doesn't exist.

Mind reading is a surefire recipe for destruction—you can destroy profits, possibilities, even people! Just say no!

Now that you have a good handle on the New Body Language cues that can indicate hot spots, you can use all those little signs—crossed ankles, crossed arms, hands over the neck, men playing with their collars because it's getting hot under there, legs wrapped around chair legs—as a series of hot spots to dig into. In the next chapter, we'll start to put the screws to them in step 5: "The Interrogation."

EXERCISING YOUR BS BAROMETER: FULL BODY SURVEILLANCE

Full body surveillance is some of the easiest homework to do on the fly. Any time you are in line at the bank or the grocery store, you can be exercising your BS Barometer.

Tube In!

Again, visit www.youtube.com/user/bsbarometer and watch one person's base-line video first, then the two corresponding stories next. You've learned a tremendous amount about liars' conscious and unconscious signals of deception. You know those telltale hot spots can show up anywhere on a person's face, body, or in their voice. Can you spot which one of the videos contains the lie based on comparing the person's verbals to their nonverbals? Once you've completed your assessment and made your guess, then click on my video analysis to reveal the truth about that person.

POWER TEAM TURNAROUND

Name: Eugene Smith

Age: 35

Occupation: Magazine publisher

(Baron Thrower II)

What was stopping you from spotting master manipulators and liars?

Prior to the DDPT [Detecting Deception Power Team] program I was only partially aware of how manipulators and liars do what they do. I believe that I would turn a blind eye to people whom I got a "bad vibe" from. Sometimes I would feel as though I was slighting them, and I would allow them partial entry to my life.

How have you changed?

This course has helped me to become more self-aware, and conscious of my body language and intentions. Now I know to ask powerful questions that will create clarity, and allow the other person to feel uncomfortable instead of me. I have discovered that most of my relationships are ultimately in my control, especially once I can truly accept the worst-possible-case scenario.

The most valuable lesson I'm taking away is how disruptive deception really is. Deception is exhausting for both the deceivers and the people who know that they're being deceived. No one is able to keep up a lie without using energy, and that use of energy shows on their face and in their body language. The search for the truth can be exhausting—but as the truth is found, energy is returned to the seeker and stripped from the deceiver!

I was deceived in the past mainly due to not providing the proper degree of consequences. I now protect myself as a CEO. I monitor my body language, and I challenge myself to always ask powerful questions. This makes my employees even more responsive, intuitive, and more likely to follow directions.

Keep Your Skills Sharp Like the Experts

Even expert private investigators need practice to keep up their skills. Marti, my private investigator friend, makes it a game. Whenever she's sitting in a restaurant, waiting in line at the grocery store, or people-watching in a park, she'll keep an eye out for people's body language. "I'll watch when a guy walks up to a woman in a restaurant or bar, and I'll watch and see if she's twirling her hair," says Marti. "Let's see how interested she *really* is in him." She'll watch their belly buttons, see if their shoulders are shrugging, if their naughty bits are out, the angles of their heads, the changes in posture—everything. Try it out during your next interminable wait at the post office or in the doctor's waiting room.

Give Your Visual Information Channel a Checkup

When in a new situation, or when you start to get a twinge of suspicion about an old one, do you attempt to get your bearings? Do you take a quick peek around you to assess any immediate dangers? Is there anything you see that should warrant concern? Or is there a glaring hot spot front and center that you are missing every time?

To fine-tune your attention to details, spot the seven differences between the set of pictures of my parents, two sisters, and me on the Royal Yacht, the Queen's Ship *Britannia* in Edinburgh, Scotland.

(Janine Driver)

(Janine Driver)

Did you spot all seven differences? No?! That's because there were only six!

When you failed to find number seven, what happened? Did you give up quickly? Were you irritated and frustrated? Or did you cheat and look at the answer section? (C'mon, just admit it! Don't lie to yourself!)

(Janine Driver)

Next time, use this technique. Take a sheet of paper and cover 90 percent of both pictures with the paper. Now, work your way down slowly, and you might spot the differences sooner. The same holds true when using your BS Barometer: visually compartmentalize the target's body into small sections; now work from the head . . . to the shoulders . . . to the knees . . . to the toes. You might be surprised what you find out!

Follow My Fingers with Your Eyes

Time to put your visual memory to the test! Set the timer on your oven, microwave, or your smartphone for forty-five seconds. Once the clock is ticking, observe the picture below and absorb as many details as possible. Once the timer goes off, turn the page and answer the questions.

Janine Driver gives her keynote speech on how to use body language to increase sales by more than 25 percent within the first month to a sales force of a leading real estate company. **(Janine Driver)**

Questions

1. Where is the EXIT sign in this picture?

2. What am I (yes, that stunning creature is Yours Truly!) doing with my hands?

3. What is the object on the wall directly above my head?

4. How many doors are in the picture?

5. Approximately how many people are in the picture (including me)?

6. Which hand am I holding the microphone in?

Answers

1. *Far left.*

2. *They're up in front of me, with palms cupped open.*

3. *The light that goes off when there is a fire alarm.*

4. *Two.*

5. *Twenty-six.*

6. *Trick question, there is no handheld mic!*

- What did you learn from this visual memory exercise?

- Did you make up an answer when you were unsure? You do realize that this sets you up to be perceived as a liar or as someone who will do anything to avoid failure?

- If you were to do this exercise again, what would you do differently? Why?

- How will what you learned from this exercise empower you as a lie catcher?

Flip the Digits

This exercise trains your brain's memory, language, and executive functions.

Step 1. Read the following numbers out loud: 7–2–1–9–4.

Step 2. Say them again, but put the book down (and no peeking).

Step 3. Turn to the next page for your next task.

Step 4. Say the numbers I gave you out loud, but do it backward. Write the numbers down on a piece of paper with the last number first and the first number last.

Step 5. Now that you've practiced, repeat the steps with the following number combinations (and score yourself):

4 4 9 2 1 7	6 7 4 3 9 2	4 3 5 8 1 9
6 4 7 2 9 3	2 1 7 5 3 6	7 2 3 1 4 3
4 8 7 7 6 1	9 9 8 2 5 1	2 3 6 7 9 5
1 7 6 2 9 8	8 9 8 9 2 7	7 8 9 2 7 1

How long does it take you to recall the numbers backward? How many numbers can you recall? All six numbers would show superior intelligence!

This exercise is important when you are listening to different chunks of a person's story. During the first interview, when the prospective employee told you about his work history with a specific company, didn't he say he interned there for six months, then worked there for one year? But the second time he told the story two days later, he said he interned for a year, then worked for six months? Which one is correct?

The truth can be found in the details, and if you aren't able to chunk information in your head from the beginning to the end, and from the end to the beginning, your job candidate might just be able to pull the wool over your eyes more often than you think!

Quick tip: think like a movie director and create an internal vision board as your frame of reference.

JUST REMEMBER . . .

- *Stay open.* Using confident, relaxed body language will keep your target feeling less stressed and more likely to share the truth.

- *Pacifiers don't indicate guilt.* They merely indicate anxiety. Some people's norm is to be a bundle of nerves. Crossed arms or wringing hands might just mean they're cold!

- *Watch that crotch!* When you see a guy lean back and spread his legs during a tense conversation, be prepared—he might be gearing up for a counterattack.

STEP 5:
THE INTERROGATION

"Three things cannot be long hidden: the sun,
the moon, and the truth."
—BUDDHA

I HAD NO IDEA WHAT was Sunhee was thinking.

She knows that I can see and hear when someone is holding something back, but that didn't stop her from tap-dancing around answering my out-of-nowhere question. I'm not sure how we got on the topic, but I asked my new twenty-four-year-old executive assistant, "Have you ever gotten into a physical fight with anyone?"

The game was on.

Sunhee responded with a right shoulder shrug, a contorted facial expression of fear and sadness, and a couple *umms*, along with a bit lower lip. Next came something like, "Maybe, but I'm not sure if I remember what happened when I was younger."

Hello, she's twenty-four!

"Well, if you *could* remember, what would your answer be?"

"Well, umm, the *fight I can tell you about* happened at an ice-skating rink, where this group of girls called my friends and me a derogatory slang word for

Asians. At first we verbally threatened and insulted one another, but in less than an hour, fists were flying, hair was being yanked, and fingernails were breaking."

I listened intently, but I was bursting inside to ask the most important question. When Sunhee was done sharing her ice-skating showdown, I said, "Sunhee, I'm sorry to hear that people are full of such hate. Now, tell me about the story that you can't tell me about.'"

She was mortified; she thought she slid that by me. What came next was deep, painful, and private.

We now know that using nonverbal signs of emotions—fear, anger, sadness, surprise—to spot a lie is less than 100 percent reliable. Even if we were fast enough to spot those fleeting microexpressions, the reality is that people feel fear, anger, sadness, or surprise for a lot of different reasons—particularly if they start to think that you don't trust them.

That's why I place so much emphasis on the verbal aspects of the BS Barometer. I want you to ask questions—lots of them! While peppering your friends or colleagues with questions may seem a bit awkward at first, you will grow to understand how to draw someone out, how to get all the information you want—and more—simply by asking the right questions and, often, just by being silent. In this chapter, we'll learn the final piece of the BS Barometer, the interrogation—how to turn up the heat with questions that will stress out the liars but leave the honest people scratching their heads like, "What's the big deal?"

START WITH an OPEN MIND

You've probably spent some time watching old cop shows or scary movies about torture at the hands of interrogators. They nearly all start with someone saying, "When are you going to tell us what we want? When are you going to admit you did it?" Researchers now know this is an absolutely counterproductive way to do an interrogation. First of all, the suspect is likely to shut down and, like a petulant child, refuse to participate: "You don't believe me anyway, so why should I talk to you?" And, if they're not that strong willed, you might get the poor soul who is so suggestible that she fesses up to a crime she didn't commit! (That happens more often than you might think.)

That's why researchers now know that an "information-gathering" style is the most effective interrogation technique. Open-ended questions (such as, "What did you do this morning before breakfast?" or "Did you run into anyone you knew at the store today?") will allow you to gather as much data and "facts"

THE TRUTH FINDER'S EMOTIONAL INVESTMENT SCALE

Every truth finder needs to have skin in the game. In an effort to separate fact from fiction, the interrogator should have between levels 2 to 6 on the emotional investment scale. Any less than 2, you could miss solid tells; any more than 6, you could be overly invested in the outcome—and ultimately your confrontation may lead to a false confession. (Or worse—a broken trust, or even a broken nose!)

Ask yourself how emotionally connected and invested you are in finding the truth with regard to *your* situation. Everyone has a different scale of what 0–10 looks like for them. Shown are three sample emotional investment scales. What does your scale look like?

Janine's Emotional Investment Scale

41, married (7 yrs.), mother of Angus (6 yrs.), owner of Hamilton (pet dog) keynote speaker and *New York Times* bestselling author

0	Someone took my pen
2	My husband is smoking cigars again
4	My employee is bad-mouthing me to my clients
6	My husband is cheating on me
8	My son, Angus, is doing/selling drugs
10	A family member of mine is murdered

Steve Facella's (Janine's Colleague) Emotional Investment Scale

28, recently engaged
cruise planner

0	Someone drank my breakfast shake
2	An employee called in sick when I know he really wasn't
4	Someone took my phone charger without asking first
6	My car was keyed
8	I was shorted on a payment owed to me
10	Violence was committed toward family or friends

(continued)

Abbey Potter's (Janine's Assistant) Emotional Investment Scale
24, single young professional; psychology graduate and assistant to Janine Driver and Body Language Institute

0	Someone drank my coffee
2	One of my roommates isn't doing housework
4	My car was broken into
6	My roommate isn't paying the rent
8	My boyfriend is cheating on me
10	Someone was violent toward my family

Now it's your turn! What does your scale look like? Copy the scale into your journal and complete it—this exercise will give you a better idea whether your head's in the right place before you confront your target. (Bonus: it can also help you put more perspective on daily annoyances, so you can avoid sweating the small stuff.)

(or lies) as you can at once. A recent review in *Psychological Science in the Public Interest* tells us why this information-gathering style works best:

1. When you get more information, you get more opportunities to drill down into someone's story and spot the weak spots and inconsistencies.

2. When you get people talking for a while, you get to see more nonverbal cues—even though they cannot be your entire "proof" of wrongdoing.

3. The more words people say, the more you can use Statement Analysis to see the changes in tense, pronoun usage, distancing language, and all the other tricks you learned in the wiretap chapter.

4. Information-gathering interviews are more conversational, so they don't feel as threatening and are less likely to cause hot spots related to anxiety.

5. If you launch into an interrogation convinced you are correct—as in the "Why don't you just admit you did it!" style—you gather less evidence and get trapped in your one-track mind. Information gathering leaves you open to other explanations you may not have even considered yet.[1]

Now that you have your mind-set in order, let's see how you can set the stage for the most honest conversation possible.

PRIME PEOPLE FOR THE TRUTH

Way before you get down to that big Yes-or-No question, you can improve your chance of getting an honest answer by "priming" your target to tell the truth. Scientists are continually finding support for this methodology. Turns out when a person is asked to "swear to tell the whole truth and nothing but the truth," it works. One study found that kids eight to sixteen years old who had promised to tell the truth before being asked about a transgression were *eight times* more likely to be honest than those who had not promised.[2] U.K. sex offenders who volunteered to be hooked up to lie detectors were *five times* more likely to confess to new crimes than were offenders who were not hooked up but were later found to have abused children.[3] Even people taking a pre-employment test only needed to be politely asked to be truthful, and they gave significantly more honest answers.[4]

I always recommend to my students that they make a big deal about being great at spotting lies. I recommend they walk into their next employee meeting and say, "I just took a class with Janine Driver, a deception detection expert— she says I'm a natural! I don't even know what that means, but evidently, I unconsciously pick up on deceptive tells." I tell the cops to do it, too. But you could do this with anyone—your teenager, your real estate agent, your broker, a car salesperson. The simple sentence, "I know you're an honest person," can have miraculous effects.

Okay, now you're ready to begin.

THE BASIC INTERROGATION TECHNIQUE

The real secret of detecting deception is to know that you have to ask lots of questions and to continue doing so until you get what you need. Start with an easy one. Ask an innocent question that you already know the answer to, or one that you know won't arouse any suspicion:

What are you doing this weekend?

How was the movie last night?

And move slowly up to the more heavy-duty ones:

Is this a picture of your wife?

Why is there a tan line on your ring finger—did you recently get divorced?

Ask Open-Ended Questions

An interrogation is not a true/false test—it's more like an essay. Yes-or-No questions are typically dead ends. You only ask those in very specific moments. (We'll get to which later.)

For now, you want to get the basics down: *Who, What, When, Where, Why, How.* Then, keep going just for sheer quantity:

1. What is it about . . . ?

2. You said . . . Tell me more.

3. What do you mean?

4. How did he show you . . . ?

5. How do you explain . . . ?

6. How long have you . . . ?

7. Tell me what happened. . . .

8. When was the last time . . . ?

9. What were you doing . . . ?

10. What you did is . . .

11. Why would you . . . ?

12. Why did you . . . ?

13. Repeat what you just said.

14. Where did this happen . . . ?

15. Who said . . . ?

16. Who did . . . ?

17. Explain. . . .

Did I mention it's all about quantity?

Really, if nothing else, I'd like you to come away from this chapter with the sense that the game Twenty Questions is for rookies—do I hear thirty? Forty? The more questions you ask, the more information you gather, the wiser you become.

And as you ask, keep your eyes open.

Maybe I'm Wrong Here

This is where the baseline comes in—you're looking for those deviations that come when people seem slightly uncomfortable. Any time anyone deviates from that nonverbal baseline, say to them, "Maybe I'm wrong here, but it seems like there's more to the story."

"Maybe I'm wrong here, but when you said your ex-girlfriend wasn't at the bar last night, you seemed happy."

"Maybe I'm wrong here, but it seems like you're pretty happy with losing your job."

"Maybe I'm wrong here, but you seem a little anxious about your meeting later."

And then you WAIT.

WAIT = Why Am I Talking?

If you take nothing else from this chapter, I want you to learn this: silence is interrogation gold. People don't like awkward silences, and they will do almost anything to fill them up (see a clip from my appearance in a Discovery Channel documentary that demonstrates the power of silence with getting a confession at www.youcantlietome.com). Your job, after the "Maybe I'm wrong here . . ." pattern of the previous technique, is to follow it with the WAIT protocol:

1. "Is there any reason why?"

Is there any reason why you're telling me this but you're showing me that? Is there any reason why you told me you're happy to be here, but you're showing me fear or contempt or disgust, or you seem a little anxious? (Note: If you recognize a true signal of fear, that's exactly the moment to dig deeper.)

2. "Really?"

Say it like you're from Boston—in other words, like you're basically saying, "I don't think so."

A truthful person has no problem if you ask them a question:

"So, where were you last night?"

"I was out with Janine, and Mike, and Jeff."

"Really?"

"Yeah [shrugging]. Really."

But a liar needs to be believed. So as soon as you say, "Really?," a liar is going to freak out: "Yeah, what do you think I am, a liar? I knew this was going to happen. I knew you weren't going to trust me. Why do you always do this? You're so insecure."

3. WAIT—Why Am I Talking?

Silence. Dead silence. Say *nothing*.

Salespeople are so good at this—so are lawyers and journalists. Whoever speaks next loses. A truthful person believes you will believe them, but a liar will immediately think the worst.

If it looks like they're getting anxious, don't be in any rush. Let them sit there and stew. Take it from a former investigator: it is torture to let someone who's lying sit in their own silence for a while—because they don't know what's going on. They're getting anxious and their heart rate is going, their blood flow is increasing—they're just freaking out.

The Question	The Truth	The Lie
"How do you think this happened?"	"I don't know."	[He/she may tell you exactly how the event occurred, as a "guess."]
"Whom do you suspect?"	"I don't know . . . maybe Joey?"	Silence, shrugs— or "Definitely Joey."
"Do you think this was hard to do?"	"I don't know."	"Nah, I'll bet it was a piece of cake."
"What should happen to the person who did this?"	"They should be punished!"	"They're probably suffering a lot with the guilt of it. . . ."
"Would there be any reason someone would say you were there?"	"Nope!"	[He will make excuses, try to explain why he may have been seen there, or give an alternate location far away.]
"What kind of a person would do such a thing?"	"A really bad/despicable/ no-good person."	[May describe herself or say the person who did it "isn't bad, just needs help."]
"How do you think the person who did this would feel?"	"I don't know."	[May describe her own feelings.]

The Rule of Three

When it comes to answering a question, there's one right way to do it—answer the question. Liars sometimes spend a lot of time talking around the question, stalling. But you can measure a person's sincerity by how many words stand between the question and his denial. More than three, and he's a big fat liar.

"Did you steal the money out of my wallet?"

"What? Seriously, Mom. Are you seriously asking me if I took money from you? How could you think I would do that? I could never do that. No, I didn't."

Busted. How would an honest person answer?

"Did you steal the money out of my wallet?"

"No, I didn't."

If people don't get to "No" within three statements, there's an 85 percent chance they're lying. You have to give them these three chances because they may take exception to something else in your question—maybe they feel you're attacking their identity, integrity, belief, or religion. Their reaction might have more to do with feeling attacked than denying the charge itself. But we draw the line at three!

Remember: No one likes to lie. But even more than that, they don't want to have to deal with the consequences of lying. Especially backsliders—they want to hide behind anything in order not to have to face the lie.

ADVANCED TECHNIQUES

The WAIT technique is usually enough to bust most of the liars in your life—the people with a conscience. But what do you do about those others, the serial offenders, the ones you just can't pin down? Let's get out the big guns.

Strategic Use of Evidence Approach

When being questioned, the truthful person has nothing to hide—it doesn't matter what the other person knows (or thinks they know), he wants to tell everything *he* knows to be true. In contrast, the liar wants desperately to find out what the other person knows so he can adjust his story accordingly. One interrogation technique—the strategic use of evidence (SUE) technique—capitalizes on this desperate need by withholding the one thing the liar wants most: information. Cops use this technique very effectively when they have physical evidence, but a manager who needs a straight answer on a deadline, a mom who finds pot or cigarettes in her son's desk, or a wife who finds lipstick on her husband's collar could use it the same way.

> *Step 1.* Same as above. Ask general, open-ended questions about the person's activities on the day in question. Stay very casual. *(Don't mention the bag of weed just yet.)*

Step 2. Ask more specific questions about contents of a drawer or where-abouts over a lunch hour. Get closer to the truth without revealing the physical evidence.

Step 3. While the standard SUE approach doesn't use this step, here's where I would inject the WAIT: "Is there any reason why you might be uncomfortable with me going in your drawer? [pause, head tilt] Really?"

Step 4. Reveal the evidence and ask them to explain the contradiction. "You said you didn't hug or kiss any female colleagues today, and your mom is out of town—so why is there lipstick on your collar?"

In one Swedish study, policemen who were trained in SUE techniques increased their accuracy rates by a staggering 30 percent. Cops who didn't receive the training identified a thief correctly 56 percent of the time; cops who did receive the SUE training spotted the guilty party 85.4 percent of the time.[5]

A longtime favorite technique of TV detective Lieutenant Columbo, SUE works on the old "give them enough rope to hang themselves" principle—by letting the person talk at length before revealing what you know, you get a whole bunch of bonus information for further analysis. But it also helps you to approach the whole situation with an open mind, so you can absorb extra information you might not be expecting if their guilt is a foregone conclusion. And, perhaps most important, it keeps the outcome of the conversation under your control. If your husband spent the afternoon at the retirement party for sweet Betty, the seventy-year-old receptionist, and she gave him a big good-bye hug and kiss—that lipstick on the collar didn't cause a marital blowup, lost trust, and major hard feelings.[6]

Ask a *"How"* Question

Earlier we talked about the fact that liars won't discuss emotions when recounting a story. They're so focused on the "facts" of the situation, they don't stop to think about *how* people are feeling. This blind spot makes *how* a great area to probe—often they haven't anticipated these questions and so aren't prepared for them.

How questions are great to catch the crazies. We saw this with two of the most notorious liars. Scott Peterson was asked, "How was Laci when you last saw her?" His response? "She was in the living room wrapping presents." Meanwhile, what was really happening: he was in the living room wrapping up her dead body with duct tape, before he threw her in the water. He didn't answer the question with a *how*—he answered with a *what*. (A fake *what,* to boot!)

Joran van der Sloot, alleged killer of American teen Natalee Holloway, was

IF YOU GIVE A LIAR A PENCIL . . .

Most liars, if given enough advanced warning, will try to work out their story ahead of time. They might even be able to work out some convincing details—what happened and why, who was there, what they were doing. But when asked to draw their story, many liars fall apart. One study found that when liars and truth tellers were given pen and pencil and asked to draw their story—as opposed to simply tell it—several differences between the liars and the honest people arose. Liars tended to depict the story from above—as if they were in a helicopter, circling the action—whereas truthful people tended to draw the story as if they were a part of the action (i.e., at "ground level"). Also, liars tended to forget the other people in their depictions—only 13 percent included them—whereas 80 percent of truthful people put both themselves and the other people into the pictures. All told, interrogators who used this picture-drawing technique improved their accuracy level, identifying 87 percent of the liars and 80 percent of the truth tellers.[7]

asked, "How was Natalee when you last saw her?" His answer: she was walking along the beach. Sorry, buddy—that's not a *how*.

Who Will You Vouch For?

If you ask a person who might be a suspect, "Who could've done this? Who could have taken the money?," a truthful person will say, "Well, any of us could've taken it."

A liar will name other people, but won't name himself: "Well, I saw Kendra, Lisa, and Julie over there—they were over by the pocketbook."

One of my students, James, a "loss prevention expert"—that is, a security guard—told me of a related tactic they use in retail theft. If an item is missing from a store, and they have a bunch of suspects but no one is fessing up, James will ask each one, "Who would you vouch for?"

An honest person will say, "Well, I can vouch for myself . . . and maybe this one other guy, but other than that, I don't know." Interestingly, James says the guilty person will *not* mention themselves. Instead, they'll say, "I can vouch for this one person," but then give a slew of other names of people who could be guilty, in an attempt to muddy the waters.

POWER TEAM TURNAROUND

Name: Minowa N. Melvin

Age: 27

Occupation: Recent graduate student / concierge

(Baron Thrower II)

What was stopping you from spotting master manipulators and liars?

Mainly it was myself. I gave off signals that others read as deception, and it was ruining all my relationships. At the same time, I wasn't going with my intuition and gut feelings about people. I got wrapped up in what people *said* rather than looking at what they *did* as well. I was afraid of losing the connection, so I let my emotional investment in the other person skew me from making the right decision.

I've had colleagues who say they'll do one thing and then do the opposite—like say they can't take my shift, and then I find out they just didn't want to help me.

Not understanding other people's intentions played a big role in how I was perceived in the past. Now that I can challenge myself to better understand why someone has problems with the truth, I can build healthier relationships in which people take comfort in telling the truth.

How have you changed?

The most valuable lesson I'm taking away is that it takes time to determine whether someone is lying and that asking powerful questions is important. If I completed the program ten years ago, I know my life would have been very different. Maybe I wouldn't have encountered abusive men who would swear they'd never put a hand on me again, or people who promised they didn't cheat but gave me an STD. Maybe I wouldn't have wasted so much money helping someone who would never help me in return, even when they said they would. Maybe I would befriend more genuine people who believe in helping one another become better people. Maybe I could be more responsible in determining who deserved to be a part of my life and who didn't.

"Maybe" stories may be just dreams, but I can say that after the program I feel like I don't have to worry about those kinds of stories anymore, and I can move forward with more confidence to spot those liars later in my life.

Look Me in the Eyes

The old "mom" technique of telling the liar to "look me in the eyes" is actually a great way to increase cognitive load.[8] When someone is creating or recalling details about a story, they often shift their gaze to look at an inanimate object in order to focus more intently before turning back to make eye contact again. But if you insist that the person maintain eye contact, he or she is going to have to work doubly hard to draw up those details with the distraction of your gorgeous face. That's when the liar's extra work will become readily apparent.

Tell the Story Backward

This baby is one of my mentor J.J. Newberry's favorite moves to use to get a liar to slip up; I learned it from him and it works sooo well (thanks J.J.!). To quickly increase a liar's cognitive load, have the suspected jerk in your life tell you her story backward.

Liars typically can't do it. They might be using every last neuron to keep their story straight—what they did first, second, last—so if you said, tell me the whole story in reverse order, something's going to crack. One study had people watch videos of others telling the truth and lying in both chronological and reverse order—and when liars were asked to reverse the order of their stories, the deception detection average shot up by nearly 20 percent.[9] People memorize the story from the beginning to the end, not the end to the beginning, so that's where people will stumble.

Now, this technique can be tricky—not everyone can use this tactic. A woman can't ask her new boyfriend to recount his whereabouts the night before in reverse order. But if a husband has been busted cheating before, and his forgiving-yet-suspicious wife has a hunch he's doing it again, she definitely *could* ask. And a person in law enforcement, or the parent of a teen who's very worried about drug use, could certainly bring this J.J. Newberry masterpiece to the confrontation party!

Ask the Same Question Three Ways

Trying to get at the same information in several ways can increase a subject's cognitive load and make the person hesitate while answering.

- How old are you?
- What year were you born?
- When did you graduate from high school?

- Whose house were you at?

- Were the parents home the whole time?

- What time did the mom get home?

Ask a Bizarre Question

People who are lying want to appear relaxed and compliant—they don't like to refuse to answer a question because they think it will make them seem deceptive. In contrast, people who are telling the truth can get exasperated by bizarre questions.[10] For example, if you ask, "What type of salad dressings did they have at the restaurant?," a liar might try to recreate a list, wanting to seem "helpful." But the truthful person would look at you like you're crazy. "Huh? Why do you want to know that? I have no idea."

Throw Them a Lifeline

This only-for-the-pros technique is extremely advanced, but nearly surefire! When liars are drowning, they will occasionally reach out for any help *you* are willing to give them to get away with their deception. So, go ahead—indulge them. Give them a way out—and turn it into a trap.

As your liar digs his hole, prepare a couple of plausible alternatives. Create explanations that seem possible and almost excusable—but while the first two are more human, the last one shows the liar in a downright cowardly light. (Check out the table for some hypothetical situations.)

As you offer the first explanation, watch his nonverbal language. If he's buying it, nodding his head, looking at you, then say, "Or . . . ," and move forward to the cowardly version right away. If your suspect is not buying your first anecdote, then move to your second story—and *then* finish him off with the cowardly version.

At the end of each one of these scenarios, once you have your "confession," you alone can decide if it's a deal breaker for your relationship. You might have had enough, or you might just decide to grant some mercy—after all, sometimes cowards need love, too.

Situation

You have some kind of proof that your boyfriend is cheating on you. You confront him.

(*Note:* A cheating partner will almost never confess unless presented with solid evidence. When you get your evidence, don't show him everything at once—use the SUE technique. He'll create a story around how he can explain your first piece of evidence. Let him run with it, then present him with more evidence.)

Power Question: "Is there any reason why I received a phone call today from a mutual friend of ours that said she saw you getting pretty intimate with another woman?" After he responds, say, "Really?" Let him speak again. When he's done, WAIT—yes, say nothing and tilt your head to the side. After he speaks again, then move on to one of the anecdotes.

It's Not Your Fault Anecdote: "Here's what I think happened: We haven't had sex in months and I've been treating you like a roommate. I have you all confused—are we dating or not? Are we friends or more than that? I don't blame you for seeing someone else. It's my fault and I accept the blame. I would have done the same thing."

You Made a Mistake Anecdote: "Or maybe it was because I was fighting a lot with you recently and I pissed you off? You had one too many drinks and bumped into an ex-girlfriend. You confided in her and she took advantage of you, like she used to do. She manipulated you and you made a once-in-a-lifetime mistake, and you regretted it immediately. It will never happen again."

You Are a Coward Anecdote: "Or you want me to break up with you. You're nervous about how I'll take it, so you are pushing me to make the decision for you. You slept with another woman, so I'll end it with you. Right?!"

Situation

After turning in a project to your boss, he finds a careless error made in the report. You later discover that your coworker (who you had completed the projected with) had blamed you for the error when really you were both to blame.

Power Question: "Is there any reason why you would tell the boss the error was solely my fault after we agreed that we had both missed the error?"

It's Not Your Fault Anecdote: "Here's what I think happened: It's all a big misunderstanding. The boss was busy when you spoke to her, and in an innocent mix-up, she misinterpreted what you were saying."

You Made a Mistake Anecdote: "I spoke to my husband about this. He thinks maybe you were under a lot of pressure and you thought you'd get in trouble if you missed the error too, and you know the boss is more forgiving if I make a mistake since we're friends. In a moment of nervousness, you avoided the blame and made a poor decision. You've felt terrible about it and wanted to immediately fix the situation, but you weren't sure how."

You Are a Coward Anecdote: "Or you no longer consider yourself my friend. You intentionally set me up to be the fall guy here and lied to the boss to make yourself look good."

Situation

You left your babysitter with your infant son, and when you return, you ask her if anything happened. She says no, but you discover that under her watch, your four-month-old son had fallen off the bed.

Power Question: "Is there any reason why the cleaning lady would tell me that my little Benjamin fell off of the bed while I was out and you didn't tell me about it?"

It's Not Your Fault Anecdote: "I think because it was late and I was exhausted when I came home and the baby was completely fine, you didn't even think to tell me about the small fall. You didn't want me to stress out about something that wasn't really a problem."

You Made a Mistake Anecdote: "I think you were nervous that I would go nuts and I wouldn't hire you back to babysit. So in a moment of nervousness, you didn't tell me the truth. It was a split-second decision and as soon as you held back the truth, you felt guilty. You wanted to tell me, but then you panicked and didn't want to look like a liar. You're deeply sorry and it's a mistake that you've learned from and it will never happen again."

You Are a Coward Anecdote: "Or it was 100 percent your fault that the baby fell off the bed. You put the baby on my bed and you were outside on the front step talking on the phone. When you came back in the house, he was on the floor crying. You didn't tell me because you didn't want me to know that you left the baby alone in the house all by himself!"

Listen for the Deep Breath

If you've really been putting the screws to someone, pause for a second—and listen for a deep breath. When people lie, they often hold their breath. As the liar watches you to see if you're buying the story, if you suddenly *appear* to let down your guard, she may as well.

I learned this trick from the great J.J. Newberry. He taught a course in questioning for Customs and Immigration officers. People who are trying to outwit Customs will often memorize answers to common questions. J.J. taught his agents to ask those common questions in a first interview, but then to listen carefully for that deep breath as the suspect turned away—those are the people they would bring in for the second interview.

If you hear that deep breath, that's a level-10 red alert that something's going on. You might use that to say, "Okay, let's back up—what was happening when I asked you that question?" Or, if you're in the middle of a heavy-duty line of questioning, and you hear a heavy sigh, you might be about to hear a confession. Stay tuned: important stuff is happening.

The "No-Nos"

Remember the rule of three—if they don't say, "No, I did not do it," in the first three responses, that's a big red flag. I call these phrases the "No-Nos":

- I knew this would happen.

7-SECOND FIX

THE CUSTOMER

(Baron Thrower II)

(Baron Thrower II)

The Problem: You're the salesman and you realize that your overly confident body language (a double-handed hook highlighting your "bits") has gone too far. Your customers completely close up with a wrist-hold and a neck dimple in hiding. Ouch!

If you're looking to increase business, you need to take action now!

The Fix: You need to act fast to get the sale! Immediately put those "bits" in lockdown mode by standing in a fig-leaf pose (hands folded in front of your "bits") or simply bury your hands in your pockets.

Be sure to send an embedded command such as, "The material you want to buy also has three free patterns with it" (assuming a fabric store), or "The patterns you need today are on the next table [as you move toward them]," or "Your search is over now; here is what you've been looking for" (in any store).

Another option: "Many people [pause and soften voice] work with me [pause and raise voice], so I can help you [pause and soften your voice] get what you want."

The Result: You might be surprised to discover that when you hide your thumbs it sends the message that you lack arrogance and may even need reassurance. This move will accelerate their trust in you and they'll begin to relax and open up to new thoughts and ideas—instantly!

- Do you want me to confess to something I didn't do?

- I would be stupid to do that.

- Are you saying you think I did it?

- Honestly, I didn't do it. I swear I didn't.

- I already answered that.

- I knew you didn't trust me.

- I would never do that.

What you're looking for in an honest person is always a "No," pure and simple. Sometimes you'll get a No, but it will be what we at ATF called a "Bad No": one that's cluttered, with stuttering or wobbling, overextending it, multiple Nos at key questions. If they keep it simple, it's likely they are simply being honest.

THE BIG GUNS: THE CLOSED-ENDED QUESTION

While most of the time, interrogation is all about starting with open-ended questions, occasionally, you just need to get to the truth. Surprisingly, sometimes a great way to get someone to slip you the truth without them realizing you are on to them is simply to ask them a Yes-or-No question. If they begin their response to a closed-ended question with the word, "Well," there's a high probability that they are holding something back.

When people use the word *Well* to answer a Yes-or-No question, they are about to send you on a fishing trip to find the truth. Now, if they use a *Well* in response to an *open*-ended question, they could be forming their answer, and most likely it is not a lie. (For instance, if you asked your boyfriend, "How was your day at work?" He may respond with, "Well, it was a bit on the boring side.") But if they answer a yes/no question with a *Well,* they are creating a smokescreen to your question—they're trying to make you think they've answered your question, but in fact, they haven't. So, what to do? Follow this example:

Step 1. You heard from a reliable source that your new boyfriend, Jeff, was bad-mouthing your sister. You calmly ask Jeff, as if you are confused, "Did you say something negative about my sister at last night's party?"

Step 2. WAIT until he finishes speaking before adding more information. Listen to your boyfriend respond, "Well, it was super-loud at the bar in

Dupont Circle last night and it was hard to hear. It was hard for people to hear what I was saying all night and people kept getting confused and misunderstanding me."

Direct Question	Well ...
Did you back my car into something?	*Well*, I noticed when I went into the grocery store to pick up some milk that there was a car parked pretty close to the back of your car.
Did you forget to lock the door to the house this morning?	*Well*, I was running late for work because you shut the alarm clock off.
Were you smoking a cigarette outside a couple minutes ago?	*Well*, I went outside to get my cell phone that I left in the front seat.

If the person doesn't use a *Well*, but begins to ramble and give anything other than a "Yes" or "No" response, you still have yourself a hot spot.

Step 3. Redirect the conversation back to your original question. Give the person one more chance to come clean.

Step 4. Listen to the person's response uninterrupted.

Step 5. Ask him or her, "Why should I believe you?" A truthful person will tell you it's because she didn't do it or because he is telling you the truth. A liar will again stall or may say, "I don't care if you believe me or not!"

Ask again. No matter what the person says, even if she says, "Because I'm telling you the truth."

Ask the same question again. "That doesn't answer my question though. Why should I believe you?"

A truthful person will once again repeat that she is telling the truth or he didn't do the act in question. The liar will stall, get overly aggressive, or become dismissive of you.

Step 6 (optional). Ask the person, "Did you expect that I wouldn't find out what really happened?" Now, the liar will say "Yes" or "No"; the truthful person will say something like, "I have no idea what you are talking about."

Step 1 (YOU): Did you back my car into something?
Step 2 (THEM): *Well*, I noticed when I went into the grocery store to pick up some milk that there was a car parked pretty close to the back of your car.

Step 3 (YOU): That answer didn't answer my question. Did *you* back my car into something?

Step 4 (THEM): Don't you think I'd tell you if I bumped your car into something? Do you think that I'd keep that from you? Absolutely not.

Step 5 (YOU): Why should I believe you?

Step 6 (THEM): I don't care if you believe me or you don't believe me.

RESULT: The probability of deception dramatically increases.

Step 1 (YOU): Did you forget to lock the door to the house this morning?

Step 2 (THEM): *Well,* I was running late for work because you shut the alarm clock off.

Step 3 (YOU): I know you were running late for work and I'm sorry I turned off the alarm, but did you forget to lock the door to the house this morning?

Step 4 (THEM): What do you think? Have I ever forgotten to lock the door before?

Step 5 (YOU): Did you think that I wouldn't find out the truth?

Step 6a (THEM): No/Yes
   Or . . .
Step 6b (THEM): I don't know what you are talking about.

RESULT for 6a: The probability of deception dramatically increases.
RESULT for 6b: The probability of them telling the truth increases.

Step 1 (YOU): Were you smoking a cigarette outside a couple minutes ago?

Step 2 (THEM): *Well,* I went outside to get my cell phone that I left in the front seat.

Step 3 (YOU): Okay, but that's not what I asked you. Were you just smoking outside?

Step 4 (THEM): No.

Step 5 (YOU): Why should I believe you? *Note:* When you ask her again, she says the same thing = most likely the truth!

Step 6 (THEM): Because I didn't smoke and I'm telling the truth.

RESULT: The probability of them telling the truth increases.

THE BS BAROMETER READING

AT THE COURTHOUSE

Duke lacrosse players stand during a media conference outside the Durham County Detention Center after being indicted on sexual assault charges on May 15, 2006, in Durham, North Carolina. **(Getty Images)**

These Duke lacrosse players were charged with raping a female stripper who'd performed for them at a party—but despite repeated interrogation by police, all insisted on their innocence. Their pacifying gestures in front of the jailhouse could suggest they are scared—but are they guilty?

BS Barometer Reading: BS-Free

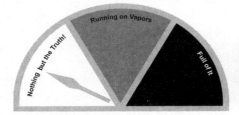

KEY

Total BS: Full of It

Partial BS: Running on Vapors

BS-Free: Nothing but the Truth!

Holding your hands in your pockets is a self-touch, pacifying gesture that could indicate an increase in stress—but be cautious of thinking that anyone who buries his or her hands in their pockets is holding back the truth. Many people stand this way as part of their baseline—Hollywood hotties George Clooney and Brad Pitt, while posing on the red carpet, can be seen with their hands in their pockets.

The lacrosse players at Duke were not guilty of rape. They were victims of a conspiracy by District Attorney Michael B. Nifong, who was so convinced of their guilt that he lied about evidence and tried to manipulate the entire investigation. Nifong was eventually disbarred for his criminal actions.

EXERCISING YOUR BS BAROMETER: THE INTERROGATION

The interrogation exercises build your confidence and develop patience. You need to have both if you're going to be able to ask powerful questions and have the courage to WAIT for the answers! I've also included some exercises for those who might be more interested in finding out what it's like on the other side of the thin blue line—the police. The police put themselves in harm's way every day to protect us. If everyone had a chance to walk in their shoes for a day, I think we'd all have a greater appreciation for how many liars they spare us from!

They Won't Have You to Kick Around Anymore!

Watch the Frost-Nixon interview (available on DVD and http://www.youtube .com/QOK3buuYMLQ). Put yourself in the shoes of Frost and literally mimic his body language to feel directly what he is feeling as he's analyzing Nixon. Also, prime your brain to look and listen for subtle and not-so-subtle body language shifts and changes in posture. When and why does Frost or Nixon lean in or lean back? What microexpressions are on their faces, in their hand gestures, and so on?

The purpose of this exercise is to sit in the posture and stance and use the same movements as one of the most extremely successful interviewers of all times. Success breeds success.

Retail Therapy Interrogation Training

In all the restaurants and stores you go to this week, ask the server or clerk the following two questions—then say *nothing*. That's right—after he answers your second question, you'll look at him, tilt your head slightly to your left shoulder, and silently spell your entire name in your head. Do this a few times, and you'll train your brain to pause and be patient—and not rush to fill the silence, cutting off your chance to get at the truth.

- *Question 1.* Is there any reason why you don't have (for example, steak on the menu, warm rolls, heated maple syrup, the tip included on the bill for large groups, the milk not in the same aisle as the yogurt, or black tank tops in a petite size, children's shoes, winter coats, bathing suits, . . .)?

- *Question 2.* [tilt head, pause] Really?

Fun Variation: Home Improvement Interrogation

Go to an auto store (or the auto section of a Walmart or Target) or go to Home Depot or Lowe's and pick up any auto part, liquid, drill, bucket of primer, or other item and ask confused questions about it.

Write down the following questions in a small notebook and begin to ask the store clerk one question at a time. Take a couple notes for each answer. Your objective is to keep them talking for a minimum of ten minutes.

- Who makes this?

- Who is the last person that bought this item?

- What is this for?

- What does it do?

- Why would someone buy this?

- How do you use this?

- Have the people who make this product ever been sued? Are you sure? How do you know?

- Do you guarantee the success of this product?

- Is there someone else here that can tell me more about this product?

Walk in a Cop's Shoes for a Day!

In most cities, local police departments offer ride-alongs to build communication within the community and to create an environment of mutual trust and respect. This means, depending on personnel resources and the number of requests a department gets for ride-alongs, you may be able to join an officer during his shift. (Note: You will have to sign a release that the department is not liable if you get injured—or worse.)

Ride-alongs can be super-exciting or super-boring—it depends on the day. But the great news is, they're an awesome way to train your brain to think like a cop, to spot danger a mile away. In some cases, you won't just be observing—the officer may have you write up tickets, complete some paperwork, or may even be open to you spotting an infraction (for example, speeding, going through a red light, expired tags, a missing plate, and so on).

To contact your local police department to request a ride-along, simply call their administrative number (never use 9–1–1 for ride-along requests).

The "I'm Super-Crazy About This Stuff and Have Some Spare Time" Exercise

Sign up at a local community college to take a basic policing course. If you are a schoolteacher and have summers off, or you're retired or even unemployed, and you want to keep yourself busy with a fascinating course of study, check out a criminal justice class. You can audit these classes, so you don't have to worry about a grade. The knowledge you'll obtain, however, will help you master the art of detecting deception at a pro's level!

JUST REMEMBER...

- *Open-ended questions are versatile.* Getting the person talking gives you more information on their story and also way more intel on their nonverbal quirks and their emotional hot spots.

- *Patience is your best tool.* When you're the one looking for the truth, you really have nothing but time. The liar will be anxious to get things over with and may trip himself up. The truthful person will just be bewildered by your odd mannerisms.

- *Ask for the truth.* Believing in people's intentions to be honest—and holding them explicitly accountable for that honesty—may be the most powerful truth serum we have.

PART 3

YOUR BS BAROMETER IN THE BIG PICTURE

PUTTING IT ALL TOGETHER

We are what we repeatedly do.
Excellence, therefore, is not an act but a habit.
—ARISTOTLE

THE FIRST COUPLE HOURS of my night out with my then-boyfriend-now-husband, Leif, it appeared like our evening was directly out of the New Year's Eve scene in the romantic comedy *When Harry Met Sally*. Leif and I were partying with more than two thousand people at a New Year's Eve gala, hosted by Washington, D.C.'s Pros in the City. *Braveheart*- and attention-loving Leif had shunned the traditional suit or tux in an effort to display his deep respect to his Scottish roots. Yes, he wore his kilt—with the green and navy MacPherson hunting tartan. Little did we know, our happily-ever-after evening would quickly take a turn for the worse when a forty-something local newsman asked Leif about his undergarments.

"Are you wearing underwear under there?" had been the most common greeting Leif had encountered that night. So when a man we'll call "Gabe," a handsome reporter, asked the same question, both Leif and I politely laughed. Within moments, we'd gotten beyond the small talk and were genuinely having a good time together. And, as almost always happens when people find out that I'm the "Lyin' Tamer," Gabe wanted to put my skills to the test. He challenged me: "Okay, ask me anything and see if you can catch me in a lie!"

Without letting him know the BS Barometer was switched on and operational, I launched right into gathering intel. "Gabe, you remind me of the kid in my neighborhood when I was growing up who sold me my first bike. Did you by any chance grow up in Waltham, Massachusetts?" I inquired.

Gabe responded, "No."

After some more small talk, I asked him, "Tell me about the day you got *your* first bike."

Gabe went on and on, consistently using pronouns, I noticed. His head would slightly tilt to his right for the first half of his sentences and then to the left for the second half, and so on. Back and forth. And although Gabe was built like a linebacker, his shoulders slumped subtly forward both when standing and sitting. His facial expressions were very animated, with frequent eyebrow and forehead movements. Imagine a cross between George Clooney and endearing actor Kevin James from the TV Show *King of Queens* and from my son Angus's favorite movie, *Mall Cop*.

Next I asked Gabe, "Before we begin this game [notice he doesn't think we had started yet], why should I believe the story you told me about your bike?"

"Because I was telling the truth," he said with his eyebrows pulled together and up, and his head tilted to the side, while he gestured again with an open-palm gesture.

I added, "Your response didn't answer my question. Why should I believe you about your bicycle story?"

Again Gabe responded, "Because I'm telling you the truth."

At that moment, Gabe's girlfriend of two years, a woman half his age, happened to walk over to see what was going on. Gabe explained that I was going to see if I could spot him in a lie. After a brief hello to Gabe's gal pal, now that I had his verbal and nonverbal baseline marked on my BS Barometer, I asked Gabe about his relationship with his girlfriend: "Tell me about how you two met."

Gabe smiled and explained how they both met. His tone, pitch, and nonverbals remained consistent with his baseline. She even smiled and subtly nodded her head "Yes," as if she was saying, "Yep, that's how we met."

I asked another open-ended question: "Tell me what you like about your girlfriend."

Gabe threw out some nice compliments in his normal tone and pitch and language. He didn't leak any microexpressions and he used his go-to open-palm gesture.

Gabe's timid gal pal smiled and tilted her head to her right.

Next, I went in for the kill: "Have you ever cheated on your girlfriend?"

"Have I ever cheated? Uh," Gabe said, his eyes closing for an extra second. He put one finger above his lip momentarily, and continued, "Michelle knows exactly how I feel about people who cheat—they're scumbags!"

I tilted my head to the side, gave him a confused look, and asked again, "Gabe, you didn't answer my question. Have *you* ever cheated on *your* girlfriend?"

What came next was a shock for Leif and me, but an even bigger shock for the young woman. Keep in mind, Gabe could have lied—we were, after all, playing a truth-or-lie game! But evidently, either Gabe felt so relaxed and was in the groove of telling the truth or he simply didn't care about that relationship—or perhaps, in an effort to beat the "Lyin' Tamer," he chose to be honest no matter what. Or perhaps the BS Barometer simply achieved its main purpose: to uncover the truth.

Whatever the reason, the truth came spilling out of Gabe's mouth.

"Well, I travel a lot for work, and we don't really have an exclusive relationship."

Gabe's seemingly introverted and reserved girlfriend went nuts! "What do you mean, we don't have an 'exclusive relationship'? Are you sleeping with other girls when you travel?" Expletives. Expletives! *Expletives!*

Right now your brain is probably beginning to automatically put the five steps of your new and exciting BS Barometer to practice. You're excited to immediately take action, turn on your tuned-up BS Barometer, and analyze my New Year's Eve debacle story above, right? Well, let's get to it! Here's the breakdown of how the BS Barometer worked here:

The Investigation

"Gabe, you remind me of the kid in my neighborhood when I was growing up who sold me my first bike. Did you by any chance grow up in Waltham, Massachusetts?" Gabe responded, "No."

> **No Hot Spots:** Gabe's baseline is not to oversell his answers when speaking the truth to a closed-ended question.

> **The BS Barometer Steps Used:** Gathering intel, interrogation, and wiretap

The Investigation

"Tell me about the day you got *your* first bike." Gabe went on and on, consistently using pronouns. His head was slightly tilted from right to left.

> **No Hot Spots:** When I tested the waters with an open-ended question, I determined that Gabe's personality appeared to be upbeat, silly, and funny—he was extremely gregarious. (Had I not seen this norm, his outsized personality might have appeared to be convincing-not-conveying.)

The BS Barometer Steps Used: Gathering intel, interrogation, wiretap, and stakeout

The Investigation

And although Gabe was built like a linebacker, his shoulders slumped subtly forward both when standing and sitting.

No Hot Spots: His nonverbals remain open throughout his norm. (Had I not seen this norm, his slumping might have appeared to be backsliding.)

The BS Barometer Steps Used: Gathering intel, full body surveillance

The Investigation

His facial expressions were very animated, with frequent eyebrow and forehead movements.

No Hot Spots: Thus far, his facial expressions have remained consistent. (Had I not seen this norm, his active facial movements might have appeared to be convincing-not-conveying.)

The BS Barometer Steps Used: Gathering intel, stakeout

The Investigation

Next I asked Gabe, "Before we begin this game [notice he doesn't think we started yet], why should I believe the story you told me about your bike?"

"Because I was telling the truth," he said.

No Hot Spots: Although Gabe looked confused about why I was challenging him on such a silly topic, his response was very direct and insistent.

The BS Barometer Steps Used: Interrogation, wiretap

The Investigation

His eyebrows were pulled together and up, and his head tilted to the side.

No Hot Spots: His facial expressions and head movement were congruent with his statement, typical of an honest person.

The BS Barometer Steps Used: Gathering intel, stakeout

The Investigation

He gestured again with an open-palm gesture.

No Hot Spots: His nonverbal gesture was congruent with his statement, typical of an honest person.

The BS Barometer Steps Used: Gathering intel, full body surveillance

The Investigation

I added, "Your response didn't answer my question. Why should I believe you about your bicycle story?"

Again, Gabe responded, "Because I'm telling you the truth."

No Hot Spots: He repeated his answer from before, not wavering on his insistence of truthfulness. (No teeter-tottering here!)

The BS Barometer Steps Used: Gathering intel, interrogation, wiretap

The Investigation

I asked, "Tell me about how you two met." and "Tell me what you like about your girlfriend."

As Gabe smiled and explained how they both met and what he liked about her, his tone, pitch, and nonverbals remained consistent with his baseline.

No Hot Spots: Gabe's word choices and pitch and tone, along with all his nonverbals matched his baseline.

The BS Barometer Steps Used: Wiretap, stakeout, full body surveillance, interrogation

The Investigation

"Have you ever cheated on your girlfriend?"

"Have I ever cheated? Uh, Michelle knows exactly how I feel about people who cheat—they're scumbags!"

Hot Spot 1: Gabe deviated in his norm with an inappropriate pause. (Teeter-tottering)

The BS Barometer Steps Used: Interrogation, full body surveillance

Hot Spot 2: Repeating the question "Have I ever cheated?" and his "Uh" are verbal fillers. (Backsliding)

The BS Barometer Step Used: Wiretap

Hot Spot 3: Ironically, he's using character testimony by saying "Michelle knows how I feel"—but she's the one he's cheating on! (Convincing-not-conveying)

The BS Barometer Step Used: Wiretap

Hot Spot 4: The phrases "people who cheat" and "they're scumbags" are both examples of distancing language. (Backsliding)

The BS Barometer Step Used: Wiretap

The Investigation

Gabe's eyes closed for a couple extra seconds and he put one finger above his lip momentarily.

Hot Spot 5: Deviation in his eye blink length and pacifying gesture (Teeter-tottering)

The BS Barometer Steps Used: Stakeout, full body surveillance

The Investigation

"Well, I travel a lot for work, and we don't really have an exclusive relationship."

Hot Spot 6: Use of the word *Well* in answer to a yes/no question

The BS Barometer Step Used: Wiretap

Hot Spot 7: The word *really* in this context indicates uncertainty. (Teeter-tottering)

The BS Barometer Step Used: Wiretap

The Investigation

Gabe crossed his arms, tilted his head to his chest, and with his right side of his lip pulled slightly up and in.

Hot Spot 8: Gabe leaked contempt and moral superiority with his sneer. (Teeter-tottering, backsliding)

The BS Barometer Step Used: Stakeout

Hot Spot 9: His closed body posture (crossed arms and head to chest) indicated that he felt exposed. (Backsliding)

The BS Barometer Step Used: Full body surveillance

The Investigation

His belly button turned to face the door, he pulled his right leg around the leg of the chair he was seated on, and he began to play with his cuticles while rubbing his hands together.

Hot Spot 10: Turning away, closing up his body posture, and using pacifiers were all signs that he was feeling severely stressed. (Backsliding, teeter-tottering)

The BS Barometer Step Used: Full body surveillance

Even though Gabe told me the truth and confessed to having sex with other women, he exhibited at least five "hot spots." Why? He later told me that he was feeling guilty and had wanted to share with his girlfriend the truth and this ended up being his time to let it out. By using my BS Barometer accurately, I took Gabe down a path of honesty, truth, and authenticity.

You might not be surprised to learn that Gabe and his girlfriend broke up that night. And as you might imagine, I felt very guilty. But I still blame the breakup on my husband and his damn MacPherson tartan kilt.

You've just seen the full BS Barometer in action in the dating world—which is only one setting of the thousands where you can use your newfound skills. In this chapter, I'll share some new pointers about how and when you can put your BS Barometer into practice in your own life.

Like the process of learning how to ride a bike, you have to learn each step of the BS Barometer as its own skill. You might learn how to balance, pedal, and steer in a step-by-step process—but when you finally get your bike up and riding for real, you perform all of those steps at the same time. You strengthen your BS Barometer in much the same way—while we've taken separate chapters to learn each of the steps individually, when you apply the BS Barometer in real time, you'll use all of the skills almost simultaneously.

When putting your BS Barometer to the test, experience is perhaps the most important teacher. The more time you spend in low-pressure situations, honing the variety of your newly polished skills, the more calm and confident you will feel and the better you'll be able to react to challenging situations. I use my personal BS Barometer in all aspects of my life: from asking my husband if he *really* mailed that check to the au pair company, to getting my son, Angus, to come clean whether or not he fed the fish, to confronting my wireless carrier about the roaming charges I incurred while overseas, to asking my OB/GYN what the likelihood is that I could get pregnant at the age of forty-one. I operate my BS Barometer every day, keeping it fine-tuned for those moments when I *really* need it.

Truthful People Are More Likely to Share:	in Statements Such As . . .
The emotions they saw in others . . .	Mary Ann appeared embarrassed because she giggled a little before she started to cry.
	You could tell that her boss was an arrogant know-it-all; he always had his chin up and his hands were behind his back.
	Kim was definitely hiding something because she would never look me in the eye. She would look scared when I'd arrive; I could see fear in her eyes.
The emotions they felt . . .	He made me very upset.
	I was pissed off.
	We were both happy that day.
Things they thought that were related . . .	Mike told me that he has ADD and when he used to work 9 to 5 jobs, he was always late.
	Sissy tells everyone that it takes a lot of discipline to train for a marathon and she has discipline up the ying-yang.
	David said that his ex-girlfriend never trusted him and he later found out she was cheating on him!
Things they thought that were unrelated . . .	Bobby's mom smelled like garlic.
	My husband clapped his hands before he opened the stroller.
	Just before your mother fell down the stairs she passed gas pretty loudly.

Truthful People Are More Likely to Share:	in Statements Such As . . .
Exact details about where they were . . .	I was going to the gas station to wash my car and when I drove by the Westin, I saw your husband standing outside with your best friend Ann and they were kissing.
	It was a Friday and in D.C. many people have Fridays off, so the traffic was pretty light on 7th Street NW, so I got into the office earlier than expected.
	After I dropped Michele off at kindergarten, I went home and watched American Idol on TiVO, which I do every Wednesday morning.
Random details about what they did . . .	I forgot to TiVO the *Dr. Oz Show* that afternoon.
	I measured four ounces of chicken on my new scale because I just started Weight Watchers Plus the week before.
	My son's name is Angus, it's a long story, but essentially, I lost a bet with my husband on the name game, but now I love the name!

THE BS BAROMETER GOES TO THE FAMILY DINNER

The BS Barometer is not just about busting cheaters and liars. Sometimes it helps you get to the bottom of sticky emotional situations, when people aren't being honest with each other, to figure out what's *really* going on behind the words. Recently, a client of mine, Marie, wasn't able to attend her family's Thanksgiving up in New England, but all she needed was a telephone and her BS Barometer to help her defuse a situation that could have gotten out of hand.

Thanksgiving was at Marie's parents' house. However, because Marie had to work, she was unable to go home for the weekend—but she was still front and center in the family drama.

Evidently, the house was full. When Marie's middle sister Ann's kids started coughing, their mom reminded Ann that because she has cancer and is on chemo, her immune system is already compromised. Ann apologized to their mom and explained that she had given her children a mini-course on how to "sneeze in their sleeve and cough in their cuff" and to stay away from whatever room Gram was in. Ann had nothing but positive intentions, and she didn't intentionally overlook her mom's situation—she'd addressed it and hoped the precautions would be enough. All went well and Thanksgiving was warm and peaceful—or so they all thought.

Two days later, it was Ann's fortieth birthday, and the family was due to celebrate at the annual "Cousins' Breakfast." Ninety minutes before the party at their cousin Caroline's house (complete with surprise cake for Ann), Ann emailed her baby sister, Mary: "Mary, are you bringing your kids today?"

Mary wrote back: "No, they aren't feeling well and I don't want to get Mom sick."

My client, the oldest of the three girls, happened to call Ann right after she received the email from Mary. The birthday girl was *not* happy and wasn't going to the party.

Marie thought, "Time to take out my BS Barometer and talk Ann 'off the ledge.'" (Her words, not mine!) She asked Ann, "Is there any reason why you are so upset?" She let Ann vent for several minutes: she had the best intentions on Thanksgiving, and she was already yelled at by their mom, and she didn't need to hear it from Mary, too! On her birthday, no less! Ann's tone of voice and word choices indicated clearly that she was upset, angry, and frustrated, a deviation from her calm, sweet-tempered baseline.

When she was done venting, Marie quietly asked, "Ann, is there something else you could've done to support your mom on Thanksgiving and still make your kids feel included?"

She paused. "I guess I could've asked Mom what she would've preferred." She took a deep breath, then added, "I feel bad for Mom and the last thing I want to do is make her sick!"

"Ann, this is your birthday. Make today about *you*. After all, who's going to miss out if *you* don't show up at the party?"

Ann responded, "Me." Shortly thereafter, Ann hopped in the car and headed to Caroline's.

Soon after, Marie called Mary and asked her why she gave Ann a hard time on her birthday. Mary was livid! She yelled, "I did not give Ann a dig, Marie! I was just telling her why I wasn't bringing the kids, and that's all! There's no more to it than that! *Enough!*"

"Mar, you could have said that the kids weren't feeling well so you were leaving them home, but you added the dig, 'So Mom won't get sick.' Is there any reason why?"

"I didn't give her a dig!" she insisted. "And, anyway, Ann didn't help me do the dishes on Thanksgiving!"

Aha! Marie had found the heart of the matter.

When a Person Is Sharing . . .	This Sounds More Truthful	This Sounds More Questionable
A description of an interaction	I called your office twice yesterday. No one called me back, so I'm calling you back again now.	Your office is not returning my phone calls.
	She tried to hold my hand, I pulled away, she was embarrassed and looked away.	She hit on me and I let her know that I'm not a cheater.
	Mom, the teacher stared at me, I stared back, then when I walked out of the room, she walked behind me and pinched my arm.	My teacher is bullying me.
The details of a conversation	I asked him why he didn't call you back. He said he sent you a text and your phone must not be working. I said, "Come on! You know that you never texted your mom yesterday!"	He claims he sent you a text message.
	I said, "Let's both take taxis home, we've had a little too much to drink." She said, "For every beer I drank, I had a glass of water, so I'm okay to drive."	She wouldn't listen to me. She drove home after drinking all night.
	When I decided to have my wedding at your hotel, your banquet manager told me, "There's no extra cost if you want to pull the red velvet drapes before you walk down the aisle." I said, "Great, I'd love to pull the red drapes, please add that to my banquet order." She said, "Great choice, almost all our brides have the drapes pulled back. You're going to feel like royalty!"	Your banquet manager told me that pulling the drapes would be free!

"Mar, tell me what happened with the dishes." She vented for several minutes. When she was done, Marie said, with a glint of humor, "Mary, you and I know damn right well, you gave Ann that dig because she didn't help you with the dishes."

Marie's normally super-sweet and patient sister Mary finally admitted it. "You're damn right, Marie!" Mystery solved.

I think we all know the true lesson of this story: always offer to help with the dishes on Thanksgiving!

By using this same model, wouldn't you agree that your BS Barometer can help you out in many different settings? When you use your BS Barometer skills to let people talk, complain, and vent, you can see how the truth will almost reveal itself.

Now, let's look at a business situation when the person did not use the BS Barometer—and how it might have changed if he had.

THE BS BAROMETER GOES TO THE OFFICE

Clyde is a very tall guy who takes up space, but he doesn't take up the room with his power. As a quality control manager for an engineering firm, he's in charge of safety when building new buildings. He had a great working relationship with all of his employees, and a high level of trust. Perhaps a bit too much.

On a major government job, one of his employees had signed a critical form indicating that the building construction had been completed according to code. Well, a government agency just happened to randomly inspect the building and—surprise!—nothing was to code.

Clyde was horrified. His reputation, even his job, was on the line. He called his employee in, and the employee insisted, "Yeah, I was there—everything was to code."

So Clyde got a little tough. "Well, let's go up together, so you can show me what you looked at."

That's when the employee came clean—he had never gone. The contractor had told *him* it was to code, so he just notated that he'd done a site visit and verified it was to code—but he never visited the site.

Clyde is so damn likable, the sweetest man you'd ever meet. And he's also a very generous man. He gave the guy another chance, which he certainly didn't have to do. At the end of the day, the error would have been on Clyde's head. That's what brought him to my class—he wanted to be able to detect deception, so that it never happened again.

Had Clyde's BS Barometer been up and running, he might have asked powerful questions and noticed hot spots right from the get-go.

For instance, when Clyde first asked his employee, "Was the building to code?," perhaps he would've gotten a glimpse of a subtle shoulder shrug, or a microexpression of fear, or a swift tongue protrusion.

Spotting those deviations from his norm, Clyde might then have asked him, "Is there any reason why you'd be uncertain about your answer?" This time

COP'S CHEAT-SHEET

Now, we know you can't use one signal to determine whether someone is lying—you have to dig way deeper. Here are some tips from a campus cop who's continually busting underage kids for stupid college misdemeanors— underage drinking, vandalism, shoplifting—in addition to much more serious crimes like drug dealing and rape. She sees the full range of accused, from the did-it-on-a-dare idiots to the more malevolently motivated. Margo Bennett, whom we met earlier, is the captain of the University of California, Berkeley's police department. In her presentation at their First Annual Compliance and Audit Symposium in San Francisco in February 2009,[1] she shared her experiences during her six years in the department and more than thirty years in law enforcement (including thirteen years with the FBI, where she taught interview and interrogation classes). Here are some of her body language observations from the presentation.

Body Part[2]	Truthful People Tend To . . .	Deceptive People Tend To . . .
Eyes	Be direct, but not overly so	Be evasive, avoid direct eye contact
	Be open, with a good portion of the whites of their eyes showing	Give a cold stare
	Be attentive, look at you	Give a tired, glassy-eyed stare
Posture	Sit up straight	Slouch in chair, preventing close contact
	Seem comfortable	Seem rigid and uncomfortable-looking

Clyde might have heard an overuse of adjectives, or maybe his employee would have tried to take Clyde off to "Never-Never Land."

What if Clyde asked him again for the second time: "Maybe it's just me, but you seem uncomfortable—is there any reason why you'd be uncertain about your answer?" Would this lying lad reply with the same answer? Or would he have started backsliding with being overly polite, or perhaps he would've dropped his *I*'s, or made fun of himself?

Body Part	Truthful People Tend to ...	Deceptive People Tend to ...
Posture **(continued)**	Lean toward you	Face belly button away from you
	Act relaxed and casual	Retreat behind barriers (other chairs, desks, purses, pillows, and so on)
		Cross arms, legs, ankles
	Hold head straight	Tilt head to side
		Fold hands in lap
		Keep elbows close to sides
		Stay in "runner" position—one leg back, like they're about to start running
		Slump head and body, eyes cast downward, and get a sad expression (when close to confessing!)
Body Movements	Have smooth, unpatterned changes in posture	Shift torso (especially in response to stress-inducing questions)
	Make occasional attempts to leave the interview	Make erratic changes, can't sit still
		Shift or "scooch" chair away from investigator
		Make occasional attempts to leave the interview

Clyde could then have drilled down: "What did you look at first? What did the contractor say about the inspection? Is there any reason why you might not have caught a violation of the code while you were on the site?"

If Clyde became even more suspicious, he could have gone in for the kill: "How do you think a person who takes the word of the contractor that everything is to code but never goes to the jobsite to see for himself would feel?"

And then, the closer: "What do you think should happen to someone who lies about the safety of a building?"

Mark my words, friends—he would have gotten to the truth a lot sooner. And that building probably would have been a lot safer.

POWER TEAM TURNAROUND

(Baron Thrower II)

Name: Jackson Peyton
Age: 58
Occupation: Forensic psychologist

What was stopping you from spotting master manipulators and liars?

As a psychologist with a specialty in children and families, most of my work is for family court. I do psychological evaluations of children and adults involved in neglect and abuse. Almost everyone, adults and children alike, is defensive when required to undergo a forensic psychological evaluation. I assume that most people are minimizing or being untruthful. Recently, I saw a depressed woman who had her children removed by the CFSA [Child and Family Services Agency] because of neglect. I had concrete evidence that she'd been neglectful, yet she denied all of the evidence. Rather than being able to do my job as a mental health professional, I found myself in the role of prosecutor, trying to get her to admit to the situation. The roles are diametrically opposed—I need to remain empathic to make an accurate mental health diagnosis. Acting as a prosecutor blinds me to a person's predicament.

In my personal life, I haven't experienced much deception—except one situation. My father lied about an extramarital affair. I was an adult and it wasn't my business, but it crystalized for me several other situations from the past when I knew he'd been untruthful. I was mad, personally and for my mother. However, it also humanized my father, who overtly held himself to extraordinary and unreachable standards.

How have you changed?

As a forensic psychologist, people are court-ordered to see me. Very few people are willing to tell the complete truth. After the training, I believe it's easier for me to maintain my empathic role while conducting psychological evaluations since I no longer have to struggle to determine if I'm being lied to.

I'm also beginning a part-time business as a real estate investor, and this will be an invaluable negotiation tool as well as a huge help in screening real estate agents, attorneys, and so on.

In my dating life, these techniques will be very helpful. If I'd known them before, I would have cut bait sooner on a relationship, and might have been more attuned to interested partners.

SHOW THEM YOU HAVE POWER—BUT NOT TOO MUCH

Clyde was in a position of power, but he wasn't using it. And in that vacuum, his employee rushed in and seized his power—and used that power to break the rules.

We've talked about how power corrupts and makes it easier for people to lie. But if you're trying to get to the truth, a judicious use of power can work for you as well. For example, in the future, using the new model we talked about, Clyde will combine his power *with* his BS Barometer to get to the truth faster.

People with more power have more control over the outcome of any situation, because they can provide or withhold resources or information; they can punish people; or they can simply choose to ignore people who are trying to influence them. In general, people with power experience fewer restrictions while simultaneously having greater access to money, information, and connections. People

AT THE AIRPORT

The Problem: You want your friend (on the left) to follow through on his promise to pick you up at the airport after your trip, and last time he forgot. You don't want to be left stranded again.

Your friend gives you a big, "*Yes,* count on me!" with a genuine smile. He's in, right? Wrong! As my son Angus would say, "Mayday, mayday . . . You are losing altitude!" Notice that your pal is literally giving you the cold shoulder and his feet are facing away from you.

The Fix: You need to move, and quickly. To reach this critical accomplishment, be sure that when you thank your buddy and ask him where you should meet him, you touch his arm. This touch creates an anchor to his commitment and to your appreciation, and he will accomplish the task this time. "I know you'll [pause and soften voice] feel motivated [pause and increase sound of voice] when you [pause and soften voice] pick me up at the airport at 1 o'clock [pause and increase sound of voice] because I'll take you out for lunch."

The Result: Now you can see his foot and belly button pointing toward you—he's in.

with less power have the opposite—more rules to govern their behavior, fewer resources to draw from.

Breaking the rules can signal to others that you have power. (I'll bet Clyde's employee felt quite ballsy and powerful when he falsified that report!) Research has shown that powerful people are more likely to:

- Take more cookies from a common plate

- Eat with their mouths open and spread crumbs

- Interrupt conversations

- Be "close talkers"

- Ignore other people's suffering

- Stereotype

- Patronize other people

- Cheat

- Take credit for other people's work or ideas

- Sexually harass low-power women[3]

- Exhibit more aggression toward other people (and have it be tolerated)

Isn't that sad? That we would look "up" to these people?

You don't have to be a boor just to prove that you have power. Just know that, if you're having trouble with an insubordinate employee, for example, little societal breaches—like entering an office without knocking, or answering a cell phone in a meeting—all of these social faux pas also unconsciously signify "power" in the mind of the person watching. Now, knowing that responding to power is a part of human nature, you can use these power signals to influence others at strategic times.

The trick with interrogation is to display supportive, appropriate power. A group of studies from the University of Michigan found that people perceive the highest-ranking officials to be less willing to cooperate than lower-ranking officials—and they based these judgments solely on their facial expression and its degree of warmth and approachability. Essentially, the grumpiest-looking person was perceived to have the highest power.[4] Your task is to walk the fine line between cheerful supplicant and angry overlord—you want your employee (or any person from whom you want the truth) to feel that you have the upper hand, but not so much power that they're unwilling to work with you.

AVOID BEING A BULLY—NO MATTER HOW SURE YOU ARE

Research has shown that when an innocent person is suspected of being guilty, more intense interrogation techniques are often used in an attempt to draw out a confession. But in some people, especially those who are shy or suffer from social anxiety, simply being the focus of so much attention is enough to turn them into a nervous wreck. Those body language signals—tension, fear, avoiding eye contact—may be misinterpreted as guilt. Always remember to keep an open mind and be open to the possibility that you are wrong—otherwise, you may stumble into bully territory.[5] When you have someone backed into a corner with a presumption of guilt, that's when they "check out"—either refuse to participate any longer or simply say whatever you want to hear. The person may "confess" just to get you out of their face and, at that point, the conversation—and the relationship—is likely over.

You want to avoid arriving at that place. The whole reason you're developing your BS Barometer is so that you can surround yourself with open, honest, caring, genuine people. You're not going to succeed if you're pushing people away with paranoia.

Maybe you've been finding yourself in that paranoid place a bit too often. Or, worse—you have been the victim of a liar more times than you care to admit. Well, it's time to take a long, hard look at what's going on with you. That's what we'll do in the final chapter: The Self-Exam.

EXERCISING YOUR BS BAROMETER: PUTTING IT ALL TOGETHER

Prime the Subject for the Examination

In step 1, we discussed the importance of determining a baseline for individuals, a critical step you must take before being able to detect deception with any degree of accuracy. And early on in step 5, we talked about how important priming is to put people in the mind of telling the truth. My go-to priming question is my line about my first bike in Waltham, Massachusetts—I can drop it into any conversation, and it feels effortless—to *me*.

That's the key—that this is a sentence you'll feel so natural delivering, no one will realize you're norming them. Develop a few priming questions that you can deliver easily to set up your baseline and prime your target to speak the truth. The sentence must be one they'll automatically answer truthfully, without thinking about it. Go for nonthreatening topics, preferably about something they haven't thought about in a while: childhood friends, high school, first car, learning to drive.

Slant Your Questions / Slant Your Results

How are you most likely to phrase your questions? Take this assessment to find out your regular M.O.—*before* you confront someone. To use the BS Barometer effectively, you have to pay attention to the way you phrase your questions. Research shows that how we word a question can significantly affect the answer we are given. For example, you would likely get a different response if you asked, "How cold is it outside?," than if you asked, "How hot is it outside?"

Ponder the following questions. Can you imagine how these minute differences may result in different answers? Even more important, can you see how even subtle changes can alter the perspectives of both the questioner and the answerer?

How long is your hair?	How short is your hair?
How fast is your car?	How slow is your car?
How formally do you dress to go to work?	How casually do you dress to go to work?
How tall is your boyfriend?	How short is your boyfriend?
How hot is it in your office?	How cold is it in your office?
How powerful is your boss?	How weak is your boss?
How cute is your friend's new baby?	How ugly is your friend's new baby?
How smart is your sister?	How stupid is your sister?
How nice is your mother?	How mean is your mother?
How relaxed was your trip?	How stressed was your trip?

Answer at least two sets of the previous questions (or make up your own).

Question 1—Positive	Question 1—Negative
Your answer:	Your answer:

Question 2—Positive	Question 2—Negative
Your answer:	Your answer:

After you have completed this task, examine your responses. How did you answer each? Did the difference in wording cause you to think of alternative aspects of your loved one, your boss, or your life? Ask yourself how you normally phrase questions. What do you think this says about you?

Getting Back to Trust

Sometimes we may have distrusted someone and called them out in a lie—and found out we were dead wrong. In those situations, it will take a while to repair the relationship—but, the good news is, it can be done. Research shows a simple apology can restore trust—so that's always worth a try. But one study[6] found that just a short series of cooperative acts can restore mutually cooperative behavior.

If you find yourself in this situation, set up a project you can do together. Maybe you and your husband can do any of the following:

- Clean the fridge

- Organize the bathroom drawers

- Install the bike rack that's been in your garage for two years

- Wax your skis

- Buy tickets to a baseball game or laser tag for the whole family

- Wash the cars together

- Get massages together at the mall (they often have small booths or salons for a dollar a minute)

- Create a garden together

Or you and a colleague can collaborate on a project, go on a site visit, or do a sales call together.

The important thing to remember is, when you are doing this to intentionally repair your relationship, you must let the other person take top billing. Allow your husband to pick the seats at the game, or what to plant in the garden, or even where you place the bike rack in your garage—and then agree with him. If it's your colleague, go out of your way to praise her ideas both when you work alone together and when you present the project to others. The study found that as few as five cooperative acts can restore the relationship, if not quite back to where it was originally, at least in a positive direction. Go above and beyond, and you'll likely be back on solid ground with the person very quickly.

Give these questions some thought:

- What are three relationships you have that would benefit from greater trust?

- What is one project you could do with each of those people?

- How can you let them "win" in each project?

Power Behind the Power

For this exercise, I'll introduce you to three very powerful and influential women who inspire me to stay focused on *my* personal and professional mission: to save lives. These are the alpha women who influence many of the world's greatest leaders and many of the top-selling brands in the world. You've more than likely seen their work or used a product they helped create, sculpt, or promote. All of these women have had to climb over, around, and through tricky roadblocks at one time or another throughout their lives, but they've somehow made it out on top. And if they can do it, so can you!

First up, the ever-gorgeous and hard-working *New York Times* bestselling author and editor-in-chief of *Cosmopolitan* magazine, Kate White. Kate is a kind soul to everyone she meets. She's also a creative mastermind. Each month, she comes up with all those edgy "I must buy this magazine now" blurbs on the cover of *Cosmo*. She's also a loving mom of two and a generous and gracious friend to all.

But don't mistake her huge heart for a weakness. Kate is ridiculously successful, powerful, and unstoppable. Everything she touches skyrockets to the top—and she's finally ready to share her secrets! Her new cutting-edge, women-focused career book, *I Shouldn't Be Telling You This: Success Secrets Every Gutsy Girl Should Know,* will reveal her tried-and-true methods to set you on a path to long-term success—even if you've failed a thousand times before.

Your first mission is to watch Kate on her numerous television appearances at http://katewhite.ning.com/video. How does she speak? What facial expressions does Kate make? How does she sit? Are her hands folded, flailing around, or open? What do her hairstyle or clothes say to you? What is it about Kate that makes you like her and respect her power at the same time?

Up next, Joanne Bradford, a former senior vice president of U.S. revenue and market development at Yahoo. Today Joanne is the chief revenue officer at Demand Media, a well-funded and rapidly growing content development company skyrocketing social media and other PR for clients such as Lance Armstrong

Foundation's LiveStrong.com, Trails.com, BF Goodrich, Kraft Foods, Lowes, and Whole Foods. Joanne is a fierce, fashionable firecracker; she has moxie, charm, and charisma.

Your next mission is to watch this video clip of Joanne: http://www.you tube.com/watch?v=4-oipMkUXaE. (Also posted on www.youcantlietome.com.)

Moving right along to Pattie Sellers. Pattie Sellers is *Fortune* magazine's editor at large and co-chair of the Most Powerful Women Summit, the preeminent gathering of women leaders in business, philanthropy, government, academia, and the arts. Pattie has interviewed everyone from Oprah to Hillary Clinton, to Meg Whitman, to Martha Stewart, to Ted Turner, to Tyra Banks.

Your final mission is to watch the following video clip of Pattie at ICAN's 2011 Women's Leadership Conference: http://www.youtube.com/watch?v=j7wL-pO2 .m4w. (Bonus points: visit Pattie's blog at http://postcards.blogs.fortune.cnn .com/.) (Also posted on www.youcantlietome.com.)

From Kate White to Joanne Bradford to Pattie Sellers, simply ask yourself these two questions:

1. What is *my* personal and professional mission in life?

2. What is it about *these* women that says . . . *"You can't lie to me"*?

JUST REMEMBER . . .

- *The BS Barometer is versatile.* You can use your new skills to keep people honest in many situations, whether in the office or around the dinner table.

- *The five steps can happen simultaneously.* The more you do the exercises and practice the steps, the more adept you'll be at getting a quick baseline and zeroing in on those deviations. Eventually, all the steps fall into place in one fluid process.

- *Your power is a tool—own it, and use it wisely.* Being disagreeable can sometimes help you signal your power to people who aren't respecting you. But no matter what your CV or your bank statement says, real power comes from knowing the truth—and how to use your BS Barometer to get it!

THE SELF-EXAM

And the day came when the risk to remain tight in a bud was more painful than the risk it took to blossom.
—ANAÏS NIN

COMEDIAN AND ACTOR DANE COOK may be one of the funniest guys around—but getting ripped off by a family member is no laughing matter. My childhood neighbor and family friend Cathy Cook's adorable little brother was robbed blind to the tune of $11 million by his own big brother, Darryl McCauley. After a decade of being Dane's business manager, Darryl, his forty-five-year-old half brother, began embezzling millions of dollars from his baby brother's bank accounts. Once, Dane's big bro even wrote out a $3 million check to himself from Dane's account. When police searched Darryl's house in Maine, there was $800,000 in cash in the safe! Darryl was sentenced to five to six years in a Massachusetts state prison, ten years on probation once he is released, and he has been ordered to make restitution to Cook in the amount of $11 million.

Let's all take a wake-up call from Dane! It's time for all of us to conduct a little bit of internal affairs, wouldn't you agree? Have you been turning a blind eye to a trusted loved one and giving them too much power over you in one area of your life or another? Or do you find that you frequently encounter deception by almost everyone in your life? Whether there is one liar or many in your life right now, it might be time to take a peek in the mirror. What mistakes are *you* making in *your* life that are stopping you from spotting that friendly phony? Or the complete opposite: Why are you attracting these losers, year after year? Why are cheating partners, lying bosses, and "frenemies" even in your world? Why are you choosing to let this poison leak into your life?

Scariest of all: If people are drawn to those most like themselves, what does their venomous behavior say about you?

Ouch. Even I don't like to think about that last sentence. Recently I was

---

WHY IS SHE A FRENEMY?

We all have one—at least one. A person who "should" be your friend, but whom you just can't bring yourself to trust. Maybe she's burned you a few times; maybe she just makes you feel uncomfortable. You might have thought women had gotten beyond that catty competition—so what's up?

That "catty competition" is not your imagination. One quantitative review of more than 272 studies, involving nearly 32,000 people from eighteen countries, found that, in general, women cooperate with men more than they do with other women.[1] Despite the stereotype of men being cutthroat competitors, when it comes to the common good, they cooperate with other men *more* than women cooperate with each other. Why?

Evolutionary psychologists believe that men's alliances tended to build resources for larger groups—together they could hunt more successfully and cover more territory. But women who might be thrown together could be co-wives, and therefore be in constant competition for sexual attention.

Well, okay—we may have an evolutionary explanation for mean girls and frenemies. But I think we can all agree that we are much better off working *with* each other than against one another! Take a good look at your immediate circle of friends, and make a list of the women you're not sure you trust, the ones with whom you feel uncomfortable, regardless of whether you think you "should" like them or not. ("We have so much in common!" is not a reason to trust someone.) Don't judge your feelings—just go with your gut. Then, make a list of those women who make you feel loved and whom you could call for help when you *really* need them. When it comes time to make social plans, focus your precious time and energy on this group of golden girls—they're your real friends.

betrayed by a trusted close friend, a betrayal that could have been avoided had *I* been paying closer attention at the time. Thank God that when I get knocked down, He helps me get back up again!

Let's turn the BS Barometer around and take a good long look at your degree of honesty with *yourself*. Do you always give people second and third chances and expect a different result—and then blame *them* when they betray you again? Have you been turning a blind eye to suspicious behavior of your longtime trusted advisor and friend—and are you anxiously waiting for disaster to strike? Or are you so busy lately that you have given someone in your life too much power over the most important areas of your life—and you just assume that they have your back?

WHAT IS YOUR INTENT?

One of the most heartbreaking things that I see over and over in my seminars is smart people (usually women) who second-guess themselves and their decisions. The average woman simply doesn't trust her gut. She might have suspicions about people or situations, but she doesn't value her own instincts. So she puts herself into bad spots—whether bad jobs, dysfunctional love relationships, or toxic friendships—over and over again, thinking, "It must be me, I must be the problem." She wants to find people who admire and trust her, people she knows have her back—but she doesn't even have her *own* back.

I know that feeling all to well—because I've definitely been that person.

When I first moved to Virginia, I moved in with a friend, Jasmine, whom I had met when I worked at the FBI. Her husband had left her and her three kids on a family-centered holiday. My heart went out to her. So when I discovered that both of us were going to be working in Washington, D.C., I offered to take my per diem moving money and finish the basement of her new townhouse, so I could live there.

After I moved in, I became like a surrogate husband to Jaz and a surrogate father to her three wonderful kids. I painted her living room, I cleaned the house, I even picked up groceries from BJs. I'd make breakfast and lunch on weekends. I'd drop her youngest son off at day care and help her oldest son with homework after school.

After I had lived with Jaz and her kids for nine months, I met the man who would become my husband. Leif lived on Capitol Hill in Washington, D.C., which was an hour and a half away from Jaz's house in northern Virginia. We started dating in October, and by late November I would stay over at his place and not come home until the next day. By May, Leif and I had bought a house together in Alexandria, Virginia.

You might already know what's coming next.

At first, Jaz was supportive—even happy for me that I'd met someone. But as things started to get more serious, Jaz became really nasty to me. She started dropping these guilt trips, trying to make me feel bad for spending time "away." "Must be nice," she'd mumble at me when I came home the next day. "Hope you had a *great* time."

At first, I felt bad. *She needs my help, and I'm not there for her.* Then, I started to think, *This is crazy.* "I'm not your husband, Jaz," I'd say. "If you need help, you need to reach out to your ex." I had a life, after all! I was a young woman in love. I wanted her to be happy for me. But more than that, I just wanted her to let me go.

Eventually, I moved in with Leif and moved my belongings out of Jaz's townhouse. Slowly, we lost touch. Then, two weeks before my wedding to Leif, Jaz called and said, "I know you're getting married soon, and I'm definitely going to be there. But I have a present for you that you have to get right now. Could you stop by the FBI building? I'll meet you outside on the curb on your way to ATF."

I was touched. I felt like, *Wow, I must've been wrong about her. She really is happy for me.* I was so relieved as I pulled up alongside her. I popped out of the car and came around and gave Jaz a big hug. I was so emotional with the wedding coming up—and so glad to share this moment of joy with all the people who cared about me.

I thanked her for the present, gave her a quick kiss on the cheek, and headed off to work. When I got to the parking lot, I ripped open the present. I sat there, stunned. In my hands, I held the book *He's Just Not That Into You.* The title page was inscribed with the words, "He does not bring out the best in you, Janine. You should reconsider—because he's just not that into you." Ouch.

Now, it's pretty clear that her intent was not, as she claimed, to help me. What was her hidden intent—to hurt me? To get me to doubt myself and my soon-to-be spouse?

And what was mine, as I eagerly rushed to her when she called me after months of silence? Was I honoring my instincts about her? Did I have my own back?

Your true intentions can spill over into all aspects of your life—and the lives of the people who cross your path. Many people who are looking to tune up their ability to detect deception and improve their communication skills skip the most important step: setting a positive and authentic intent—such as success,

THE BS BAROMETER READING

WITH THE LAWYER

Once a sweet, odd, and shy high school boy who disappeared in the back of the class, Adam Wheeler later conned his way into Harvard with claims of a perfect 4.0 from MIT and 1600 on his SATs. Wheeler became a muscle-head, a scholarship-winning, plagiarizing poet, and a young con man. Busted when he applied for a Rhodes scholarship, Wheeler was eventually indicted on twenty counts, including larceny and identity fraud. Wheeler had already made off with nearly $45,000 in grant and prize money, all won from plagiarized work.

Convicted thief and plagiarist Adam Wheeler talking to his lawyer during his arraignment in May 2010. **(Associated Press)**

BS Barometer Reading: Full of It

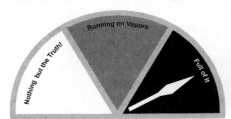

Running on Vapors

Nothing but the Truth!

Full of It

KEY

Total BS: Full of It

Partial BS: Running on Vapors

BS-Free: Nothing but the Truth!

However overly confident he once was—straight, strong posture, chin up and shoulders pulled back—that powerful body stature disappears quickly in court. Notice how Adam's shoulders are slumped forward, making him a smaller target; his head is tilted to his right, and instead of looking his lawyer "straight in the eyes," he peers out the sides of his eyes. This sideways glance could mean that Adam processes his world through primarily an auditory process (he is a poet, after all), "lending his lawyer an ear," or it could indicate that he feels threatened or skeptical. As for Adam's puckered lips, they send a signal of uncertainty.

love, or truth. Instead, they often set a negative one, such as "The next guy better not be a cheater!"

Or "I hope I don't appear nervous."

Or "I hope people don't think I'm a liar!"

When people focus on what they *don't* want to happen, it's as if their ability to honestly communicate and genuinely connect with other people just deflates. We've seen it happen: it's clearly possible to have a super-polished speech (hello, Tiger Woods), armed with some pretty confident gestures, and people still won't buy it. That's because the "intent" is to fool others into believing one thing (that you are worthy of authentic, real, honest relationships, for example), when you yourself don't even believe it's true.

SHOWING UP—OR SHUTTING DOWN?

I'll never forget the chilly winter night when my out-of-the-ordinary instructor grabbed a chair and started walking around the room dragging it behind him. "Hi, so nice to meet you," he cheerfully said to a woman in the audience. "I'm sooooo excited to be on this super awesome date with you! You are sooooo pretty!" He whispered that he'd like to give her a kiss goodnight—and suddenly the chair floated off the ground and moved between both of their faces. As you might imagine, the student immediately "broke up" with her imaginary perfect blind date.

Next, the instructor began rambling around the room dragging two chairs. "Hi, so nice to meet you. I'm sooooo excited to be on this date." There were at least four chairs that caused four breakups that night. The class: the Landmark Forum (www.landmarkeducation.com); the discussion: how we recycle our formerly damaged relationships.

The Landmark Forum leader explained that the chair-dragging is a perfect metaphor for our emotional baggage, the stuff we lug around from one relationship to the next. Once we've lived through a painful experience, we now look at life through a different lens. Maybe your lens says, "I was left at the altar." Or maybe it says, "I've had two guys cheat on me." Who knows—maybe your lens even says, "I cheated." You now look at every relationship through that lens—especially when you look in the mirror.

Those lenses not only color every interaction—they sometimes blind us entirely. As we do the self-exam, we need to take a good hard look at all the deceptive lenses we use to view the world and how they can block us from creating genuine, authentic relationships with ourselves and others.

Denial

As we talked about at the beginning of the book, one of the three main reasons that people don't detect lies is very simple: because they don't want to. We all have certain realities that we don't want to face. Maybe you suspect your boyfriend of cheating—but you're thirty-five and want to have a baby soon. Maybe you think your employee is skimming off the top—but she's great with the customers and the losses aren't that much. Maybe you think your husband is gay—but you can't bear to think what it would do to the kids if you were to confront him.

In some industries, reality is kept from the CEOs in order to give them "plausible deniability"—they don't want to know what they don't want to know. But for common folk, run-of-the-mill denial is usually the cause. Denial can prevent us from seeing the truth that's right in front of our eyes. Paul Ekman even has a name for this: the Ostrich Effect.[2] We bury our heads in the sand rather than confront uncomfortable truths. Denial is the mac-daddy of all lenses that prevents us from having a genuine, honest life.

Prejudices

None of us likes to think of ourselves as a racist. Or a sexist. Or an anything *–ist*, for that matter. But even the most forward-thinking person can be swayed by difference. Several studies have found that we read people who share our same race more accurately than we do those of other races. We tend to attribute more complex mental states to them, we look at them holistically, we pick up more subtleties, and we remember their expressions longer. Brain scans have shown that our reptilian brain—the amygdala, the seat of our most basic emotions—responds more intensely to expressions of fear of people who share our race.

One study found that both Japanese and white Americans experienced the same phenomenon—more brain activation in response to emotions from people of their own race versus those of the other race. When asked to verbally identify emotions, both groups were 10 percent better at identifying the emotions of those who shared their race.[3] We might say we "don't see color"—but saying that is just another very socially acceptable form of denial.

Now, this heightened sensitivity to the feelings of our own race is not necessarily caused by closed-mindedness. Scientists believe we evolved that way because we likely had strategic alliances with other people within our "group," so that any lies or betrayal from within that group would be more serious and threatening to our survival. In other words, we might have these biases precisely *because* we realize how much we need other people and how much they need us.

That doesn't excuse us from questioning these biases—let alone making decisions about people's trustworthiness or honesty—based on race.

Stereotypes

As a plus-size woman, I have dealt with my share of stereotypes—but I've perpetuated them, too. For example, when I'm out in public, I'm always subconsciously looking for someone heavier than me. Then I can think, *At least I'm not that heavy.* I do understand that our brains are evolutionarily programmed to prefer beauty, and to a certain degree, that knee-jerk anti-fat bias is not our fault. But we do need to remain aware of this powerful "beauty bias"—and never was that more apparent to me than with Casey Anthony. I firmly believe that had she not been a beautiful, fit young woman, there would have been a different verdict.

This bias for beautiful faces has been documented by science. People believe they can judge the "trustworthiness" of a person almost instantly—within the first 100 milliseconds of seeing the face for the first time. But one study showed this bias to be as wrong as they come. A group of study subjects believed their ability to judge a person's trustworthiness was unshakable, yet they were completely unable to tell the difference between generous philanthropists and dangerous criminals from *America's Most Wanted*. This "facial appearance heuristic" is a clearly documented bias that people believe men and women with attractive, symmetrical faces are the most honest.[4]

I followed the Casey Anthony trial every day of testimony. As a mother of a child who is about the same age as Caylee, and as a former federal law enforcement official, the case hit me on all levels. Casey Anthony, the smoking-hot girl, was found not guilty—but imagine how different the trial would've gone if she'd been 300 pounds and had a few teeth missing. If you ask me, had that been the case, she would not be free today.

Power Lust

We've talked about the fact that power corrupts, and corruption brings more power—which can be an intoxicating cycle that can get people caught up, almost like an addiction. We would hope that when someone lies or cheats it would decrease that person's power, but it actually *enhances* it in the eyes of those who are watching. One study of 169 people found that, when told a story about a bookkeeper who bent the rules versus one who followed them, the rule bender was more often seen as someone who could influence other people's pay level and promotions, "make life difficult," or "make things unpleasant at work." The rule

THE BS BAROMETER READING

ON THE STAND

Na-na-na-na-na, you can't catch me!

For this BS Barometer challenge, you'll take Casey Anthony's emotional pulse through analyzing three of her many childlike gestures. Casey's legendary moody disposition allowed her to vacillate between being enraged and petulant (yelling in her jailhouse call, "They just want Caylee back. That's all they're worried about right now, is getting Caylee back,") to being happy (to see the brother who supposedly molested her) to seething

with contempt, anger, and teeth-flashing rage (in court, no less). Is that behavior suspicious? Let's see.

Here you'll notice Casey, during a recess in her murder trial on June 30, 2011, tilting her head, squinting her eyes, playfully gesturing to someone in the courtroom, as if she is motioning for a toddler to get over here before the scary

Get over here or I'm going to tickle you! **(Getty Images)**

tickle monster gets you. Casey had many "imaginary friends"—such as "Zenaida," the nanny who supposedly kidnapped Caylee; "Jeffrey," the friend who referred the nanny; and "Juliette Lewis," her coworker at the job she told her parents she still held at Universal

Studios, despite having not worked there since Caylee's birth.

On June 8, 2011, Casey is spotted leaning back in her chair sulking, with a tense jaw, her chin pulled in, and a pout on her face, next to her attorney Dorothy Clay Sims. When people stare straight ahead daydreaming, they are often having internal dialogue, a.k.a. self-

(continued)

Nobody wants to play with me anymore. **(Getty Images)**

talk. If only we could be a fly inside what many psychologists have called her "sociopathic brain." When her brother first asked why she wasn't bringing

Caylee home after thirty-one days, she said, "Because maybe I'm a spiteful bitch!" before spinning the tale of the kidnapping nanny.

On July 7, 2011, during Casey's sentencing on charges of lying to law enforcement, she is seen with a smile of "Duper's Delight," giving herself a massage by stretching her fingers and bending them backward. This self-touch gesture relieves stress and increases plea-sure by decreasing the pressure in

Did I just get away with murder, or what? **(Getty Images)**

the capsule inside the joint. A week later, George Anthony, Casey's own father, said on *Dr. Phil* that he believes Casey should be held responsible for Caylee's death.

BS Barometer Reading: Full of It

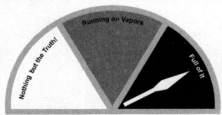

Casey is the prima donna of master manipulators. She can lie quickly and with ease! She lied about a nonexistent nanny, the nanny's address, her job, her friends, her boyfriends, her whereabouts, her child's father—she even stole a checkbook from her best friend. She may have been acquitted for the murder, but we can safely call her a liar—as deception was the only charge that actually stuck in this sad case.

bender was seen as a person more in command of his own actions and the situation. This result has been duplicated in dozens of studies: people who lie, cheat, steal, and break the rules are seen as having more power, and may influence us, even if we consciously disapprove of their behavior.

You also might think that "rude" people would be seen as lower class, but rude signals also indicate that those people have power. When we consciously know that, of course, we can try to remain vigilant for those signs and signals and watch our own reaction to them. Do you overtly disapprove of the loud-mouth at the bar but secretly admire his or her confidence?

Could it be that you keep falling for the same kind of lying jerk because he gives off the bad-boy/I'm-in-charge kind of vibe? What may be understandable from an evolutionary point of view—our genes want a Cro-Magnon man who can defend us and bring home the bacon!—can be totally destructive in this day and age.

Make sure you are clear about your relationship to power. Know the nonverbal and status-enhancing signals that may be influencing you outside the realm of your awareness. Always ask yourself, "What does this person want? What do they gain—and what do I give up—if I give it to them?"

WHAT'S YOUR PaYOFF?

In the movie *Up in the Air,* George Clooney plays a professional hatchet man, a guy whose job is laying people off. What makes him so good? He's a master at "reframing" the horrible situation. George's character would ooze empathy and say, "Don't think of this as a layoff—think of this as an opportunity to follow your life dream."

Now, we all know this is BS—but this is the *good* kind of BS. The essence of what George is saying is true: we can decide how we deal with the outcome of any situation. We can decide what our payoff will be.

Will you be a victim of a bully boss? Or will you use that situation to work up the nerve to quit and start your own company?

Will you wallow in self-pity for a relationship that didn't work out? Or will you be grateful that you saw the warning signs and were "relieved" of that connection before you had invested more time?

Will you take this last deception as yet more evidence that you can only get hurt? Or will you use it to create stronger boundaries, to recognize the warning signs, and to focus on the qualities you *do* want in your relationships? Honesty. Strength. Integrity. Compassion.

7-SECOND FIX

THE NEIGHBORHOOD DOORMAT

(Baron Thrower II)

(Baron Thrower II)

The Problem: You're sick of being the neighborhood doormat for dog watching, yard watering, and babysitting, and you're ready to create action.

The Fix: Become a "short fat candle" (your feet are between one and two feet apart) and hold your chin. This move arouses in others the belief that you have power and confidence. "Believe me, [pause] my schedule is so packed right now, I can barely walk my own dog. I think [pause] you'll agree with me [pause and soften voice] that there are other people in the neighborhood with more time on their hands who will be able to help you."

The Result: Your neighbors will be more respectful of your time and start asking someone else to do their chores.

It's up to you to decide. What's *your* payoff? Is there a bigger payoff in confronting the liars in your life? Or is the bigger payoff to remain a victim? Make no mistake—you're getting something out of both choices.

Everything we do in our lives has a payoff. Take a look at this chart to consider some examples of perceived versus hidden payoffs. As you read, consider what your hidden payoffs might be.

Example

Your mom put her foot down, and she won't let you borrow $500 (again) to pay your overdue cell phone bill.

Action: You throw a "Poor Me" pity party (that is, you have an adult tantrum).

Perceived Payoff: You show your mom how selfish she's being and prove that people aren't helping you.

Hidden Payoff: You get to feel like a victim, which helps you rationalize why you can't land a job.

Example

You discover that your boss has cooked the books, and you confront him.

Action: He offers you a promotion in return for your silence. You decide to turn him in.

Perceived Payoff: You get to look like a hero.

Hidden Payoff: You feel proud that you've done the right thing and acted ethically. You can sleep at night!

Example

Your seven-year-old son begs you to forgive him after he calls you a bad name, so he can play another round of his favorite Wii game.

Action: You give in.

Perceived Payoff: Your son gives you a big kiss and a huge hug, and you feel appreciated and connected to him. You get to feel in control, and you feel loved.

Hidden Payoff: You don't have to think about why he called you that bad name or what kind of precedent you're setting with his behavior.

Example

You discover a mistake on your tax form—that nets you an extra thousand bucks.

Action: You call your accountant and point it out.

Perceived Payoff: A negative payoff—you're out $1,000!

Hidden Payoff: You won't get charged with tax evasion. You can breathe easy with a clean conscience.

Example

Your wife wants to have sex tonight—but last night you wanted to have sex, and she was too tired.

> **Action:** You refuse to give in and deny her advances.
>
> **Perceived Payoff:** You get to get her back—now instead of feeling powerless, like you did last night, you feel powerful.
>
> **Hidden Payoff:** You maintain the distance in your relationship, so you don't have to feel vulnerable or think about why you're not "in sync."

Example

Without asking you, your significant other promises her family that you'll both be spending Christmas with them in Connecticut.

> **Action:** Your partner tries to persuade you with compliments and small gifts. After careful consideration, you decide to agree.
>
> **Perceived Payoff:** Compliments and small gifts! And you feel like "the good guy."
>
> **Hidden Payoff:** Ultimately, you both feel respected—and your initial resistance ends up bringing the two of you closer.

Example

You are overweight and you know it, and now your health is really being affected.

> **Action:** You continue to do nothing to get healthier.
>
> **Perceived Payoff:** Being heavy gives you a way to judge people: if they still like you, they're true friends. If they don't, they're just "superficial."
>
> **Hidden Payoff:** Maybe deep down, you use your weight as a way to keep people at a distance, so they never know the "real" you and they can't hurt you.

Example

You see your friend's boyfriend out with his ex for lunch.

> **Action:** You snap a photo with your phone, and break the news to your crushed BFF.
>
> **Perceived Payoff:** You protect your friend from this horrible man.
>
> **Hidden Payoff:** You feel like a good friend. And you get your Friday night happy hour pal back!

CHaLLeNGe YOUR INNeR LIaR

We are extremely connected to other people in ways we are only just beginning to grasp. We *feel* our connection to other people very acutely—when we are rejected socially, it activates the same neural pathways as when we experience physical pain. Even when we feel embarrassment for someone else, our brains experience this physical pain. When it comes to our relationships, whether with other people or with ourselves, there is no mind-body "connection"—it is, quite literally, all the same thing.[5]

When we continue to lie to ourselves, we are fooling no one, and that denial is taking a physical toll on our bodies. We have to look at it like a metaphorical Band-Aid—and rip off that denial. The harsh pain we experience in the short term, when we face up to the deception we've "known" but ignored for weeks, months, or even years, is much better than the buried pain that festers and eats away at us from the inside.

When you rip off that bandage, and admit the deceit—he is cheating, she is trying to get your job, you don't love her—the skin underneath might, indeed, be raw and exposed. But you've just opened yourself up to more—more honesty, more connection, more authenticity. By being willing to face the pain

NeeD TO GeT IT OFF YOUR CHeST?

When it comes to lies and deceit, some would say that Catholics have it made—the confessional is the ultimate lie cleanser. There are other places where you can anonymously release the lie and feel unburdened.

Postsecret.com. People send in postcards with their most closely held secrets. See many confessions of infidelity, theft, and other lies.

Dishonestylab.com. People email/tweet their biggest lies, from toddler shoplifting incidents to tearing up a parent's will in order to get a bigger slice of the inheritance pie.

Grouphug.us. A simple site that allows you to just log in and confess—and then forget it. Each poster is tagged with a number—no other identifying details. Freedom is just a click away!

now, you're saying "Yes" to the beautiful thing to come. You now know how to recognize truth and even more important, you know how truth feels: Lighter. Easier. More free.

TURN THE BS BAROMETER ON YOURSELF

You've learned a great deal about lying in this book—how it shows up, what it looks like, even why people do it. Now it's time for you to turn the BS Barometer back on yourself, and dig deep: Where are you in all of this? Here are some hard questions I'd like you to consider. Consider this your own personal interrogation:

What's at stake for you? What issues brought you to this book? Were you interested in getting a leg up on dishonest salespeople? Sneaky teens? Suspicious caregivers? Or have you had a series of dishonest friends and lovers? Or, is it possible that you suspect others without cause—because the dishonest person is you?

What is the intel someone could gather on you? How have you been interacting with people around truth and honesty? Do you lie to your mother? Your kids? Are you honest in your business dealings? Do you return extra change?

What would a wiretap show about you? Is your résumé 100 percent legit? Do you gossip about friends or casually lie to get out of social engagements?

What would the stakeout and full body surveillance show about the "real" you? If someone used the stakeout and full body surveillance on you, what would they see? Would they see someone who takes pride in his or her appearance? Someone who stands strong in his or her own power?

And, finally,

What would a true interrogation reveal about you? Are you someone who would rather hide her true self than feel vulnerable and exposed? Are you ready to stop hiding and to start living your life out loud?

To create a life you love, you must first imagine how you want your life to be and the steps you need to make any necessary changes. Start by simply visualizing your goals and committing to writing them down. The self-exam exercises will help you on your way.

As you look to your future, take a few minutes to reflect on how far you've come and where you want to go next. You will be far more likely to succeed this year and in the years to come! And wherever your path will take you, know that your BS Barometer will help you build the caring, honest, authentic connections that make life worth living.

POWER TEAM TURNAROUND

Name: Erin Gelzer

Age: 34

Occupation: Real estate developer

(Baron Thrower II)

What was stopping you from spotting master manipulators and liars?

I can be guilty of deception in relationships. I try to be very honest, but I frequently lie by omission. I don't tell people what my real motivations are, or I don't tell people what I am really thinking. I also think it works the same way in reverse. I don't feel that people typically lie to me—more that they skirt the truth, or gloss over what they are really thinking, or tell me what I want to hear.

How have you changed?

I think strengthening my BS Barometer will make me feel stronger and less afraid in relationships. Sometimes the unwinding of a relationship has just been due to freaking out about what I don't know. Having more confidence in my ability to detect when I am being duped will probably help me have more stable, carefree relationships.

I used to be so focused on myself in a conversation—what I thought, what my reaction was to what someone was saying, how I was coming across. I now realize I was missing a lot of cues from those around me. I was focusing on their words and was blind to the other nonverbal signals people were giving off. The BS Barometer training helped me to become more present, which helps not only in detecting lies but also in being a better friend, daughter, employee, and so on. I learned to not hold back or play it safe, to say what I think in my gut regardless of opposition.

I think this program will make me much more powerful and confident in both my relationships and my career. It has already given me more confidence that I can trust my instincts in a situation, protect and stand up for myself, and have the insight to know whom to trust. Beyond just detecting deception, the program has also taught me to be others-focused, to play life full out and be fully engaged, and to express gratitude.

EXERCISING YOUR BS BAROMETER: THE SELF-EXAM

Set Your Best Intentions

To help you get started, here is a short list of some positive intentions you can choose. I love to choose two or three at a time. Some of my favorite combos include "success, opportunity, and abundance"; "joy and serenity—no matter what"; and "love, forgiveness, and trust":

Abundance	Generosity	Patience
Acceptance	Gentleness	Peace
Beauty	Honesty	Reliability
Caring	Honor	Respect
Commitment	Humility	Serenity
Compassion	Integrity	Service
Confidence	Joy	Strength
Courage	Justice	Success
Creativity	Kindness	Tact
Enthusiasm	Love	Thankfulness
Excellence	Loyalty	Tolerance
Flexibility	Magic	Trust
Friendliness	Moderation	Truthfulness
Forgiveness	Modesty	Understanding

Circle one to three of the intentions listed, or create your own, and then kick it up a notch by adding the word *ridiculous* in front of it! For example, "My intent is for ridiculous amounts of love, forgiveness, and trust."

Strike a Power Pose

A recent study suggests that standing in a powerful pose for as little as one minute can help you perceive yourself as more powerful, decrease the level of stress hormones in your body, and even increase your tolerance for risk.[6] Use a few of these basic power moves the next time you're feeling unsteady or insecure. Stand and sit in confident poses at the office to show that you mean business—you're not a pushover and you take your work seriously. If you've been burned in the past, these moves can be especially helpful to rebuild your confidence before you take the leap and trust again. (For more Power Poses, check out "Tune Up Your Power Gestures" in my first book, *You Say More Than You Think*.)

The Steve Jobs Hand-on-Chin Power Pose

On May 2, 1985, at the Tavern on the Green in New York, co-founder of Apple Inc. and inventing superstar Steve Jobs displays the Steve Jobs Hand-on-Chin Power Pose while sharing the spotlight with another computer genius, co-founder of Microsoft, Bill Gates. **(Getty Images)**

When speaking with someone in person and they ask you a question or for a favor and you have a burst of uncertainty or an increase in stress, avoid rubbing your temple or neck or playing with your cuticles! Instead, simply grab your chin. Then say something like: "Let me think about it and I'll get back to you tomorrow with more information." In less than three seconds, you can look so much more intelligent!

The Elbow Power Pop Position

When seated, relax, take up space, and pop your elbow over the back of the chair. Immediately you'll look and feel confident, yet likable. This is a great power move to initiate during your next office meeting, while waiting for your

On February 20, 1957, with her arm over the back of her chair, Hollywood's Golden Age actress Elizabeth Taylor glamorously demonstrates "The Elbow Power Pop" position. **(Getty Images)**

blind date to arrive, or when your kids come home after they have snuck out of the house! This little baby is one of my faves—it packs a punch of power, while at the same time leaves you looking cool, calm, and confident!

Face Yourself

Take out a piece of paper, and at the top, write the one issue in your life that you would love to change. Shine a light on this difficult part of your life and ask yourself, "Where is my denial undermining my success in resolving this situation or circumstance?" Write down some possible solutions that would work if you had unlimited time, resources, and will. Look in the mirror each morning and ask yourself, "When I think about this issue, am I being honest with myself and others?"

What Will Be *Your* Legacy?

This visualization exercise helps you quickly zero in on the three biggest changes you need to make in order to achieve your goals and bring more honest, open, and genuine relationships into your life. Ask yourself probing questions.

- How is your current lifestyle helping to create your destiny?

- How will you be remembered after you are gone?

What are you actively working toward achieving or becoming? What kind of life do you *really* want? What are your top personal and professional goals?

Take a few moments to gather these thoughts together. Now, imagine you have achieved them all. From your point of view, how would you commemorate your life on your tombstone?

_____

_____

_____

_____

Now write down how you would like *other* people to remember you.

_____

_____

_____

_____

- What changes will you *really* make to create the legacy you desire?

- When do you plan to make these changes? Be specific: commit to the year, month, day, and time of the day to increase the likelihood you will stick to the goal.

- How do you intend to hold yourself accountable to these plans?

- What roadblocks do you see that may prevent you from following through on this commitment to yourself?

- What proactive steps can you take *now* to ensure these potential difficulties will not negatively affect your success?

- How did these exercises (and this book) make you feel?

Can You Judge a Book by Its Cover: Serial Killer or Corporate Queen?

Based on their faces, their clothing, and their expressions, can you identify how many serial killers or corporate queens are pictured below?

A   (Getty Images)   B   (Pekka Sakki/AFP)   C   (Getty Images)

Answers

A: Serial Killer. On November 18, 2003, seventy-two-year-old Elfriede Blauensteiner, who always dressed in black, and was dubbed "Black Widow," died in jail, while serving a life sentence for murder. She confessed to killing five fellow elderly people she took care of, for their assets.

B: Serial Killer. On December 22, 2010, Finnish nurse Aino Nykopp-Koski was sentenced to life in prison for murdering five patients between the ages of seventy and ninety-one and attempting to murder five more elderly. Her apparently motiveless killing spree was done by giving her patients drugs they had not been prescribed, including sedatives and opiates.

C: Corporate Queen. On November 2010, Carol Bartz, former CEO of Yahoo!, Inc., speaks at the Web 2.0 Summit in San Francisco.

Did you guess correctly? This exercise demonstrates why you can't judge a book by its cover. Sometimes during my ninety-minute corporate keynote presentations, I'll have the audience participate in a playful interactive first impression exercise. They each tape a piece of paper on their backs and walk around introducing themselves to five strangers. After a quick hello, they write on each other's backs their initial thoughts about one another. Surprisingly, some people will write on these complete strangers' backs such powerful words as "trustworthy," "kind," "honest," and "truthful."

Really?

Can you really trust someone within minutes? How about in hours? Years? A decade? Unfortunately, no—at least, not 100 percent!

Just ask Dane Cook! And Dane's not alone. One year while I was being a mom, going through an intense medical treatment, training a new employee as the director of education at the Body Language Institute (BLI), and flying from one end of the country to the other for speaking engagements, my stress level was ridiculously high! I was distracted and desperate for serenity and certainty, and I couldn't add any more responsibility to my plate. I was so overwhelmed that without me consciously knowing it, my BS Barometer was occasionally on the fritz.

That year, on Christmas Eve day, within a four-hour span of time, everything came crashing down on me: I discovered I'd lost a fledgling pregnancy. I had a major project land in my lap right before a planned vacation with my family. And I discovered that my good friend, whom I had trusted with my most intimate secrets, ideas, and dreams, had taken advantage of me during my most difficult days. This woman had been a trusted friend for years. I admired her. I looked up to her. I sang her praises to my family, my friends, and even my clients. However, when I was emotionally overloaded, she took advantage of me, and I was devastated.

After I finished crying and kicking myself that someone in my inner circle would betray me, I dusted off my smile. I reset my intention to "Love, Success, and Serenity—no matter what!" Wouldn't you know it—within the next five days, the phone never stopped ringing with new business. I reconnected with an old friend. And my son got his dream present from Santa: the Star Wars LEGO Death Star!

Life is good.

Why am I telling you about my personal deceptive sucker-punch to the gut? Because maybe by sharing my story, you'll take a look at the checking account your husband manages for the family, or you'll move your investments into someone else's hands, or you'll find out that you really aren't getting paid as much as the guy down the hall doing the same job you do, or you'll simply make smarter decisions about who you have protecting your assets—and I don't just mean your money.

While the nurse watching *your* grandfather might not be a serial killer, and *your* older brother might not be embezzling from you, and *your* good friend might not have betrayed you, it's crucial that you be cautious about giving the people in your life too much power. Now, remember: I'm not telling you not to trust people. I'm just reminding you to ask questions, be nosy, make surprise visits, and conduct random audits of whoever is managing your money or the care of the people you love. If it can happen to Dane and it can happen to me, it can happen to you. Be smart. Trust your gut and, when you're in a crisis, look around: Whose life could receive a high payoff as a result of you being buried deep in your crisis?

Now fetch your BS Barometer and investigate anyone who just came to mind. You know more than you think you know, so do something about it! You are so worth it! When you discover whatever it is you discover, breathe deeply, then set a powerful and positive intention and believe it with your heart and soul.

Finally, be grateful for something, anything—even if it's that Santa brought your son his dream toy and he says to you what Angus said to me: "Mom, this is the best day of my life—ever!"

JUST REMEMBER . . .

- *Every aspect of communication begins with intention.* You can choose whether that intention is positive or negative. Negative intentions break down relationships, opportunities, and self-esteem. Positive intentions create possibilities, growth, confidence, and love.

- *We all view the world through our own lenses.* Taking time to examine your own prejudices will help open you up to alternatives you've not even considered.

- *The biggest lens of all is our own denial.* What are you hiding from? And how would your life improve if you faced your biggest fears head-on?

EPILOGUE: USING YOUR POWERS FOR GOOD!

The only thing needed for the triumph of
evil is for good men to do nothing.
—EDMUND BURKE

WHEN MY MOM FOUND OUT she had triple-negative breast cancer, she gathered up all her PET scans and medical reports from a year earlier. The tests had been taken at a different hospital, after doctors spotted a couple small spots on her lungs, which ended up being some chemicals she must have inhaled years earlier. Prior to her doctor's appointment at Massachusetts General Hospital for breast cancer, she came to my house in Alexandria, Virginia, for a weekend visit with her sister, my aunt Geraldine, and my cousin Joey. While we sat on my screened-in porch, I could tell that something was on my mother's mind. Cautiously, I asked, "Mom, how are you feeling?"

"Fine." She didn't look me in the eye.

I said, "Mom, how are you *really* feeling?"

She immediately burst out crying. I thought it was because of the breast cancer. Turned out, she was carrying a much heavier burden.

She'd gone through the whole file from the last hospital, reading the results with her nurse's eye. Turns out the written report from a year earlier said that my mom had "abnormal cells in the throat typical of metastasizing."

My poor mom was completely blinded by one thought: *The cancer started in my throat—and has now spread all over my body. I am going to die.*

She wasn't just about to fight a battle with breast cancer, she thought—now she had an even harder fight ahead of her. I was confused. Why hadn't we known this before? Why hadn't any doctor mentioned it? Wouldn't she have had a sore throat or been spitting up blood if she had throat cancer for a year? Nonetheless, Mom made me swear not to tell my two sisters. She asked me not to bring it up again.

Two weeks later, when Mom met with the team of doctors at Mass General, I flew to Boston to join my parents and two sisters. After the first doctor came in, spoke, and left, I softly said to my mom, "Mom, are you going to ask the doctor about the report from Mount Auburn?"

She shot me the dirtiest look, as if I had just dropped an f-bomb around the Thanksgiving table. "Janine, I can only fight one cancer at a time. I just don't want one more piece of bad news!" Mom was terrified; she didn't think she could handle it.

This reaction is the textbook definition of denial as a coping mechanism. Denial prevents us from facing the truth, from finding out what is real, from moving forward. I see this all the time, in all walks of life. You could be a cancer patient. You could be a fraud victim. You could be a single mother, working two jobs, barely getting by, raising four kids on your own, who doesn't have the strength to confront your teenager who might be having sex or doing drugs.

We all have so much on our plates, we're sometimes afraid to know the truth about these big things. They're so big that we're afraid to ask, because we think we can't handle it. We can, of course. And we must. But sometimes, we just need some help understanding that we're stronger than we think.

I disobeyed Mom. She didn't mention her worry to the doctor during her exam. So I seized my opportunity. When the oncologist arrived, the oncology nurse pulled the curtain and began to take Mom's blood pressure and ask her a few questions. I whispered and gestured to the oncologist, "Can I speak to you outside?"

Out in the hallway, I mentioned the report to the doctor and asked if it were possible that the cancer started in Mom's throat and was now throughout her body. He shook his head and said, "No, there must have been an error." He said he'd look into it, and we both stepped back into the exam room.

An hour later, the oncologist came back and asked to see only me in the hallway. Mom shot me another look—she didn't know what was going on and, as you might imagine, she was nervous and not happy.

The doctor explained to me that it had been a mistake—a typo.

These days, doctors read their patient notes into handheld recorders and then those tapes are transcribed. The transcriptionist for my mother's oncologist's report had made a mistake. The word that was missing was *No:* "*No* abnormal cells in the throat typical of metastasization."

That night, we went out and celebrated—because now she was only fighting one cancer! Sadly, Mom had been tormented for two and a half months, believing the cancer had spread throughout her entire body. She just couldn't bring herself to ask.

I think many people are struggling with denial in one form or another. *I'm barely holding it together. One more thing and I'm going to snap.*

I hope that by tuning up your BS Barometer, you're creating the courage and the confidence to do what's right, to get to the truth of the matter faster, and more directly. I urge you to continue to work with the exercises—the more you practice the skills, the greater your confidence will become. Instead of spending months or years denying your gut feelings, you'll have the tools to know right up front. Using your BS Barometer won't even be a conscious thing anymore—the more you use it, the more highly trained your brain will be to instinctively seek out the truth. Then, right when confusion or dishonesty pops up, you're going to catch it.

You'll automatically create more authentic relationships. You'll trust yourself and your own gut more.

Which is important—so important. Because, ultimately, I want you not only to fight for yourself—but to fight for the other people who might need you even more. Your student, who needs you to confront him about drugs. Your mother, who needs you to watch out for a dishonest caregiver. Your young son or daughter, who needs you to stay vigilant to the predators in your midst.

That's what I want for you: to have open, trusting relationships. To enjoy genuine connections with people who deserve your respect and your love. To approach the world with confidence and without fear.

And now that you know what signals you're looking for, I want you to put a finger on the scale of justice and start taking a stand for those who need a helping hand. So when you think your sister's husband is having an affair, when you are suspicious that your boss is on the take, when you think that pillar of the community is touching little boys—you'll face the truth head-on. You'll fight for those who are too weak, young, or scared to fight for themselves.

In the moments you need it most, you'll listen to your fine-tuned BS Barometer and you'll act fast. You'll walk with your head up high, knowing that not only can others count on you, but that *you* can count on you, too!

ACKNOWLEDGMENTS

Thank you to all the courageous victims of deception and betrayal who have shared your stories, which ultimately protects other innocent people from future injustices. I applaud your bravery. You have more power than you know. You make a difference.

To J.J. Newbury, thank you for writing your generous and thoughtful foreword, for sharing your "Truth Wizard" secrets with me, and for demonstrating the virtues that make a great friendship: trust, integrity, and love.

This book would've never found its way into this world without my unstoppable literary agent, Dan Lazer—thank you. As for my dangerously awesome partner in crime, my co-writer, Mariska Van Aalst, it was you who made this book a mission possible. You are a creative genius with a continuous source of ideas. I love you.

Much appreciation goes to my amazing editor, Jeanette Perez, who was flexible, encouraging, and made numerous valuable suggestions. Jeanette, few surpass your mind-blowing kindness. Also, thank you to the HarperOne team: Mark Tauber, Gideon Weil, Lisa Zuniga, Jacqueline Berkman, Ralph Fowler, and Molly Birckhead. A huge hug goes out to HarperOne's Melinda Mullin, director of publicity, you're extraordinary. As for the ever-wonderful Heather Jackson, my former editor, thank you for keeping the light on for me and being so willing to shine your brilliance on the crucial early phases of this undertaking.

Next, my deepest gratitude goes to my Body Language Institute's (BLI) past and present creative team: Jerusalem Merkebu (imagine the letters "Ph.D." here soon), Sunhee Yoo (you still scare me a little), Janine Sidarous (love your beautiful first name), Rebecca Maguire (writing superstar), Lindsay Scarff, Adam Yi, Vanessa Collins, Nikki Sims, Abbey Potter, Bridgette Turner, and my new executive assistant Valerie Medina (you scare me more than Sunhee). You are helping change the way the world will unlock the truth.

This book wouldn't have been possible without the inspiration from my work husbands, Chris Ulrich and Aaron Brehove. I love you guys! Infinite respect is reserved for my other dear friends: Terence Noonan, Dr. Oz, Anderson Cooper, Terry Moore, Sissy Bray, Brian O'Shea, Frank Marsh, Kathy Trahan, Chief Jim Williams, Henry Lescault, Michelle Dresbold, Ed Villavicencio, Stuart Boslow, Lori Conrad, Ken Foote, Jeff Jamison, Michael Karlan (www.prosinthecity .com), and Gloria Rossi, who believes that "mentors change lives!"

As for the Detecting Deception Power Team (DDPT), I'm impressed with your unrelenting determination to fill the world with the truth: Anja, Clyde, Jackson, Marina, Minowa, Caroline, Edward, Michelle, and Eugene. Erin Gelzer, thank you for touching my heart with your kind words. I'm also incredibly grateful for DDPT members Oscar Rodriquez, for creating the "Instant Replays"; my new trusted confidante Blanca Cobb (www.truthblazer.com), who challenges us all to "live our possibilities"; and Tim Smith, my dependable business manager.

To all the television and radio networks, national interest magazines, and producers and editors who have trusted me as your "go-to" body language expert, thank you! You guys ROCK!

Above all, I want to thank my loyal husband, Leif; my incredibly lovable son, Angus; my devoted parents, Lorraine (BLI "Employee of the Month") and Charlie (Mom's unpaid intern); and my sisters, Kerry and Caileen, and their families, who supported and encouraged me while I wrote this book, despite all the time it took me away from them.

I love you all.

APPENDIX

Free Online Resources

Scan with RedLaser

← Website for this book:
www.youcantlietome.com

Save your seat in Janine's next *You Can't Lie to Me* 5-Day Train-The-Trainer Program: www.lyintamer.com/bodylanguageinstitute/register

Scan with RedLaser

← Download the free *You Can't Lie to Me* app
on your Smartphone:
www.youcantlietome.com/apps

Scan with RedLaser

← Test your BS Barometer mad skills at Janine's
You Can't Lie to Me YouTube channel:
www.youtube.com/bsbarometer

Scan with RedLaser

← Download your free audio "Instant Replay"
for each *You Can't Lie to Me* chapter:
www.youcantlietome.com/instantreplay

Scan with RedLaser

← Book Janine as your next keynote speaker:
www.lyintamer.com/book

See if you qualify to attend Body Language Institute (BLI) *now:*
www.lyintamer.com/blog/do-you-meet-our-requirements-to-apply-to-
attend-blis-elite-certification-tr/

View the schedule for upcoming BLI classes:
www.lyintamer.com/bodylanguageinstitute/schedule

Like the Body Language Institute on Facebook:
www.facebook.com/BodyLanguageInstitute

Follow the Body Language Institute on Twitter:
@BLInstitute

Follow Janine on Twitter:
@janinedriver

NOTES

Introduction

1. N. L. Carter and J. M. Weber, "Not Pollyannas: Higher Generalized Trust Predicts Lie Detection Ability," *Social Psychological and Personality Science* 1 (July 2010): 274–79.
2. Carter and Weber, "Not Pollyannas."
3. B. M. DePaulo, D. A. Kashy, S. E. Kirkendol, M. M. Wyer, and J. A. Epstein, "Lying in Everyday Life," *Journal of Personality and Social Psychology* 70 (May 1996): 979–95.
4. Kaja Perina, "Who Are You—and What Do You Think of Me?," *Psychology Today,* January/February 2011.
5. K. Williams et al., "Identifying and Profiling Scholastic Cheaters: Their Personality, Cognitive Ability, and Motivation," *Journal of Experimental Psychology: Applied* 16 (2010): 293–307.
6. http://www.nytimes.com/2008/10/28/health/28well.html.
7. http://www.nytimes.com/2008/10/28/health/28well.html.
8. http://www.usatoday.com/yourlife/sex-relationships/2011-01-22-monogamy-young-couples_N.htm.
9. DePaulo et al., "Lying in Everyday Life."

Chapter 1
The Truth About Lying

1. http://www.bloomberg.com/news/2010-07-30/galleon-bp-visa-new-star-kebble-eu-budweiser-westlb-in-court-news.html.
2. D. Carney et al., "People with Power Are Better Liars" (working paper, Columbia Business School, March 2010).
3. http://hbr.org/2010/05/defend-your-research-powerful-people-are-better-liars/ar/1.
4. E. Tahmincioglu, "People in Power Make Better Liars, Study Shows," March 15, 2010, http://www.msnbc.com.
5. D. Carney, "People with Power."
6. Timothy R. Levine, "The Impact of *Lie to Me* on Viewers' Actual Ability to Detect Deception," *Communication Research* 3 (December 2010): 847–56, first published on June 17, 2010.

7. Aldert Vrij et al., "Pitfalls and Opportunities in Nonverbal and Verbal Lie Detection," *Psychological Science in the Public Interest* 11 (2010): 89–121.

8. Vrij, "Pitfalls and Opportunities."

9. C. F. Bond, A. Omar, A. Mahmoud, and R. N. Bonser, "Lie Detection Across Cultures," *Journal of Nonverbal Behavior* 14 (1990): 189–204.

10. D. Matsumoto, H. S. Hwang, L. Skinner, and M. Frank, "Evaluating Truthfulness and Detecting Deception," *FBI Law Enforcement Bulletin,* June 2011.

11. http://www.magarchive.tcu.edu/articles/2005-01-AC2.asp.

12. Vrij, "Pitfalls and Opportunities."

Chapter 2
How the BS Barometer Process Works

1. H. M. Schaefer and G. D. Ruxton, "Deception in Plants: Mimicry or Perceptual Exploitation?," *Trends in Ecology & Evolution* 24 (December 2009): 676–85.

2. "Detecting Lies," *BBC Edited Guide,* http://www.bbc.co.uk.

3. S. A. Spence, "The Deceptive Brain," *Journal of the Royal Society of Medicine* 97 (January 2004): 6–9.

4. V. Reddy "Getting Back to the Rough Ground: Deception and 'Social Living,'" *Philosophical Transactions of the Royal Society B: Biological Sciences* 362 (April 29, 2007): 621–37.

5. V. Jaswal et al., "Young Children Have a Specific, Highly Robust Bias to Trust Testimony," *Psychological Science* 21 (October 2010): 1541–47.

6. M. F. H. Schmidt and J. A. Sommerville, "Fairness Expectations and Altruistic Sharing in 15-Month-Old Human Infants," *PLoS ONE* 6 (2011): e23223.

7. T. Ruffman et al., "Age-Related Differences in Deception," *Psychology and Aging,* April 2011.

8. B. Verschuere, A. Spruyt, E. H. Meijer, and H. Otgaar, "The Ease of Lying," *Consciousness and Cognition* 20 (September 2011): 908–11.

9. Matsumoto et al., "Evaluating Truthfulness."

10. C. Bond and B. DePaulo, "Accuracy of Deception Judgments," *Personality and Social Psychology Review* 10, no. 3 (August 2006): 214–34.

11. Matsumoto et al., "Evaluating Truthfulness."

12. Aldert Vrij, *Detecting Lies and Deceit: Pitfalls and Opportunities,* 2nd ed. (West Sussex, UK: Wiley-Interscience, 2008).

Chapter 3
When to Use the BS Barometer

1. N. O. Rule et al., "Face Value: Amygdala Response Reflects the Validity of First Impressions," *Neuroimage* 54, no. 1 (2011): 734–41.

2. N. Ambady and R. Rosenthal, "Half a Minute: Predicting Teacher Evaluations from Thin Slices of Nonverbal Behavior and Physical Attractiveness," *Journal of Personality and Social Psychology* 64 (1993): 431–41.

3. http://www.nytimes.com/2010/09/07/health/views/07mind.html?_r=1&ref=education.

4. F. Zeidan, S. K. Johnson, N. S. Gordon, and P. Goolkasian, "Effects of Brief and Sham Mindfulness Meditation on Mood and Cardiovascular Variables," *Journal of Alternative and Complementary Medicine* 16 (August 2010): 867–73.

Chapter 4
Step 1: Gathering Intel

1. Kaja Perina, "Secrets of Special Agents," *Psychology Today,* January/February 2011, p. 56.

2. "Wizards Can Spot the Signs of a Liar," Associated Press, October 14, 2004, http://www.msnbc.com.

3. "Detecting Lies."

4. DePaulo et al., "Lying in Everyday Life."

5. R. B. Lount Jr., C. B. Zhong, N. Sivanathan, and J. K. Murnighan, "Getting Off on the Wrong Foot: The Timing of a Breach and the Restoration of Trust," *Personality and Social Psychology Bulletin* 34 (December 2008): 1601–12.

6. Lount et al., "Getting Off on the Wrong Foot."

7. A. Vrij et al., "Pitfalls and Opportunities in Nonverbal and Verbal Lie Detection," *Psychological Science in the Public Interest* 11 (2010): 89–121.

8. M. Weisbuch, M. L. Slepian, A. Clarke, N. Ambady, and J. Veenstra-VanderWeele, "Behavioral Stability Across Time and Situations: Nonverbal Versus Verbal Consistency," *Journal of Nonverbal Behavior* 34 (March 2010): 43–56.

9. C. Remsberg, "Final Findings from Force Science Exhaustion Study," *Force Science News,* April 25, 2011.

10. E. Goode and J. Schwartz, "Police Lineups Start to Face Fact: Eyes Can Lie," *New York Times,* August 28, 2011.

11. A. L. Shelton et al., "Should Social Savvy Equal Good Spatial Skills? The Interaction of Social Skills with Spatial Perspective Taking," *Journal of Experimental Psychology* (July 2011), 0–7.

Chapter 5
Step 2: The Wiretap

1. http://www.nydailynews.com/sports/college/jerry-sandusky-i-seeking-young-person-sexual-helped-article–1.977730#ixzz1dvgjovfC.

2. J. T. Stanley and F. Blanchard-Fields, "Challenges Older Adults Face in Detecting Deceit: The Role of Emotion Recognition," *Psychology and Aging* 23 (2008): 24–32.

3. N. Ambady, D. Laplante, T. Nguyen, R. Rosenthal, N. Chaumeton, and W. Levinson, "Surgeons' Tone of Voice: A Clue to Malpractice History," *Surgery* 132 (July 2002): 5–9.

4. C. B. Zhong, V. K. Bohns, and F. Gino, "Good Lamps Are the Best Police: Darkness Increases Dishonesty and Self-Interested Behavior," *Psychological Science* 21 (March 2010): 311–14. Epub Jan. 29, 2010.

5. Zhong et al., "Good Lamps Are the Best Police."

6. L. Shu et al., "When to Sign on the Dotted Line? Signing First Makes Ethics Salient and Decreases Dishonest Self-Reports," Harvard Business School (working paper no. 11–117, 2011).

7. P. Fraccaro et al., "Experimental Evidence That Women Speak in a Higher Voice Pitch to Men They Find Attractive," *Journal of Evolutionary Psychology* (March 2011): 57–67.

8. D. Larcker and A. Zakolyukina, "Detecting Deceptive Discussions in Conference Calls" (working paper no. 83, Rock Center for Corporate Governance, Stanford, CA, July 29, 2010).

9. http://www.npr.org/2011/07/14/137868888/judge-declares-mistrial-in-roger-clemens-case/.

10. http://www.deceptionanalysis.com/truth_tools_lexicon.html.

11. N. Carlson, "At Last—The Full Story of How Facebook Was Founded," March 5, 2010, http://www.businessinsider.com.

12. J. Schafer, "Reading People by the Words They Speak," June 17, 2011, http://www.psychologytoday.com.

13. J. Hancock et al., "Hungry Like the Wolf: A Word-Pattern Analysis of the Language of Psychopaths," *Legal and Criminological Psychology,* first published online: September 14, 2011.

14. J. Pennebaker, *The Secret Life of Pronouns: What Our Words Say About Us* (New York: Bloomsbury, 2011).

15. Larcker and Zakolyukina, "Detecting Deceptive Discussions in Conference Calls."

16. http://transcripts.cnn.com/TRANSCRIPTS/1106/01/ltm.02.html.

17. http://www.nydailynews.com/sports/college/jerry-sandusky-i-seeking-young-person-sexual-helped-article-1.977730#ixzz1dvhoMIPn.

18. http://newsroom.ucla.edu/portal/ucla/how-to-tell-when-someone-s-lying-202644.aspx.

19. M. Newman et al., "Lying Words: Predicting Deception from Linguistic Styles," *Personality and Social Psychology Bulletin* 29 (May 2003): 665–75.

20. Pennebaker, *Secret Life of Pronouns.*

Chapter 6
Step 3: The Stakeout

1. N. Ambady, J. Koo, R. Rosenthal, and C. H. Winograd, "Physical Therapists' Nonverbal Communication Predicts Geriatric Patients' Health Outcomes," *Psychology and Aging* 17 (September 2002): 443–52.

2. M. Stel, E. van Dijk, and E. Olivier, "You Want to Know the Truth? Then Don't Mimic!" *Psychological Science* 20 (June 2009): 693–99.

3. Vrij et al., "Pitfalls and Opportunities."

4. M. Bennett, "Who's Lying?," University of California's First Annual Compliance and Audit Symposium, San Francisco, February 2009.

5. Z. Hussain, A. B. Sekuler, and P. J. Bennett, "Superior Identification of Familiar Visual Patterns a Year After Learning," *Psychological Science* 22 (June 2011): 724–30. Epub May 17, 2011.

6. Bennett, "Who's Lying?"

7. Vrij et al., "Pitfalls and Opportunities."

8. D. Benjamin and J. Shapiro, "Thin-Slice Forecasts of Gubernatorial Elections," *Review of Economics and Statistics* 91 (August 1, 2009): 523–36.

9. Matsumoto et al., "Evaluating Truthfulness."

10. P. A. Stewart, "Presidential Laugh Lines: Candidate Display Behavior and Audience Laughter in the 2008 Primary Debates," *Politics and the Life Sciences* (September 2010): 55–72.

11. B. Chakrabarti and S. Baron-Cohen, "Variation in the Human Cannabinoid Receptor (CNR1) Gene Modulates Gaze Duration for Happy Faces," *Molecular Autism* 2 (2011).

12. K. J. Haley and D. M. T. Fessler, "Nobody's Watching? Subtle Cues Affect Generosity in an Anonymous Economic Game," *Evolution and Human Behavior* 26 (2005): 245–56.

13. M. Bateson, D. Nettle, and G. Roberts, "Cues of Being Watched Enhance Cooperation in a Real-World Setting," *Biology Letters* 2 (2006): 412–14.

14. Bennett, "Who's Lying?"

15. http://www.magarchive.tcu.edu/articles/2005-01-AC2.asp.

16. R. B. Adams et al., "Cross-Cultural Reading the Mind in the Eyes: An fMRI Investigation," *Journal of Cognitive Neuroscience* (January 2010): 97–108.

17. T. Neal and S. Brodsky, "Expert Witness Credibility as a Function of Eye Contact Behavior and Gender," *Criminal Justice and Behavior* 35 (December 2008): 1515–26.

18. Vrij et al., "Pitfalls and Opportunities."

19. Bennett, "Who's Lying?"

Chapter 7
Step 4: The Full Body Surveillance

1. Bennett, "Who's Lying?"

2. H. A. Marano, "How Much Control over Me Does This Person Really Have?," *Psychology Today* (January/February 2011): 55.

3. G. A. Van Kleef et al., "Breaking the Rules to Rise to Power: How Norm Violators Gain Power in the Eyes of Others," *Social Psychological and Personality Science* (September 2011): 500–507.

Chapter 8
Step 5: The Interrogation

1. Vrij et al., "Pitfalls and Opportunities."

2. A. D. Evans and K. Lee, "Promising to Tell the Truth Makes 8- to 16-Year-Olds More Honest," *Behavioral Sciences & The Law* 28 (November–December 2010): 801–11.

3. D. Grubin, "A Trial of Voluntary Polygraphy Testing in 10 English Probation Areas," *Sex Abuse* 22 (September 2010): 266–78.

4. J. Kuroyama, C. Wright, T. Manson, and C. Sablynski, "The Effect of Warning Against Faking on Noncognitive Test Outcomes: A Field Study of Bus Operator Applicants," *Applied H.R.M. Research* 12 (2010): 59–74.

5. M. Hartwig et al., "Strategic Use of Evidence During Police Interviews," *Law and Human Behavior* 30 (2006): 603–19.

6. Vrij et al., "Pitfalls and Opportunities."

7. A. Vrij et al., "Drawings as an Innovative and Successful Lie Detection Tool," *Applied Cognitive Psychology* 24 (September 2009): 587–94.

8. Vrij et al., "Pitfalls and Opportunities."

9. Vrij et al., "Pitfalls and Opportunities."

10. Vrij et al., "Pitfalls and Opportunities."

Chapter 9
Putting It All Together

1. M. Bennett, "Who's Lying?" Presentation at University of California's First Annual Compliance and Audit Symposium, San Francisco, February 2009.

2. Bennett, "Who's Lying?"

3. Van Kleef et al., "Breaking the Rules."

4. P. Chen et al., "The Hierarchical Face: Higher Rankings Lead to Less Cooperative Looks," *Journal of Applied Psychology* 14 (November 2011).

5. Vrij et al., "Pitfalls and Opportunities."

6. Lount et al., "Getting Off on the Wrong Foot."

Chapter 10
The Self-Exam

1. D. Balliet et al., "Sex Differences in Cooperation: A Meta-Analytic Review of Social Dilemmas," *Psychological Bulletin* (November 2011): 881–909.

2. Vrij et al., "Pitfalls and Opportunities."

3. Adams et al., "Cross-Cultural Reading."

4. Vrij et al., "Pitfalls and Opportunities."

5. S. Krach et al., "Your Flaws Are My Pain: Linking Empathy to Vicarious Embarrassment," *PLoS One* 6 (April 13, 2011): e18675.

6. D. Carney et al., "Power Posing: Brief Nonverbal Displays Affect Neuroendocrine Levels and Risk Tolerance," *Psychological Science* (in press).

Index

Page numbers in *italics* refer to illustrations.